ENGAGING
—*the*—
CIVIL WAR

Chris Mackowski and Brian Matthew Jordan, Series Editors

A Public-History Initiative of Emerging Civil War
and Southern Illinois University Press

THE SPIRITS OF BAD MEN MADE PERFECT

THE LIFE AND DIARY OF CONFEDERATE ARTILLERIST WILLIAM ELLIS JONES

Constance Hall Jones

Southern Illinois University Press
Carbondale

Southern Illinois University Press
www.siupress.com

Copyright © 2020 by Constance Hall Jones
All rights reserved
Printed in the United States of America

23 22 21 20   4 3 2 1

Cover illustration: interior of notebook William used to record his 1862 Civil
    War diary (cropped). *Image courtesy of Clements Library, University of
    Michigan.*

Library of Congress Cataloging-in-Publication Data
Names: Jones, Constance Hall, 1964– author.
Title: The spirits of bad men made perfect : the life and diary of Confederate
    artillerist William Ellis Jones / Constance Hall Jones.
Other titles: Life and diary of Confederate artillerist William Ellis Jones
Description: Carbondale, IL : Southern Illinois University Press, [2020] |
    Series: Engaging the Civil War | Includes bibliographical references
    and index.
Identifiers: LCCN 2019009180 | ISBN 9780809337613 (pbk. : alk. paper) |
    ISBN 9780809337620 (e-book)
Subjects: LCSH: Jones, William Ellis, 1838–1910. | Confederate States of
    America. Army. Virginia Artillery. Crenshaw's Battery—Biography.
    | Soldiers—Virginia—Diaries. | United States—History—
    Civil War, 1861–1865—Campaigns—Virginia. | United States—
    History—Civil War, 1861–1865—Campaigns—Maryland. |
    Jones, Thomas Norcliffe, 1800–1864. | Richmond (Va.)—History—
    Civil War, 1861–1865—Biography. | Virginia—History—Civil War,
    1861–1865—Regimental histories. | United States—History—
    Civil War, 1861–1865—Regimental histories. | United States—
    History—Civil War, 1861–1865—Personal narratives.
Classification: LCC E581.8 C9 J67 2020 | DDC 973.7/455092 [B] —dc23
    LC record available at https://lccn.loc.gov/2019009180

Printed on recycled paper ♻

This paper meets the requirements of ANSI/NISO Z39.48-1992
    (Permanence of Paper). ∞

FOR THOMAS ELLIS JONES,
who showed me through example
that it's never too late to try.

FOR ANN BENN WYCHE JONES,
who made trying possible.

Aetas parentum peior avis tulit
nos nequiores, mox daturos
progeniem vitiosiorem

—*Q. Horatii Flacci*
Carminum

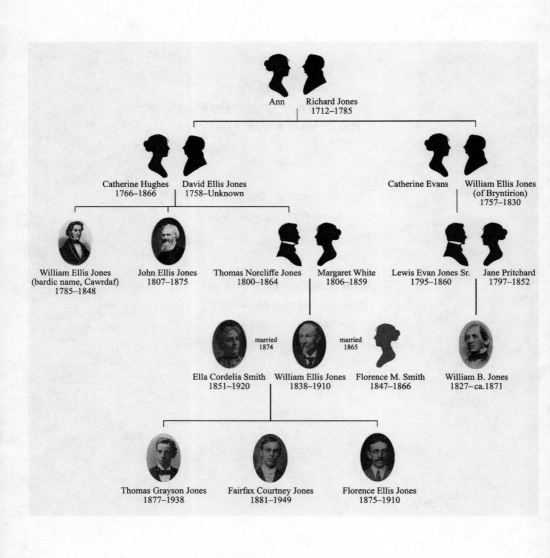

Ann   Richard Jones
1712–1785

Catherine Hughes   David Ellis Jones
1766–1866   1758–Unknown

Catherine Evans   William Ellis Jones
(of Bryntirion)
1757–1830

William Ellis Jones
(bardic name, Cawrdaf)
1785–1848

John Ellis Jones
1807–1875

Thomas Norcliffe Jones   Margaret White
1800–1864   1806–1859

Lewis Evan Jones Sr.   Jane Pritchard
1795–1860   1797–1852

Ella Cordelia Smith   married   William Ellis Jones   married   Florence M. Smith
1851–1920   1874   1838–1910   1865   1847–1866

William B. Jones
1827–ca.1871

Thomas Grayson Jones
1877–1938

Fairfax Courtney Jones
1881–1949

Florence Ellis Jones
1875–1910

Contents

Illustrations

Maps

Plates

Preface

Between March and December 1862, William Ellis Jones, a twenty-three-year-old private serving as an artillerist in Crenshaw's Battery, Pegram's Battalion, Army of Northern Virginia, maintained a journal of his daily experience and his battery's participation in the Peninsula Campaign, the Second Battle of Manassas, the Maryland Campaign, the Battle of Fredericksburg, and others. William's journal offers a previously unpublished, primary source account of the war as experienced by an educated, articulate participant in events that shaped American history. While the journal alone provides a valuable firsthand account of these events, its value is enhanced by the addition of extensive research into the background of its author and his family; their social, commercial, and political connections; and their rapidly rising position within the complicated strata of antebellum Richmond, Virginia, society.

William Ellis Jones was, as his journal reveals, a figure who grappled with contradictory views of his place in the Confederate army, the greater purpose of the war, and his self-identification as a Christian and a white Southern gentleman. In undertaking the work of transcribing this journal and researching every aspect of William's life, my goal has been to discover what influences and life events pressed his decisions, molded his opinions, and ultimately forged the character of the man William became after the war concluded, and what that understanding reveals to us in the twenty-first century.

The project is entirely unique on at least one account, in that it presents the story of how a Welsh immigrant family experienced the American Civil War from the Confederate side of the conflict. Previously, the Welsh immigrant to antebellum America has been portrayed as a monolith of Union sentiment and loyalty. (See Jerry Hunter's *Sons of Arthur, Children of Lincoln: Welsh Writing from the American Civil War*. It's a well-researched volume and one of the few ever published on the subject.)

The perspective of the Welsh immigrant as a universally pro-Union loyalist is reinforced by countless articles and letters published in the Welsh-language press in Wales and America during and after the war. There has been little serious investigation into the experience of Welsh Confederates prior to the undertaking of this project. Generally, Welsh immigrants to the United States tended toward progressive politics, from supporting organized labor actions to unflinching support for abolition. William's Welsh forebears were no different; however, after they arrived in Richmond and found a new world with great opportunity for social advancement and economic gain, a change in their political and moral leaning occurred, which is examined in depth in the chapters covering William Ellis Jones's family and his youth.

While the Jones family of Richmond may not be entirely representative of the experiences of all (or even most) Welsh immigrants in the Confederacy, it is this author's position that they provide a fascinating contrast to what is conventionally understood about the Welsh immigrant experience before, during, and after the American Civil War. This book should provide a valuable resource for consideration when studying the immigrant's role in the war and in the contentious peace that followed.

Acknowledgments

At the beginning of this undertaking I had only the base text of the Civil War diary made by my great-great-grandfather William Ellis Jones, with precious little knowledge of the man himself and even less understanding of the antebellum South or the American Civil War. In truth, I did not know what I did not know. My ignorance of the material is likely what made the project seem reasonable at the time I began. Had I known then the challenges, setbacks, brick walls, and adjustments in worldview that lay ahead, I may have been too discouraged to continue. What got me through all the challenges was the encouragement, assistance, and patience of a handful of individuals who recognized the value in this endeavor. If there's anything novel or insightful offered here, I promise the credit lies with one or more of these contributors. All remaining fault in the work I'll claim as mine alone.

While they remain anonymous to me, the manuscript reviewers at Southern Illinois University Press deserve gracious thanks, as they rendered much-needed scholarly critique of the originally submitted text. They gently but firmly offered clear guidance on where to turn for deeper research on issues requiring more comprehensive analysis. Their advice was necessary, and it markedly improved this work. Similarly, the production and copyediting teams at SIU Press also deserve a sincere "thank you" for their efforts with the manuscript. Sylvia Frank Rodrigue, Jennifer Egan, Wayne K. Larsen, and Julie Bush all contributed immeasurably to ensuring this project finished on schedule and applied the highest degree of polish they could to the rough work I gave them. Every author should be so fortunate to have such a dedicated group of perfectionists propping them up!

John Hennessy deserves tremendous thanks for providing me with detailed information about little-documented aspects of the 1862 campaigns. His unparalleled knowledge of the geography and events of the Civil War in Virginia proved invaluable in helping me put context to the challenges the soldiers of Crenshaw's Battery faced and understand how the soldiers' presence in the Virginia countryside affected the civilian residents. John never failed to recommend more sources to consider, new perspectives to investigate, new people to turn to for help. More than all this, however, John staunchly refused to allow me to fall back on "moonlight and magnolias" notions of my ancestors' motivations. He challenged me to dig deeper into the history, to think and write critically rather than accept the romanticized story of the antebellum South with which I was reared. At times his challenges were painful to confront, but having confronted them, I have a far more accurate and nuanced understanding of the nineteenth century and of William Ellis Jones's world. What's more, John's challenges have led me to a better understanding of myself and my place in the twenty-first century. His efforts with me on this project not only informed the work but also informed my life. My worldview is transformed as a result. I can never repay John's contribution to my growth as a human being.

Jeffry Burden, board member at the Friends of Shockoe Hill Cemetery, contributed substantially to this project by helping me confirm familial and social relationships between William's extended family and network of friends. His knowledge of Richmond history and its antebellum and Civil War–era geography is extensive. His generosity of time and attention in showing me around Richmond during the 150th Civil War anniversary events proved invaluable to my understanding of William's geographic world both before and after the war. Beyond this, his advice and recommendations have assisted tremendously in improving the final text. Jeffry's enthusiasm for this project kept me going when I felt most discouraged. I can't thank him enough for his generosity and his boundless energy and ideas.

Mike Gorman, with the online research project Civil War Richmond, deserves a very special thank you for bringing to my attention a crucial piece of primary source material: the letter written by an anonymous soldier of Pegram's Battalion and published in the *Richmond Whig*. This letter, while seemingly a random scrap of peripherally relevant material, provided me with answers to questions I could not have found elsewhere. The letter revealed a great deal about the character of the man William Ellis Jones was as the war wore him down. This letter propelled me over a brick wall that seemed insurmountable for many years prior to its discovery. Credit goes to historian and author Peter Carmichael for pointing out the existence of this letter.

Jayne Ptolemy, curatorial assistant at the William L. Clements Library, University of Michigan, Ann Arbor, was so generous and so resourceful in her assistance with the physical diary manuscript. I cannot adequately express my gratitude for her patience with me and this project. Kelly Powers, digitalization specialist at the Clements Library, did an outstanding job providing high-resolution scans of this fragile document. Austin Thomason, senior photographer with University of Michigan Photography, provided beautifully composed studio shots of the diary for inclusion in this book. Their care and craft are more appreciated than they will ever know.

Buddy Secor is due my thanks for his fantastic photographic work that he has generously provided for this project. In addition, I owe him a debt of gratitude for getting me to "Eastern View" and showing me the place as William and his fellow artillerists saw it. His magical camera work closes the gap of more than 150 years between what William witnessed and what we fail to properly imagine today.

Mike Tomey provided me with the firsthand account of his great-great-grandfather's march across the Blue Ridge with the Indiana 27th (Union) at the same time William recorded the grueling march in his own diary. I'm indebted to him for this supporting perspective and forever thankful for his encouragement and correspondence.

Dr. Michael Trahos and his wife, B. L. Trahos, owners of Mulberry Place at Bowling Green, Virginia, deserve a sincere and special thank you for their hospitality and generosity with their time. They are a remarkable couple with an unwavering devotion to the preservation of one of the most important properties in Virginia.

I cannot overlook Pat North, co-owner with her husband, Jack North, of Mayhurst Inn in Orange, Virginia, who brought me into their home for a tour of this historic and beautiful house. While we enjoyed iced tea in the main parlor, I read William's diary entry concerning his stay there in 1862. Mrs. North was understandably moved by William's words and the fact that we were standing in his footsteps.

Many others assisted me with this project either directly or indirectly. Doug Bond, George Psomas, Ed Neely, Scott Mingus, Linda White, Christina Lujin, Robert Krick, Linda Morris Mann, and Aldo Perry all deserve generous thanks for their contributions and time taken in review of the material and feedback. Chris Mackowski, Eric Wittenberg, and John Cummings, in particular, earn special thanks for speaking up for this project (to the right people) when it felt like there was little hope it would ever see the light of day.

Brian Slyfield in West Sussex, UK, deserves generous thanks for providing me with background and sources for my Welsh ancestors, including their professional and political histories. I am eternally in the debt of my brother,

William Ellis Jones (the fifth of that name in our line), for all the time and careful attention he put into scanning documents in advance of this project. I need to thank my cousin Penny Warden Minton for the photographs of William Ellis Jones and William B. Jones. They are priceless!

My dear friend the late Margaret Robertson deserves the warmest gratitude I can extend for her gracious generosity in opening her home on multiple occasions so that I could visit Richmond and locations in central Virginia "on the cheap." She fed me and made me laugh, she encouraged me, and she reminded me of all I have missed by not having had a sister. I'm saddened that Maggie did not live to see this project, which she so enthusiastically supported, come to fruition.

My best friend, Jon Rowland, must be acknowledged and thanked for his limitless patience over the last eight years as I talked of the Civil War, old Wales, my ancestors, and all the odd details that pricked at my brain as I puzzled through this project. He never failed to provide a springboard for good ideas or be a conscientious judge of bad ones. He never failed to listen carefully and objectively. He supported my ambitions when others felt I was wasting time and treasure on a dream no one else cared for. I can never repay his patience or his belief in me.

My father, Thomas Ellis Jones, deserves a special acknowledgment for all the books and primary source material he preserved and gave to me and my brother, and for the stories and facts he communicated to me about his family in Richmond. My father did not live long enough to see this project begin or end, but I hope he would have been proud of my efforts.

I must extend the greatest debt of gratitude to my mother, Ann Wyche Jones. Without her material support there is no way this project would have come together. Sadly, my mother passed as I was preparing the final manuscript for publication. She never had an opportunity to see the fruits of my labors, but my memories of her will always motivate me to finish what I start and do my best.

Aside from family, the person who has known me the longest and whose encouragement has had the most impact on the trajectory of my life is my dear longtime friend Bill Adler. Bill took an interest in my future when I was very young, encouraging me to raise my expectations for myself. Without his intervention and belief in me, I never would have conceived that I could undertake a project like this one, much less that I might have the right to do so.

To all of you, I hope I have done justice to your sacrifices on my behalf and your belief in me.

ENGAGING
—*the*—
CIVIL WAR

For additional content that will let you engage this material further, look for unique QR codes at the end of the introduction and at the start of each section. Scanning them will take you to exclusive online material, additional photos and images, links to online resources, and related blog posts at www. emergingcivilwar.com.

A QR scanner app is readily available for download through the app store on your digital device. Or go to www.siupress.com/spiritsofbadmenlinks for links to the digital content.

The Spirits of Bad Men Made Perfect

1. ❄ Prelude to Soldiering

Came off guard at eight o'clock. Soon after coming off the Yanks opened up on us. I went down to the battery from the house to see the fun . . . and just as I passed in the yard around the house a shell came over my head and killed two of our horses. The shell broke the back of one and entered the other, exploding while in him. I don't think I ever saw such a sight before in all my life.

—From the Civil War diary of William Ellis Jones, June 25, 1862 (prelude to the Battle of Mechanicsville)

Wednesday, June 25, 1862, was the first day of the war for Private William Ellis Jones. Prior to that day, he and his comrades in Crenshaw's Battery only played at the notion of soldiering. Late in the evening, with the sun setting over the hills behind him, William heard the pounding throb of battle not far from his picket. Once relieved of his watch, he wandered nearer the lines to get a better view of the "fun." Yards away, dueling artillery teams hurtled cannon shot over hillock and tree top, making a horrendous racket—none of it to any tactical result, as both sides were still novice at ranging their guns or aiming to any effect.

Then one of those Union boys discovered his art.

A cannonball as hot as Vulcan's temper flew past, just feet from William's head. He never had time to duck. The ball was not aimed at him but at a big iron gun nearby. It missed its mark, tearing instead through a horse attached to the gun's caisson. After it ripped the first horse in half, it lodged in a second, and there it exploded into a thousand angry shards.

In the blink of an eye, William found himself standing in a sticky red and green soup of horse entrails and gore. A mist of bloody glaze spritzed him and everything else within yards of the impact. The ground glistened with bile and the twisted lights of dead animal.

William stood frozen, his feet locked to the ground, his mind trying to process the scene or blink it away as if it was a dream.

1

That exploded horse certainly had a name, but William couldn't recall it amid the thunder erupting all around him. As William looked on, the creature was no more than bloody paste and steaming bowels in the dirt. The instant comic cruelty of it touched him in a place he hadn't known existed just seconds before.

That is war. That is what it does. It reveals an absurd truth that you didn't know existed before it bruises you deep and for all time, imprinting a vision that so thoroughly fouls you, you'll never be able to scrub it off or wish it away. It comes again and again, piling up layers of filth and fatigue so heavy and thick that if you keep your eyes open and take it all in, it will break you in half or make you laugh like a madman.

In the early fire of the Seven Days' Battles, the boys in blue and gray laughed. They laughed in the shadow of the gallows and facing the guns. They laughed so they couldn't hear the screams of the wounded and dying in the woods and swamps around them. They laughed because the only alternative was a rapid descent into sobbing lament. Lament would come, but on that night in June 1862, many of the young men on both sides of the battle lines believed this war would be a short-lived adventure that was going to be grand, noble, and "fun."

That night, William got his first glimpse of war. In the coming days, the minié ball and cannon shot would demonstrate the full range of their gifts. He got a close look at the "fun" of death in the blasted flesh of comrade and enemy alike. That first night, warfare's instruction was paced, piecemeal, almost comic in its cruelty. What came in the days, weeks, and months after was a baptism in hell, disabusing twenty-three-year-old William Ellis Jones of the idea that this war would be over in a month or that the "Yanks" would skedaddle and everything would go back to the way it was before. For William and those who survived the perdition at Mechanicsville, Seven Pines, and Second Manassas, nothing would ever be the same again.

* * *

Before we go forward to those hot days and beyond, we must go backward in time, before William was a soldier, before spies swung from the gallows at Richmond's parade grounds to a cheering audience of thousands. We must retreat to a time before every young man in Virginia sang "Dixie" with a raised glass and a grin, before the days when every old man—men who had never seen a real war—cried for glory, for honor, and for blood.

2. ✵ Stumbling in the Shadows of Giants

John Donne observed in *Devotions upon Emergent Occasions*, "No man is an island." The principal subject of this project, William Ellis Jones, was no island. His life and character, before, during, and after the American Civil War, were defined by the people who influenced him, the places that played pivotal roles in his and his family's journey, and the unfolding events of the era that affected individual lives, landscapes, and global geopolitics. When examining William's life within the context of these, he is rendered in full dimension. Without this context, William exists only as a flattened character type, out of time, lacking depth or breadth.

A handful of Civil War historians know William Ellis Jones as a Confederate artillerist who served without distinction in Crenshaw's Battery, Pegram's Battalion, in the Army of Northern Virginia, a young man without a past or a future who just happened to have kept a detailed account of his wartime experience over the first ten months of his service, March to December 1862.

Similarly, a handful of antiquarian booksellers and collectors know William Ellis Jones as the postwar printer and publisher of Richmond. His firm, which operated under a variety of imprints, published many hundreds, perhaps thousands, of titles between 1869 and 1919. The firm is best known to collectors as one of the most prolific publishers in the American South of Virginia Civil War histories, colonial Virginia histories, the *Southern Historical Society Papers*, and the *Virginia Magazine of History and Biography*.

Beyond these narrow facts, few if any persons now living know anything about William Ellis Jones or his associations, either before or after the Civil War. In all my inquiries to Civil War scholars and antiquarian booksellers, not one of them managed to connect the two historical figures, even while they referenced his publications and quoted liberally from his diary in their own dissertations, books, and articles.

While William Ellis Jones is the principal subject of this work, to understand him we must explore his influences. As a youth his mind and character were shaped by an immediate and extended family with a colorful and often controversial history. He was influenced by his dearest friends and peers, a generation that came of age in Virginia during a period of tremendous social, political, and technological upheaval. No less important than these are the physical geographies of the places he, his friends, and his family members occupied and the events of the day that formed their characters, challenged their decisions, and ultimately made and remade their belief systems.

The story of William's earliest origins begins in the tiny town of Dolgellau in the northwest of Wales more than one hundred years prior to his birth. In the eighteenth century, this remote region of the British Isles was considered by Englishmen to be a foreign land, sparsely populated by strange people who spoke a language wholly unlike their own and who stubbornly clung to ancient customs and superstitions, even as the world itself grew smaller and ever more English as every year passed. It was a land, at least in the view of colonial-minded Englishmen, in dire need of "civilization."

Dolgellau, with its surrounding mountains, river valleys, and tidal estuaries, was the homeland of William Ellis Jones's most remote ancestors. William's grandfather David Ellis Jones was born and raised under the shadow of one of Wales's most famous mountains, Cadir Idris ("The Seat of the Bard," loosely translated from the Welsh), speaking no other language except Welsh until he, along with his brother, was sent to a boarding school for the express purpose of learning the English language.[1] In England in that era, it was commonplace for wealthy families to send their children away to school. In Wales, however, such a thing was almost unheard of. David Ellis Jones and his brother, William (commonly referred to as William Ellis Jones of Bryntirion), were probably among the first in their community to thoroughly learn English as a second language. This skill would serve them well throughout their lives, as English influence and eventual domination of Wales increased and rapid industrialization of the once pastoral countryside transformed the native Welsh economy, its landscape, and the demographics of the local population.

It is easy to assume that the parents of these two boys were progressively minded, even prescient in their anticipation of how Wales would evolve over their sons' lifetimes. It is unlikely they were fully capable of envisioning the world these boys would inherit as they matured. Before the passing of two generations, the Welsh language, most of the old customs, and an entire way of life that had flourished unchanged for centuries was swept away in a choking black tide of industrial-scale coal mining and iron making.

Unregulated industrialization on a scale that defies imagination recast the Welsh landscape, devastating the environment and overwhelming the small country with wave after wave of migrants from all over Europe seeking work in the coalfields and iron foundries. Amid the environmental, social, and technological upheaval, the native Welsh people were pressed to near cultural extinction.[2]

The Jones clan reacted the way many native people react when their lands are savaged, their way of life is broken, and their language is corrupted and ultimately outlawed: they spawned a few generations of radicals and revolutionaries who fought back, using any means at their disposal in an attempt to preserve and protect their land, their culture, their religious traditions, and their native tongue. The primary weapon the Jones family employed in their war against the English Crown, the Anglican Church, the mine owners, the ironmongers, and the absentee landowners was the printing press. The first press was brought to Dolgellau, Wales, in 1798.[3] The ammunition employed in this weapon was the Welsh language, the Welsh religious tradition, and a uniquely Welsh, socialist-style cultural bent that the Joneses' presses distributed in defiance of English government authority.

By the middle of the nineteenth century, the Jones family of Dolgellau, as well as apprentices and journeymen printers trained in their shops, operated a syndicate of publishing firms, from the far north of Wales at Caernarfon to the far south at Merthyr Tydfil, from their home base at Dolgellau, and from numerous presses in cities and towns from the west coast to the marches in the eastern border country. The Jones dynasty of printers and publishers used their influence to spread political radicalism, anti-establishment religious thought, early principles of organized labor, and the preservation of the Welsh language through editorials, storytelling, and the long tradition of Welsh literature and poetry.[4]

From this backdrop of radical cultural transformation and defiant Welsh nationalism emerged four men of particular importance to the life and development of William Ellis Jones: his father, Thomas Norcliffe Jones; Thomas's brother William Ellis Jones (who took the Welsh bardic name Cawrdaf); their cousin Lewis Evan Jones Sr.; and Lewis's son William B. Jones. Each of these men was profoundly ambitious. Each of them boasted strong personalities and aspirations, setting them apart from many of their contemporaries. Individually and collectively, they set a standard for William Ellis Jones that he struggled to live up to or walk away from for his entire life.

Thomas Norcliffe Jones (born c. 1800 in Denbigh, North Wales; died 1864 in Nova Scotia) was the second son of David Ellis Jones (one of the two previously mentioned brothers sent off to school to learn English). He was raised, as were all his brothers and cousins, in the family business. He was a printer by trade and training, a Methodist in his faith (at least early in his life), extremely well educated (if not formally) by the standards of early nineteenth-century Wales, and progressive in his politics and philosophy. Thomas, after his immigration to Richmond, became father to William Ellis Jones, the subject of this biography.[5] In succeeding chapters we will learn a great deal more about Thomas Norcliffe Jones and his relationship with his adopted home.

Thomas's older brother, William Ellis Jones (Cawrdaf) (born 1785 at Tyddyn Sion, North Wales; died 1848 at Cowbridge, near Cardiff, Wales), also played a significant role in this story. In his day, Cawrdaf was a celebrity—a celebrity bard in the Welsh tradition. He was also a political radical and an outspoken opponent of the Anglican Church. In his lifetime he was a vociferous supporter of the nascent organized labor movement in Wales. Cawrdaf was an ardent Welsh nationalist who worked tirelessly for the preservation of the threatened Welsh language and culture. He was also a deeply religious man who adhered to and preached the still relatively fresh Wesleyan faith across Wales. Among many other things, he wrote and published in support of the early temperance movement and against the African slave trade in the English colonies as well as in the United States. In his lifetime he attained the status of cult hero among the Welsh-speaking working classes for his honest and gritty portrayal of the real lives, joys, and brutal suffering of his people. He was, if we can take the liberty of drawing such comparisons, an early nineteenth-century equivalent of a Welsh Woody Guthrie in theme, fame, and popular longevity.[6]

Cawrdaf's greatest dream, early in his life, was to immigrate to America, to the home of Thomas Jefferson and James Madison.[7] His romanticized image of America was of a place and a people who successfully threw off the yoke of English tyranny, founding a nation based upon the basic, God-given human rights of liberty, equality, and justice for all men, regardless of class or religion. It was William the bard who encouraged his younger brother Thomas Norcliffe Jones to migrate to America, and to Virginia, in particular. And it was William, the famous Welsh bard and political radical, for whom Thomas Norcliffe Jones, after arriving in Virginia in 1830 and starting a family of his own, named his only son.

Thomas Norcliffe Jones's cousin Lewis Evan Jones Sr. (born 1795 in Dolgellau; died 1860 in Caernarvon) was the son of William Ellis Jones of Bryntirion, near Dolgellau (brother to David Ellis Jones, both previously mentioned).

Working from his busy publishing firm in the bustling port city of Caernarvon in the far north of Wales, Lewis Evan Jones Sr. used his press and his wickedly sharp editorial pen to align the Welsh people to his overt antiestablishment, anti-English government, pro-organized labor brand of militant radicalism. While Lewis Evan Jones's name is still recalled in some radical Welsh circles, much of his published work has been lost. His publications were suppressed by the English government, even as his life was threatened by his much more powerful political opponents.[8]

Over the course of his career, Lewis Evan Jones wrote and published countless works against British and American slavery and the transatlantic slave trade while simultaneously decrying the horrendous working conditions and paltry wages of "free labor" in his own country. He was so controversial a figure in both Wales and England that his eldest son, Lewis Evan Jones Jr., wrote that the primary reason he left Wales and immigrated to the United States was to escape the "heat" his father attracted due to his political affiliations and radical activities.[9]

Lewis Evan Jones Sr. sired four sons, three of whom migrated to America.[10] His second son, William B. Jones (born January 21, 1827, in Caernarfon;[11] died c. 1871, presumably in Richmond, Virginia),[12] followed his cousin Thomas Norcliffe Jones to Richmond around the year 1855. By 1856 he and Thomas Norcliffe Jones were co-engaged in a business partnership, operating as grocers and wholesale commission merchants.[13]

Together, Thomas Norcliffe Jones and William B. Jones represent the fruit that fell as far away from the family tree as one can imagine, given their origins. We'll learn a good deal more about William B. Jones in succeeding chapters; however, it is worth noting that this man left his mark on Richmond to such a profound and distasteful degree that the city—not to mention his nearest blood relations in both the United States and Wales—have all but written him out of history. His existence was completely omitted from the oral and much of the written family histories of both the Richmond (Thomas Norcliffe Jones) and Welsh (Lewis Evan Jones Sr.) lines. His presence in the family was resurrected only through research into historical newspaper, legal, and real estate records, relevant to his presence in Richmond before, during, and slightly after the U.S. Civil War.

The city of Richmond played a central role in this and nearly every Civil War story. Its history is well documented in its complexities and contradictions, from the social, to the political, to the economic. While it is not within

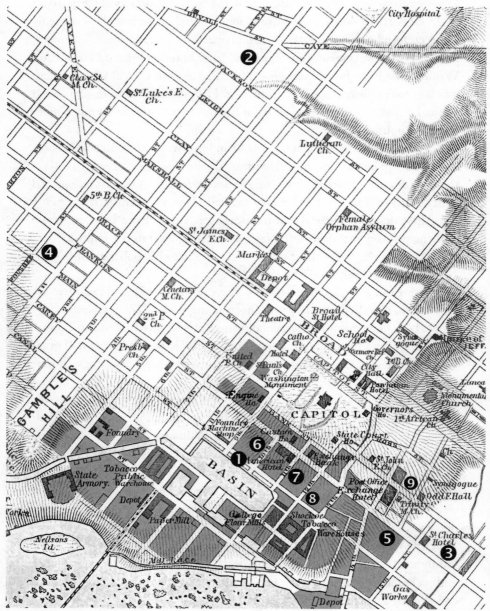

U.S. Coast Survey's map of the city of Richmond, Virginia, during the Civil War era, with locations relevant to William Ellis Jones. Gray-shaded areas represent the burned district from the evacuation fire of April 3, 1865. (1) Basin Bank: location of the Crenshaw Battery first muster, March 14, 1862. (2) 2nd Street between Jackson the scope of this work to render a history of antebellum Richmond, it is necessary to touch upon aspects of Richmond's development during that period to better understand the character and motivations of our subject, William Ellis Jones. Richmond was his hometown, and he was wholeheartedly invested in its well-being on multiple levels, from the purely sentimental to the social, cultural, and economic.

and Duvall Streets: Thomas Norcliffe Jones and family residence (and business, for a time) from 1840 until 1859. (3) 30 Main Street: Thomas Norcliffe Jones and Company business address in 1856. (4) 8 Main Street: Thomas Norcliffe Jones's business, from early 1861 through late 1862. After 1862, Thomas Norcliffe Jones used this building for tobacco manufacturing. (5) Cary Street, between 14th and 15th: occupied by Thomas Norcliffe Jones as primary business from 1862 until his death in 1864. (6) 140 Main Street: printing offices of William Clemmitt in 1864. (7) 11th Street, between Main and Cary: printing offices of (William) Clemmitt & (William Ellis) Jones in June 1877. (8) South 12th Street (by the sign of the Mint): printing offices of William Ellis Jones in July 1889. (9) 1207 East Franklin Street: printing offices of William Ellis Jones from 1902 until his death in 1910. *Washington, DC: U.S. Coast Survey, 1864. https://www.loc.gov/item/99448334/.*

3. ✤ Before Dixie

William Ellis Jones was born on May 15, 1838, somewhere in the city of Richmond. He was the first child of Thomas Norcliffe Jones and his wife, Margaret White. Both of his parents were, like a growing minority of Richmond's white population, recent immigrants with little money and even less status. Thomas was Welsh. Margaret was Irish. Neither nationality was held in particularly high esteem by the natives.[1]

In Virginia in that era, the only people who could cast a vote in elections were property-owning white male citizens of the Commonwealth. Virginia's suffrage laws in the early nineteenth century disenfranchised the greatest majority of people living in the state. Thomas Norcliffe Jones was not yet a property owner in 1838, nor was he a citizen, two deficits in his civic and economic status he worked with diligence to overcome in the impending decades. While his prospects may have appeared slight in the late 1830s, Thomas Norcliffe Jones was a remarkably ambitious man.

Before their son, William, was two years old, Thomas and Margaret purchased an undeveloped lot in a newly planned section of town, then called Duvall's Addition (modern-day Jackson's Ward).[2] Thomas built a structure on 2nd Street between Jackson and Duvall Streets, which served double-duty as the family's principal residence and as a retail grocery store. On June 1, 1840, Thomas filed a formal request for naturalization as an American citizen, taking the Oath of Allegiance to the United States. Three years later, on June 21, 1843, his request for citizenship was approved.[3] From that point forward Thomas was considered a true citizen of his adopted home. As a landowner and a citizen, he was entitled to vote, a fact that distinguished him among the overwhelming majority of Richmond's immigrant population. Henceforth, Thomas Norcliffe Jones invested his energy and his money into growing his business interests and increasing his stature in Richmond.

By 1840, Richmond's population had swelled to 20,153, half of whom were black slaves.[4] The greatest increase in the white population was a result of European migrants moving to the city, as well as skilled tradesmen and their families relocating from the American Northeast, most seeking work in Richmond's busy factories and mills. The suburbs around Richmond expanded in response to the population increase. The 1840 census records the household of Thomas Norcliffe Jones in the Duvall neighborhood with a wife (Margaret), two children (William and Mary, their daughter, who died just a year or two after the census was recorded), plus two nonfamily underage dependents and one slave who is indicated as being female, over fifty-five years of age. There is no way to determine who the two nonfamily dependents were. It is possible they were relations of Margaret White Jones or perhaps live-in apprentices or employees of the grocery store. This is all speculation. What is not speculation is that Thomas—while not yet a United States citizen until 1843—was a Virginia slaveholder by 1840. The emigrant from Wales, whose family back home railed against slavery, had gained an incremental toehold in the Old Dominion lifestyle less than a decade after his arrival in Richmond.

The decade of the 1840s brought forth in large measure the city of Richmond we can still see and, to a certain degree, experience today. The city William Ellis Jones grew up in enjoyed the strongest economy in the antebellum South fueled by its most productive industries: flour milling, tobacco manufacturing, iron foundries, locomotive works, railroads, waterworks and canals, warehouses, docks hosting substantial domestic as well as international trade, textile manufacture, coal mining, and industrial-scale slave trading. Richmond also saw a steady, year over year increase of both the white and enslaved black populations in relatively equal proportion. The geography of the city was gradually tamed throughout the 1830s and 1840s, transforming Richmond from a series of rustic, semi-isolated hilltop neighborhoods, separated one from the other by deep gullies and marshy creeks, into a graded, cobbled-lane business district at Shockoe Hill. The business district was fed by residential communities surrounding it on three sides, all connected by reasonably well-maintained thoroughfares lined with busy shops, horse-drawn carriages, and fashionably attired pedestrians.[5]

A building boom got underway in this period that has left its mark to the present day. Many of Richmond's grandest residential homes were constructed on Shockoe and Church Hills during this period, while at the same time the first of Richmond's famous wood frame and brownstone townhouses went up in newly established suburbs to the west and north of Shockoe (like Duvall's Addition, where Thomas Norcliffe Jones first set down his young family's roots).

Despite its booming economy and expanding industrial footprint, Richmond had no museum, no public library, no parks, no university or college, no public schools for children, and very few properly trained physicians. And although the city had no book publishers, authors, or artists, it did host a few broadside printers, a great many lawyers and legislators who frequented Capitol Square, and a great many more taverns, wharves, warehouses, gambling establishments, theaters, hotels, boardinghouses, and brothels.[6] Richmond was a city dedicated to commerce and to the demonstration of its economic and political pedigree on the global stage.

From what most people in the Western world considered a distant backwater of civilization, eighteenth-century Richmond produced Revolutionary War–era statesmen, United States presidents, and millionaires, in unequal proportion to the rest of the young nation. Virginians of a generation or two older than William elevated the ranks of those early statesmen to the position of mythical gods. In Virginia, and in Richmond in particular, Thomas Jefferson, James Madison, and George Washington were deified to a degree rivaling Christ himself.[7] Plantation millionaires, whose wealth was wholly tied to landholding and slaves and who claimed Jamestown and pre–Revolutionary War family lineages, became the high priests of the cult of America's creation story. Richmond's rising civic architecture, capped by its neoclassical capitol building (designed by founding father Thomas Jefferson), stood proudly as an example of citizens' ambition to see Richmond elevated to a world capital on par with Athens or Rome.

Beyond all this worshipful attention to the nation's founders, there was another competing religion in Richmond: the church of the almighty dollar. The high priests of this cult were men of somewhat newer establishment in the city from Richmond's expanding merchant and skilled trade class. Already competing by the early to mid-nineteenth century with native Virginians for majority population status, a large percentage of this emerging class was made up of recent immigrants.[8] Their great temples of worship were the sprawling blocks of warehouses and flour and tobacco mills, built sturdy of simple red brick, ordered neatly and packed together in an efficient grid of commercial production. The temple complex spread from the fall of Shockoe Hill below the capitol, all the way to the waterfront at Rocketts. It wove into and then beyond the slums of Shockoe Valley, splaying finally into the busy shipping docks on the mighty James River, southeast of Richmond proper, then spilling across the James's southern shores into the community of Manchester.

It was from this merchant neighborhood, dubbed "Shockoe Bottom," that the lion's share of Richmond's antebellum wealth emerged. While it is true that Virginia's heart and soul was made from agriculture, the state's backbone was transportation, and Richmond was Virginia's transportation head and shoulders. The James River, below the last cataract just above Rocketts, offered an open, deepwater run downriver to Portsmouth, Norfolk, and the Chesapeake Bay. In the early nineteenth century, it was as common to see Russian, Dutch, English, and French flags flying from the tall-masted ships docked at Rocketts as it was to see a vessel bound for New York, Boston, or Philadelphia.[9] The Kanawha Canal brought cotton, grains, tobacco, and increasingly coal and iron ore from the western counties of Virginia to Richmond, either for direct export or for processing in its various factories and mills.

Rail lines extended westward from Richmond and east toward the Chesapeake Bay. The rails flew north toward Baltimore, Philadelphia, and New York and south across the North Carolina state line to Atlanta and eventually to Richmond's only real Southern rival, the great port city of New Orleans. Railroads enabled a fast and affordable transfer of people, goods, and money from every part of the Deep South into the commonwealth of Virginia and then on to the industrialized cities of the North. The rapid growth of the rail system ushered in even greater industrial opportunities for Richmond as the city rolled forward into the economic boom of the 1850s.[10]

Beyond a storied history of Revolutionary War heroes and a slowly industrializing economy, another outsized industry thrived in Richmond: the largest and busiest slave markets on the Atlantic coast. In North America, their supremacy was only barely eclipsed by the international slave market at New Orleans, which serviced much of the Caribbean and Central American (French and Spanish) trade, as well as the growing Mississippi valley region, upriver from its busy port.[11] About half of Richmond's population was made up of slaves of African descent existing in an inescapable state of generational bondage. Most labored in the homes of white Richmonders as domestic servants;[12] however, a large percentage also worked as hostlers, blacksmiths, and craft carpenters; on the canals and in warehouses; in the myriad sugar, flour, and textile mills; in tobacco factories; and in the iron foundries.[13]

At the foot of Richmond, below the city's seven sparkling hills adorned with handsome houses and storied neoclassical buildings, in the neighborhood known as Shockoe Bottom, sinking and wet in the sticky mud on the banks of the James River, the busy slave markets of Richmond boiled like a cauldron, steaming with misery, burning white-hot with profit. The money made there in that era would make late nineteenth-century robber barons and the wolves of twenty-first century Wall Street blush with embarrassment.

Antebellum Southern wealth was built on rice, tobacco, cotton, and sugar; the raw material of agriculture was the foundation from which prosperity and power bloomed. The slave markets at Richmond effectively demonstrate that there would have been no rice, cotton, tobacco, or sugar were it not for the forced labor of millions of slaves who toiled, generation after generation, under the relentless Southern sun, wresting those globe-shaping commodities from the dirt.

Between 1830, when Thomas Norcliffe Jones arrived in Richmond, and 1860, roughly 10,000 slaves per month were sold or traded from the markets at Shockoe Bottom.[14] They were imported, methodically bred like livestock, bought and sold to work on tobacco and cotton plantations inland in Virginia, or sent into the Deep South to work in cotton, rice, and sugar. Slaving in this period was Virginia's most lucrative industry. It was bigger than tobacco, iron, or cotton. Slavery made the antebellum South (and therefore America) wealthy, and it made Virginia among the wealthiest regions in America.[15]

This is the city of William Ellis Jones's boyhood and youth. It was an optimistic time in Virginia for those with white skin, money, and ambition. William Ellis Jones's father had no shortage of the latter. It appears that carefully cultivated relationships, luck, and prudent investments assisted him with the pursuit of material wealth. How Thomas Norcliffe Jones managed to form his business associations remains a mystery. His son's earliest friendships are better known, if only because many of them persisted throughout his long lifetime.

Among William Ellis Jones's earliest and most fortuitous friendships was with Edgar Alonza Smith, the son of John Wesley Smith and Francis Sephronia (née Osgood) Smith. The Smiths were a well-established merchant family in Richmond, having given up the farming of tobacco either late in the eighteenth or early in the nineteenth century.[16] Their home, which was reputed to have been a grand old manor house built in the eighteenth century, was located on St. Stephen's Street, between Baker and Charity,[17] not far from Shockoe Cemetery and next to the city's powder magazine, just a few hundred yards from William's childhood home on the corner of 2nd and Duvall Streets.[18] It is likely that ancestors of John Wesley Smith farmed this property prior to the city of Richmond growing up around it and that the old house was the original plantation house built by an earlier generation. The Smiths were well respected in town, maintaining society among the city's best families. They attended St. James's Episcopal Church, and later St. Mark's, along with other prominent residents of Shockoe Hill. There were four children in the Smith family, three daughters and a son. Edgar, the eldest, was two years younger than William. The proximity between their homes and the fact that they both attended St. James's probably contributed to their early bond.

Another childhood friend was Edward "Ned" Virginius Valentine. The Valentine family was a venerable Old Virginia planter family originally of King

William County.[19] Ned's father, Mann Satterwhite Valentine Sr., came to Richmond as a boy, following his father's untimely death. Early in life, Mann Valentine demonstrated tremendous business acumen and quickly became one of Richmond's most successful merchants, competing enthusiastically with British merchants who generally dominated trade in Virginia in that era.[20] His youngest son, Ned, showed an early passion for collecting, fine art, and reading. His parents, people of genuine means, were able to provide Ned with the best of educations available in that era, sending him to Europe to study with fine art masters in Paris, Italy, and Berlin.[21]

William's dearest childhood friend was Robert Alonzo Brock. Like William Ellis Jones, Robert Brock was descended from Welsh lineage, a people who are notoriously obsessed with family genealogies and history in general. Also, like William, Robert was dedicated to reading and collecting books. The Brock family had plantation roots in Virginia going back to the eighteenth century, but due to his family's financial difficulties, Robert was compelled to leave school and join his uncles in the timber merchant business at about twelve years of age.[22] His childhood home was located just yards away from William's, also in the Duvall Addition neighborhood. As children these two played together, studied together, and collected.[23] Along with their early shared passion for books, history, and reading, they also shared the common experience of having their educations abruptly halted, being routed instead into apprenticeships in fields it is unlikely either of them would have selected for themselves had they been given an option.

Edgar Alonza Smith, Ned Valentine, Robert Alonzo Brock, and William Ellis Jones were typical among the generation of young men of their class and education. They came of age in a period of economic, political, religious, and technological transition that challenged nearly every notion of what it meant to be manly, a gentleman, and a Virginian.

In the decade between 1850 and 1860, they witnessed Richmond in its boom years, when the city's population increased dramatically, property values skyrocketed, speculation was rampant, and million-dollar fortunes were made and lost in a single day's trading. It was also a period of political upheaval, where rife divisions formed between older, native Virginians who clung to the "cavalier tradition" (men who were content to allow Virginia to rest on its slaveholding, agricultural, elitist laurels) and a new generation of men born after 1830 who had limited prospects for becoming landed slaveholders. These men, the last to come of age in a society where slaveholding appeared "to be as permanent a fact as the Rappahannock River," felt their future social, economic, and political power would be derived from individual accomplishment and embracing innovation. They pushed what they viewed as a hopelessly anachronistic society forward with progressive policies that were forward-looking but also still included slavery and white male supremacy as integral to the natural order.[24] Such men decried the fact that Virginia had been allowed to languish, underdeveloped (compared to Northern states), despite their belief that the Commonwealth contained vast natural resources, intellect, and—perhaps the most important asset of all—a generation of ambitious young men who were the natural heirs of the energetic and visionary founders of the United States.[25]

This generation came of age politically when, on the national stage, the antislavery Republican Party emerged from the wreckage of the more moderate Whig Party, which imploded due to intraparty disputes on the divisive subject of admitting new territories to the Union as slave states. The aftermath of that split left a chasm that extremists on both sides of the slavery issue fled to, leading to a sectional crisis. As Peter Carmichael states, "No other period in American history witnessed such political divisiveness or extreme expression of Southernism. It is tempting to assume that the decade of sectionalism weakened the bonds of Union to such an extent that . . . [young white Southern men] had no difficulty imagining an independent Southern nation."[26]

Throughout the 1850s, Upper South states like Maryland, Virginia, North Carolina, and Tennessee, which had close economic ties to the North and were not as dependent upon slave labor as Deep Southern states, were not as easily tugged to the secessionist side of the gulf as their Deep South cousins, whose entire existence was predicated upon plantation agriculture, and therefore upon slavery. Nevertheless, tensions grew between the North and the South and became increasingly more tenuous as every year of that fateful decade passed.

The vitriol and rhetoric of abolitionists in the North irritated and frightened many white Southerners, especially the younger generation, as described by Carmichael:

> When Northern attacks intensified against the South, condemning everything in the region from slavery to speech habits, young Virginians felt an overpowering need to defend Virginia's honor. . . . *Harper's* contributor David H. Strother, a "Virginia Yankee," found the Commonwealth in a shocking state of disrepair. "I have myself considered the Old Virginia people as a decadent race," Strother opined. "They have certainly gone down in manners, morals, and mental capacity. There seems to be nothing left of their traditional greatness but a senseless

pride and a certain mixture of dignity and suavity of manner . . ." Strother predicted that the Civil War would "wipe out this effete race" and give the Old Dominion "a more active and progressive generation." He expressed a basic Northern assumption that Virginia had fallen from national grace and become a decrepit, degenerate place.[27]

Young Virginia men felt—even more so than their elders—under personal attack by a foe determined to emasculate them and destroy the only way of life they had ever known. On the cusp of the 1860 elections, many of the old cavalier generation dug in, determined to hold Virginia to the Union. The younger generation was far more enthusiastic about secession.[28]

As the sectional crisis intensified in the latter years of the 1850s, optimists of every generation remained confident that those holding opposing positions could be brought to reasonable compromise. In Richmond, successful merchants like John Minor Botts, Horace L. Kent, and Jacob Bechtel remained pro-Union men, even as the October 16, 1859, Harpers Ferry raid inspired by John Brown and a small group of coconspirators galvanized extremists on both sides of the slavery question.[29]

While Thomas Norcliffe Jones's business opportunities expanded and his profile as a Richmond merchant waxed large, it is clear by his actions in 1860 and 1861 that he, like many of his middle-class merchant peers in Virginia, saw the raid at Harpers Ferry as a turning point regarding the question of Virginia's secession and the inevitability of Civil War. Unlike many Richmond residents and most native Southerners, Thomas Norcliffe Jones had been to the North.[30] He knew the Northern states were decades ahead of the South in terms of industrial development and infrastructure improvements, such as heavy manufacturing, railroads, canals, and roads. He knew the North possessed a large population that could both finance and provide manpower for a nearly limitless armed force.

For a man who appears at first glance as no more than a petty Richmond shopkeeper, Thomas's business and political associations and the decisions he made in the lead-up to Fort Sumter are remarkable if not downright prescient. Where the less well informed (or at least less well traveled) white Southerner saw an easy victory over perceived Northern tyranny, or those with patriotic and economic ties to the Union saw imminent catastrophe, Thomas saw opportunity. Opportunity must be seized, and in the truest spirit of the shrewd opportunist, Thomas Norcliffe Jones put his effort toward harnessing the rising tide and riding it through the oncoming storm. To do so, he aligned himself with men who possessed inside knowledge of the issues as well as of the decision process while hedging his bets against reversals, which is part and parcel of every successful gambler's plan.

Shifting Political Landscapes / Shifting Political Bedfellows

By 1860 foreign immigrants and Northern transplants composed half of all white workingmen in the city of Richmond. The Constitutional Convention of 1850 brought about important changes in Virginia politics, chief among these being white male suffrage. Every white male in the state who was a citizen could vote after the ratification of the new constitution. This change created a wave of naturalization through Virginia's vast and growing population of immigrants. White male suffrage altered Richmond's political landscape, which played itself out in elections for local offices from mayor to sheriff to county alderman. On the state level, as was observed by Gregg Kimball in *American City, Southern Place*, "although many authors assume the hegemony of Southern (land-owning, slave-owning) elites, workers pushed state leaders like [Joseph] Anderson [of Tredegar Iron Works] and Governor Henry A. Wise toward a conception of politics that included white workingmen."[31]

With this shift of power toward the citizenry and away from the aristocrats who ruled Virginia for two centuries, native-born Virginians of the slave-owning caste bristled. From their perspective, their entire way of life was under assault by a "Yankee" pathogen sweeping into every aspect of Southern life, from fashion to speech patterns, education, and manners, and even in the way Southern merchants eschewed Southern-made goods for items imported from the North.[32] The infection was inflamed by the insults of Northern and Midwestern abolitionists who spared no opportunity to denigrate the South, even as they wore Southern cotton on their backs, drank Southern whiskey, enjoyed their cakes made with Southern sugar, and smoked and chewed Southern-grown and Southern-manufactured tobacco. White Southerners' indignation grew with each perceived insult. And yet the Democratic Party, which enjoyed substantial support among white slaveholding Southerners, developed an antislavery plank that rapidly gained support at the national level.[33]

Pro-slavery progressives, who wanted to see Virginia move forward into the modern era in regard to industry, trade, and investment in infrastructure, turned toward a tactic that promised—at the very least—to inspire a great deal of controversy and debate among members of the increasingly influential merchant class, who were inexorably bound to slavery for their livelihoods.[34] The Central Southern Rights Association of Virginia was born with a manifesto laying bare, in a manner similar to the Declaration of Independence, all the ways that the North had violated Southern rights, taxing the South beyond the bounds of equity and extending its vast patronage to foreign powers while denying the South its financial due. It then laid a series of challenges to all white Southerners to prove their loyalty and their very *Southernness* by severing economic ties with the North, investing instead in Southern industry, infrastructure, and ingenuity.[35]

At some point not long after its organization in 1851, Thomas Norcliffe Jones became affiliated with the Central Southern Rights Association of Virginia. By 1860 Jones, who was essentially an outsider among this group of Virginia insiders, climbed to the executive committee;[36] therefore, it is to be assumed that his tenure with this body was a lengthy and deliberate one.

The Central Southern Rights Association sought to strengthen ties between merchants and planters and to motivate both merchants and their fellow industrialists to forge stronger relations with the city's working classes and tradesmen against the threats of an empowered black working class as envisioned by the Northern abolitionists. Industrialists like Tredegar Iron Works' Joseph R. Anderson had good reason to want to convert their largely immigrant workforce into a body that more closely identified members' interests with management's interests (and therefore Richmond's interests), rather than self-interest and the prospect of organized trade-unionism, which threatened owners' ability to effectively control their own workforce.[37]

Scholars have proposed that the goal of the Central Southern Rights Association of Virginia was to stay in the Union, if that was possible, and if not, to lay the groundwork for a sustainable, slaveholding South following peaceful secession. While there is ample evidence to support this theory, particularly early in the organization's incarnation, one only needs to consider the members of the 1860 executive committee to see that many (though not all) of these men were agitating aggressively for secession and war.

In order to establish where Thomas Norcliffe Jones stood politically and ideologically in the face of these shifts, we must look first at the company he kept and at the decisions he made. Among the men he was most closely aligned with—if not socially, then certainly economically and politically— were his fellow executive committee members on the Central Southern Rights Association of Virginia.

Daniel H. London was a fabric merchant in Richmond and an ardent secessionist, who since the early 1850s actively courted foreign commerce into Southern ports in defiance of United States trade policy. On January 5, 1860, he appeared before the Virginia House of Delegates, delivering a speech prepared by the Central Southern Rights Association of Virginia, promoting Southern independence from the Union.[38]

Horace L. Kent was a native of Connecticut who became a successful Richmond merchant, cofounding the firm Kent, Payne and Company. He was active in Richmond politics and civic life, including becoming a principal in the development of Hollywood Cemetery in the 1850s. He was an economic progressive and a dedicated Unionist until the assault on Fort Sumter forced him to take sides. He reluctantly chose secession, but even so, many hard-core Confederates leveled accusations at him, questioning his loyalty to the Confederate cause.[39]

Charles Y. Morriss was half-owner of the Tredegar Roller Mill in the 1850s and a sugar mill operator in Richmond. During the Civil War, a great portion of Morriss's considerable wealth flowed from contracts with the Confederate War Department. He was a quiet secessionist who was moved by the events at Harpers Ferry to choose sides, casting his lot with the rebellion.[40]

Joseph H. Crenshaw owned the Spotswood Hotel in Richmond. Through family connections he maintained business and investment interests on a global scale. He was the brother of Lewis D. Crenshaw, a wealthy flour merchant with Haxall, Crenshaw and Company (the largest flour milling operation in North America, and arguably the largest in the world at the time), and William Graves Crenshaw, one of Virginia's wealthiest shipping, import, and export merchants, who owned a fleet of ships and maintained business and financial interests all over the world.[41] During the war William Graves Crenshaw became one of the most successful blockade-runners operating for the Confederacy. Both he and his brother Joseph were pro-secessionists prior to the war. Both men risked and lost a large portion of their personal fortunes in support of the Confederate cause, only to reconstitute their immense wealth working between New York and England in the years following the war.[42]

Charles Dimmock, born in Massachusetts and educated at West Point, was a career U.S. Army officer. Today he is best known for constructing the "Dimmock Line" of defensive earthworks around besieged Petersburg, Virginia. In 1860 he was captain of the Virginia Public Guard, a distinguished position in prewar Virginia. After Harpers Ferry, he was a secessionist who wholeheartedly supported rebellion.[43]

George W. Gilliam was a prominent tobacconist in Richmond, a partner in the firm Gilliam and Matthews. He was also a slave owner who, in 1854, had a slave who was involved in an "Underground Railroad" operation at Rocketts, smuggling fugitive slaves onboard Northern-owned ships to be spirited away to ports above the Mason-Dixon Line. The case became a high-profile news story in Richmond, causing much irritation at abolitionist ship owners and captains who flagrantly defied Virginia law, using the city's ports to encourage runaways and insurrection.[44] Gilliam was active in Richmond politics throughout the 1850s and early 1860s. He became a Confederate soldier once the war began.

William B. Newton owned Summer Hill plantation near Richmond. He was a slave owner and a member of one of Virginia's most eminent families. He was a Democrat, elected to Congress in 1859, and a vociferous writer of proslavery, pro–states' rights, pro-secessionist material. His works often appeared in the *Richmond Examiner* under the pseudonym "Virginius."[45]

Charles T. Wortham, proprietor of C. T. Wortham and Company and the Charles T. Wortham Forwarding and Commission Merchant / Auctioneer, was a prominent Richmond slave trader, a Freemason, and a member of the Southern Baptist Convention Foreign Mission Board. He was a pro–states' rights secessionist whose entire livelihood depended upon the continuation of slavery, with the hope of expansion of the practice into new U.S. territories and Central American regions under the influence of the United States.[46]

William F. Ritchie was a printer and publisher in Richmond who served as the public printer for the state of Virginia. His father, Thomas Ritchie, founded the oldest newspaper in Richmond, the *Enquirer*, for which his son William served as editor for a period. The *Enquirer* was renowned for its "restrained and balanced" reporting, earning a reputation as the "Democratic Bible."[47] While the paper gradually turned pro-secession under the editorial leadership of O. Jennings Wise (son of former Democratic Virginia governor Henry A. Wise), William F. Ritchie maintained a political middle ground until the raid at Harpers Ferry.[48]

Lewis Edwin Harvie was an ardent secessionist and Virginia state senator who introduced the first bill of secession in the Virginia state legislature.[49]

Edward Fontaine was the superintendent of the Virginia Central Railroad and from a wealthy plantation family with properties located near Beaver Dam, Virginia. He was the first great-grandson of Revolutionary War hero Patrick Henry and a close friend of the J. E. B. Stuart family. He personally delivered the news of Stuart's mortal wounding to the general's wife, who resided with the Fontaine family during the war. He was an ardent, early secessionist and dedicated Confederate.[50]

In terms of social and political influence and general dedication to the slave-based economy of Richmond, these men represented the ideal of what a "true Virginian" ought to be: civic-minded and, above all, wealthy. This was not trifling company for a recent immigrant and shopkeeper like Thomas Norcliffe Jones. These associations show Jones to be a shrewd operator in the complex world of Richmond's political and social relations. His association with men of rank and wealth, with connections far outside Richmond, would prove instrumental both financially and personally as the war commenced. The fact that an immigrant—with no prior connections and little start-up money when he arrived in 1830—had climbed the social and economic ladder to this height by 1860 is demonstrative of Thomas's remarkable intelligence and talent, as well as his ambition.

What is interesting to note, in contrast to this association, is that at the same time Thomas Norcliffe Jones put himself on record as supporting complete Southern independence, eschewing the import of goods from Northern ports and encouraging investment in a sustainable, slave-based Southern economy, there is strong evidence that he was engaged in purchasing large quantities of imported goods and warehousing them outside the South, ostensibly for the purpose of enjoying large profits if and when the Confederacy failed to emerge victorious from the inevitable devastation of war. Jones was not alone in this sort of double-dealing; it was common among merchants, bankers, and industrialists on both sides of the Mason-Dixon Line. In the South, however, and particularly in Richmond, among the average citizens who were generally unaware of the conspiratorial machinations going on behind the scenes, hypocrisy of this sort was viewed as loathsome and dishonorable, especially once the war began and deprivation set in.

Thomas's motivations are clear enough. His goal was to survive whatever came with his financial footing intact and with profitable connections on whichever side of the battle line emerged victorious.

4. ❈ A True Virginian

It might have been the stones in his pockets. Not pebbles, but stones—fist-sized, sharp-edged, suitable only as projectiles. They had the look of objects shaped by the imaginations of warlike men—or the unruly, vagabond boys of Richmond who regularly assembled in empty lots and at the bottom of the city's worst neighborhoods. There in the muck, Richmond's boys clashed in ferocious battles verging upon the medieval. The local newspapers were filled with their violence, these gangs of unsupervised boys who roamed the city looking for mischief, finding fights, stealing from defenseless women and sassing grown men. These youthful gangs advertised names like the Hill Cats, the Basin Cats, the Union Hill Boys, the Church Hill Boys, and the Butchertown Cats.[1] They were a plague on the city's decent people and an embarrassment to their families, as it became ever more notoriously reported that white boys from otherwise good backgrounds brawled in the trash heaps of Shockoe Valley, scrumming in the filth like savages.

It might have been the stones. It might have been something else. Whatever it was that convinced Thomas Norcliffe Jones that his son's idle childhood was over, the decision was a profound one that would forever alter the course of William's life.

You may think that a self-made man who had grown wealthy in the span of just a few years would admire the bravery and pluck of a small boy willing to skirmish with rough, streetwise orphans who fancied themselves the Basin Cats. Was Thomas proud that his son stood tall with the aristocratic Church Hill Boys, looking down his nose at the Butchertown Cats, boys who fought dirty and swore like their swarthy fathers did on Saturday nights, after the taverns turned them out in tumbling scuffles, reeking of mud and offal, to blindly feel their way back to shacks stacked on the boiling streets in the gut of Shockoe Bottom?

Maybe he admired his son's pluck. Perhaps he also understood that even as these boys played and fought, young William was his only son, his only surviving child. Thomas was not having it. His son was not going the way of the savage or to the grave as a result of childish pranks. William was destined to work in the family business—not his father's commission merchant establishment—following in the footsteps of his cousins, uncles, and grandfather. He was going to become a printer.

William H. Clemmitt's new printing office was located in the heart of Richmond's Shockoe business district, down the street from the venerable old capitol building, on Printers' Row. Clemmitt's professional life as a printer began early in Richmond. He was apprenticed at ten years of age, learning the trade from the floor sweepings to the binding press.[2] In 1844, at just twenty-one years old, he went to work at the *Richmond Whig* under John Hampdon Pleasants, a social progressive who wrote disparagingly in his paper about the institution of slavery, in support of a public school system, and in support of both white male and white female suffrage.[3] Pleasants was a cornerstone of early Richmond society, a man who took ideas seriously and believed in the obligation of civic engagement. He was a shrewd journalist who understood that controversy cloaked as editorial or genuine reporting is what sold newspapers. He cultivated a reputation as a gentleman and a scholar who just happened to be a successful businessman.

While at the *Whig*, Clemmitt undoubtedly came into close contact with many of Richmond's merchant, political, and social elite. While he was born and bred a Virginian and grew up in the employ of one of Virginia's premier citizens, Clemmitt was no aristocrat. He started out life as a child of the lower working class, a social designation he never shrugged off or tried to climb above. Throughout his long life, Clemmitt managed to maintain an air of political neutrality, a skill that served him well in the turbulent 1850s. In 1854, Clemmitt, with two other partners, went into business for himself.[4] His first apprentice was William Ellis Jones.[5]

How Thomas Norcliffe Jones managed to secure for his son what would have been a valuable apprenticeship with Richmond's newest, best-connected printing and publishing firm is a mystery. As one of Richmond's up-and-coming commission merchants, Thomas frequented the offices of the *Whig* and the city's other newspapers regularly, placing advertisements for his wholesale wares—everything from sides of beef offered by the ton to barrels of fine wines and spirits imported from Europe and the Caribbean.[6] He and Clemmitt certainly knew one another, but how well is a matter of speculation. What is certain is the two men had one thing in common: by early training, Thomas Norcliffe Jones and William H. Clemmitt were both printers. Jones may have purchased the apprenticeship for his son with a promise of a certain amount of business trade, or perhaps even a cash payment. It is impossible to know.

What probably puzzled Clemmitt is why Jones did not put his son to work in his own firm, bringing him up to take over the commission mercantile operation the boy should one day inherit. Perhaps it was the nature of his work, which took Thomas Jones frequently to the North and even occasionally beyond America's ports. Perhaps Jones did not feel comfortable taking William abroad. As a commission merchant, following in a father's footsteps and with the right training, a young man might become extremely wealthy. There was no great wealth to be made in printing broadsides or books.

Was this decision a purely sentimental one? The decision to apprentice William to a printer made little sense beyond the sentimental, unless Thomas Norcliffe Jones never intended to bequeath his mercantile operation, with its lucrative import business, to his son.

Clemmitt took William Ellis Jones under his wing and made of him an excellent apprentice. William learned fast and worked hard, swiftly mastering the basics of the craft. Clemmitt may have found that his charge responded well to an approving hand on his shoulder and a warm compliment sincerely delivered. Yet he was just a boy. Sometimes he scurried out with his friends at quitting time, a lightness in his step and an air of adventure about him.

Was it the stones in his pockets that made him light? William, Robert Brock, Ned Valentine, Edgar Smith, and a handful of other boys, all of whom were bitten hard by the collecting bug, scoured the creek beds and the exposed mud walls of Richmond's labyrinth of eroded gullies for relics of Powhatan's warriors. William came back with pockets full of arrowheads and broken ax blades. He proudly displayed them on the window ledges of the printshop like treasures. Richmond's boys, at least the bright ones with brains brimming with curiosity and imagination, had for generations made "Indian archaeology" an early profession. Richmond's boys—the best kind—knew how to spend their idle time after the work was done.[7]

As the boys matured, so did their interests. Ned Valentine continued with his formal education, but instead of studying stones, he took up the study of the human figure and fine art. Robert Brock, like his friend William, was compelled by necessity to go to work. Brock was sent to his uncle's lumber business and taught the trade everyone assumed he would follow the rest of his life. As soon as the whistle blew at the end of the day's work, young Brock made his way downtown, where he and William poured themselves into their next—and as it turned out, lifelong—passion. Clemmitt often found the two youngsters sitting quietly in the storage room, studying among the many printed items lining the warehouse shelves. Overruns and back stock of pamphlets and books filled carefully marked and ordered boxes. The warehouse contained copies of almost every book, broadside, and pamphlet produced since Clemmitt first opened the doors of his own establishment. It was quite a library for two young minds to absorb, but they gave it their best effort. Like printer's ink, books were also in William's blood. His father brought a substantial library with him from Wales, and the boys readily devoured its contents.[8]

Thomas Norcliffe Jones's business took him frequently to New York and as frequently downriver to the Chesapeake region, where he enjoyed access to the full variety of imports arriving daily from all over the world. In 1856, at about fifty-five years old and possibly hoping to curtail some of his travels, Thomas took on a new business partner, twenty-nine-year-old William B. Jones from Wales, the son of his cousin Lewis Evan Jones Sr.[9]

William B. Jones appeared even more ambitious and determined to succeed in the mercantile business than his sponsor and partner. Rather than renting rooms, taking a house of his own, or even residing at the Jones residence on 2nd Street, William B. Jones moved into the Thomas Norcliffe Jones and Company warehouse at 30 Main Street.[10] The arrival of this cousin seemed to guarantee that William, Thomas's son, would have little to no involvement in the company his father founded, a fact that was almost unheard of among the city's merchant class who, to a man, groomed their sons to take over hard-fought-for family businesses.

William B. Jones cut a striking figure around Richmond; he was a tall, handsome young man who dressed stylishly and carried himself with pride. His early business success should have guaranteed his acceptance into Richmond's largely immigrant merchant class. One would assume that many young ladies of that society sought to catch his eye. It is possible that Jones was more focused on business than developing social contacts, or perhaps upon closer inspection the young ladies of Richmond might have found his manner aloof or disinterested. For whatever reason, William B. Jones remained a bachelor who devoted himself entirely to commercial interests. He rarely engaged himself in social activities, which is notably odd behavior for a young man of means in antebellum Richmond.[11]

Thomas Norcliffe Jones used the newfound freedom that having a young, energetic business partner offered him. He turned a portion of his attention to matters at least as important as commerce—politics. Along with his activities with the Central Southern Rights Association, Thomas became involved with the local Democratic Party.[12]

While Thomas Norcliffe Jones split his time between business and politics and William B. Jones traveled and worked at expanding Thomas Norcliffe Jones and Company into one of the largest and most successful commission merchants in Richmond, William Ellis Jones spent his teens honing his skills as a printer while forging friendships and social relationships that would carry him through the most trying years of his life. William spent six days a week at Clemmitt's printing shop in an environment infused with the scent of black ink that stained his fingers as he worked. William learned to read backwards and to compose clean, careful, well-set prose from unedited handwritten manuscripts, and to do so fast and error-free.

Unlike his father or single-minded cousin, William was not the sort who focused exclusively on work. He loved books and reading, and he saved his money to acquire new volumes, beginning in his late teens to build the foundation of a library that in the decades to come would become the envy of his peers. Equal to his passion for books was his fondness and deeply ingrained loyalty toward his friends.

While Thomas Norcliffe Jones worked to align himself politically with Richmond's elite, he may have observed that his son naturally cultivated a circle of friends from that class, based not on money or quid-pro-quo politics but on genuine affection. By his early twenties William's dearest friends were still Robert Alonzo Brock, Ned Valentine, and Edgar Alonza Smith. They must have cut a gallant entrance at many of Richmond's public balls and private parties. William may have been the son of an immigrant, but in his heart and in his head, he was a true Virginian and made in the same mold as others of his class and generation. He was hardworking, devout, educated, and curious. He was also, like many other young white males of his generation and class, impatient, often disrespectful of authority, ambitious, and occasionally arrogant.[13]

His father and cousin were recognized as successful businessmen whose commercial and political connections could not be overlooked, but they possessed the sharp manner and accent of foreigners. William's accent, by contrast, was that of the cultivated young gentleman, and his manners reflected the genteel bearing of a native Virginian. William distinguished himself from his relations even in the area of religious denominational preference. When his father attended church (irregularly), it was the Duvall Street Presbyterian assembly he visited, probably because it was the church most convenient to his Duvall Street home.[14] William attended regular Sunday services at St. James's

Episcopal Church in the company of his friend Edgar Smith and family.[15] The credit here likely goes to Edgar's younger sister Florence, for whom William developed an early fondness.

While many of the young men of Richmond joined one or another of the city's militias, donning uniforms and parading around the Capitol Square demonstrating their manly affectations of patriotism, these four gathered together to trade books and discuss history, exchanging their thoughts on politics and religion, Virginia's place in the Union, and the Union itself. They assuredly participated in raucous debates, but it seems unlikely they allowed disagreements on politics to get in the way of their friendship. These four young men found camaraderie not in a uniform or under a flag but between the pages of shared books and in the open debate and discussion of ideas.

They were naive, young, and idealistic. They all had enough money and social status to live comfortably among Richmond's upper-middle classes. The world, so far as they knew it, was their oyster. The year 1859 was the year these headstrong, swaggering young Virginians began the difficult march-step into manhood and into a history that would rip their comfort to shreds, turning their world on its head.

William was perhaps the first to taste the bitterness of disillusionment that often initiates one into adulthood. On June 1, 1859, his mother, Margaret White Jones, died. He was twenty-one years old. She was just fifty-three. Years later he would recall her to his grandson as a patient, sweet-tempered woman who endured a great deal of disappointment in her life but who never complained and who never failed to show her love and affection for her only surviving child. She believed in a benevolent God and transferred that belief to her son, not knowing that his faith would one day be tested more profoundly than she might ever have imagined or that the faith she gave him would carry him forward when everything else around him shattered.[16]

The most profound bitterness of this loss arrived within days of Margaret's death, when William had to confront the painful truth about his father's cool ambition. There was no period of mourning. There was nothing decent or proper in the way Margaret's memory was honored. Thomas Norcliffe Jones placed a one-line announcement in the *Richmond Daily Dispatch* on the day after her death, advertising her bare-bones funeral at the Duvall Street church.[17] Seven days later he placed a second advertisement, announcing the auction of every single possession she and the small family had acquired over the years for the comfort of their tidy home: "Genteel Household Furniture at Auction. On Monday, 13th inst, at 10 o'clock. I will sell at the residence of Mr. Thomas Jones on 2d near Duvall street. All his household Furniture, embracing the usual variety of well-kept articles. At the same time will be sold, one negro Woman who is a good Washer, Ironer, and Cook. Said slave to remain in the city . . ."[18] Even Margaret's house slave was auctioned off like a piece of worn furniture.

The only home William had ever known was broken up like so much merchandise to be liquidated within days of his mother's death. William's boyhood roots on Duvall Street were severed as his mother's china, crystal, and dining room table were carted off by strangers. Margaret's cook was taken away to work for another family.

The truth of the matter was revealed: Thomas Norcliffe Jones intended to remarry as quickly as possible, propriety be damned.[19]

William's mother was dead but not yet cool in her grave, and his father was about to marry someone he had kept hidden away for who knew how long and who knew where. The blow must have been crushing. More than that, though, the realization that all his youthful assumptions were completely false may have called every other notion he held sacrosanct into equal question.

William packed his few possessions—his books, his clothes—and headed to the safest place he knew: William H. Clemmitt's printshop, down the street from the capitol on Shockoe Hill. There in the familiar comfort of the printing company, he might have taken a few moments to meditate upon the collection of sharp stones still neatly arranged on the windowsills. Those stones, which once filled his pockets and his imagination, may have given him some measure of solace.

As political tensions throughout the South grew more inflamed with each passing week, Thomas Norcliffe Jones divested himself of his real estate holdings throughout Richmond.[20] During those months, states in the Deep South began to talk of seceding from the Union, while an undercurrent of anti-Northern sentiment boiled to the top of street corner conversations and congressional debates. Throughout Virginia, and in Richmond in particular, there remained a solid belief that the talk was all hotheaded rhetoric and cooler heads would prevail once everyone came to realize what an absolute economic calamity disunion—not to mention a war—would bring to the South.

In Richmond, conservative governor Henry A. Wise and pro-Union politician John Minor Botts took potshots at one another in the newspapers and from the lectern, while the conservative proslavery elites in Virginia tried to consolidate the immigrant, working-class citizenry along racial lines, thereby bringing them into the secessionist fold.[21] All over Richmond, people gradually began to see the writing on the wall. Some welcomed the prospect of secession and even war, believing it when politicians told them the South would sweep over Washington, DC, in weeks or months. Others quietly packed up, closed their houses and businesses, and left town, departing to the homes of friends and family in Maryland, Philadelphia, and New York to wait out what they hoped would be a short conflict. Some, like the Crenshaws, who owned and operated a massive, loosely affiliated collection of flour mills, textile mills, and shipping interests, with tentacles reaching all over the world, quietly sent vast quantities of tobacco, textiles, cash, and other goods to warehouses in the North, to England, and to the Caribbean for safekeeping until the situation was ultimately resolved.[22] And some did nothing, thinking that nothing would come of all the talk.

Ned Valentine's parents, who were conservative and wealthy and who stood among the city's most respected old families, quietly sent their son to study abroad in Europe—indefinitely. Ned left Richmond in 1859 and did not return to the city until after the conclusion of the Civil War.[23] Among William's closest friends, Ned Valentine was the only one who never tasted the bloody bitterness of the Civil War. Years later Ned tried to make his amends, but his avoidance of the conflict must have haunted him for the rest of his life; his life's work stands as testament to that claim. Ned Valentine is best known today for his fantastic busts and life-size sculptures of the Confederate army's most eminent officers, including the stunning sculpture *Recumbent Statue of Lee*, which rests in the Lee Chapel of Washington and Lee University.

In those final days before John Brown's raid on Harpers Ferry, William Ellis Jones and Robert Brock went to work every morning and watched the militia parades in the evening. Both young men paid close attention to the speeches and searing newspaper headlines that ever more divisively debated the issue of whether (and how) to preserve the Union or leave it under a flag of rebellion.

Robert Brock and Edgar Smith, like many young men in Richmond's upper-middle classes, vowed that if Virginia seceded and war came, they would join the army immediately. William was more reticent. Perhaps it was the moderating influence of William Clemmitt and the work at the print-shop that cooled William's ardor for battle. In 1860, Clemmitt bought out his original business partners, leaving just himself and William to run the place. William's primary responsibility was as journeyman printer, overseeing several compositors, a pressman, a binder, and one or two apprentices. Clemmitt oversaw it all while handling the main office work of securing new projects, estimating, billing, and payroll. There was plenty of work to go around. Between broadside announcements of slave auctions (a mainstay of every job printer in town) and pamphlet reprints of popular political speeches, along with all the regular subscription, commercial, and agricultural work, they likely had more than they could keep up with. Despite the workload, Clemmitt did not contemplate hiring more men or adding another press. He had never seen a war before, but the air smelled of something foul. He paid his bills and began stockpiling paper, ink, glue, and tooling for his presses.[24]

Thomas Norcliffe Jones spent more time abroad, presumably making his own wartime preparations. Curiously, despite remarrying shortly after the death of his wife Margaret, his new wife never appeared in Richmond. Thomas stopped placing advertisements for wholesale goods in the papers and issued a notice of cessation of business in March 1862 (the same month his son joined the Confederate army).[25] He filled his company's warehouse at 8 Main Street with commodities that would be easy to liquidate if war came to the city. When Thomas Norcliffe Jones was in Richmond, his primary professional focus appeared to be devoted to political rather than commercial endeavors.

It is worth restating that among the white working classes of Richmond in the years and months leading up to the war, the prevailing sentiment was with the Union rather than the secessionists. Workingmen and tradesmen had little in common with wealthy slave owners and every economic incentive to eliminate the slave labor system, which depressed their wages. The working classes acquiesced to the Confederate cause only when their emotions were struck by the events of Harpers Ferry; by the fiery speeches of Henry A. Wise, which elevated workingmen above the dehumanized ranks of the black population; and by the opening shots of the war fired upon Fort Sumter. After Fort Sumter, every Virginia university, street corner, and mill shop floor was suddenly rife with ardent secessionists, young men chomping at the bit to get to war, as if they had an inkling what war really meant.[26]

Robert Alonzo Brock joined the ranks of the Confederate cause as soon as Virginia seceded, enlisting in Company F, 21st Regiment, Virginia Infantry.[27] This regiment is notable as it was the home regiment of some of Virginia's earliest volunteers from established Virginia families.[28] Edgar Alonza Smith joined the 41st Regiment of the Virginia Infantry as a sergeant.[29] Interestingly, neither of these young men saw much in the way of direct violence, as both were reassigned to less hazardous duties after the First Battle of Manassas.[30] Meanwhile, William remained in Richmond, still working for Clemmitt, still holding out for a quick conclusion to the conflict.

While William Ellis Jones waited and watched the developments of the earliest parts of the Civil War unfold, the Thomas Norcliffe Jones and Company partnership between his father and William B. Jones was legally, if not materially, dissolved.[31] William B. Jones quickly became his own corporate entity operating under the moniker "William B. Jones & Company."[32] The purpose of this disunion is unclear, except perhaps as a legal maneuver to protect each party in the event of one or the other's capture by Union forces or ultimate demise. After 1865, research reveals that the two men still operated very much in unison in at least some of their business dealings. Once the war came, William B. Jones showed himself as a brilliant operative in the world of wartime procurement, blockade-running, and war profiteering. Utilizing high-level connections most likely facilitated by Thomas Norcliffe Jones and relations back in England and Wales, he served the Confederate War Department as a principal supplier and was assigned to the important position of Confederate mail carrier between Fredericksburg and Brunswick Hall, near Lawrenceville, Virginia (close to the North Carolina border).[33]

William B. Jones obtained and stockpiled supplies, selling them to the public only when prices reached an irresistible apex or when political expediency demanded it. He made money by selling wholesale goods in bulk quantities into an inflationary market. His principal products were cigars and tobacco, alcohol, and sugar, all hard-to-come-by luxuries in Richmond's spiraling wartime economy. He had many buyers, most bearing Confederate dollars. His largest customer was the Confederate War Department. His warehouses were occasionally broken into, and the newspapers of that era advertise court cases where he prosecuted thieves.[34] Through a couple of revealing notices placed in the *Richmond Daily Dispatch*, we also catch a glimpse of the brash young man who, during the war years, built the largest wholesale mercantile supply business in Richmond and who was recognized as having become one of the wealthiest men of that city.[35] One of the advertisements read, "Substitute Wanted—A liberal price will be paid for a SUBSTITUTE. He will have the privilege of joining any company he may wish. Apply to Wm. B. Jones, 15th st. betw. Main and Cary."[36]

The "substitute" William B. Jones sought was someone willing to join the Confederate army in his place. This was legal in the era, and many wealthy young men paid others to serve in their stead. This advertisement was placed on September 2, 1862, just after the Confederate Conscription Act was passed and about to go into effect. The line in the advertisement "He will have the privilege of joining any company he may wish" indicated that not only was

William B. Jones willing to generously pay his substitute, but also he was willing to pay off the commanding officer of the selected unit to secure a place for that substitute, regardless of the unit's requirements. This too was common in the era, causing substantial problems for the Confederate army in the area of personnel placement. Some prestige or low-risk units were overmanned and underequipped, stuffed with socially well-connected volunteers and substitutes, while many infantry units ran short of qualified, willing recruits.

A second and equally revealing advertisement of a somewhat later period read, "Twenty Dollars Reward—Lost on Main Street, between Fourth and Custom-house, a Link Button, set with a carbuncle in Etruscan gold, with a linen cuff. The finder will be liberally rewarded by leaving it at William B. Jones & Co's. Fifteenth Street."[37]

A "carbuncle in Etruscan gold" refers to an unusually large piece of revival-style jewelry, often gaudy in size and ornamentation, fashionable in the Victorian period. This advertisement was placed on November 30, 1864, when even Richmond's best families suffered on the brink of starvation, walking shoeless, breaking up heirloom furniture for the hearth to keep their children warm. It is difficult to imagine the callous degree of privilege the author of this advertisement maintained in the face of so much deprivation and suffering in his midst.

William B. Jones cast his lot squarely with the war profiteers who made fortunes while hundreds of thousands of soldiers died and millions more citizens of Virginia and the Confederacy suffered grave shortages of basic essentials. During the worst period of Richmond's wartime deprivations, Jones ran ads in the *Daily Dispatch* advertising everything from cotton sheeting and cognac to "very fine whiskey," cigars, tobacco, and flour (a particularly hard-to-come-by commodity in a city made famous for its wartime bread riots). A postwar news article described William B. Jones's operation as "the largest wholesale grocer in the city at the time."[38] In addition to his wholesale grocery business and the import business he operated throughout the war, there is also evidence that Thomas Norcliffe Jones and William B. Jones co-owned a tobacco manufacturing company in Richmond, as well as a distillery for the production of domestic whiskey.[39]

What this background on Thomas Norcliffe Jones and William B. Jones establishes is that William Ellis Jones was, at least by 1862, from a family that had quickly developed significant financial resources, if not an established Old Dominion reputation. The family's newly acquired wealth and his father's business and political connections almost certainly factored into some of William's decisions and his behavior early in the war years. William was, in the parlance of the Southern aristocracy, "nouveau riche," and he often behaved more like an entitled brat than the Christian gentleman he imagined himself to be.

The war, however, had plans for remolding William's self-image, reforging the character of an entire generation of young white Southern men, and forever altering the city of Richmond, as well as the whole nation. The lessons would be painful; the scars, everlasting.

5. ❊ Prelude to War

William Ellis Jones didn't sign up to join the Confederate army in April 1861, when the war opened at Fort Sumter, South Carolina. He didn't sign up when Virginia finally voted to secede from the Union in May of the same year. He didn't sign up after the First Battle of Manassas in July 1861, which all the papers declared was the beginning of the end for the Union, causing another wave of volunteers to pour into the Confederate ranks. He didn't sign up as Virginia's politicians and preachers began riling up their constituents at the capital, in church services, and in the papers, crowing about cowards and Union sympathizers. He signed up only when they started talking about conscription[1] and talking about hanging people.[2]

In his fascinating and comprehensively researched book *Reluctant Rebels*, Kenneth Noe examines the motivations of soldiers like William who didn't automatically follow the drumbeat to war in 1861, when roughly half of all the men who would ever serve in the ranks of the Confederate forces rushed in headlong to enthusiastically volunteer.[3] William never expressly discloses in his diary why he remained outside the Confederate ranks for so long.

We know through sentiments revealed by William in his diary that he was no ardent abolitionist. Like most young men of his class from Richmond, William accepted slavery and white supremacy as a fact of life; therefore, it is a safe assumption that William was not laying out of the army on ideological or political grounds.[4] Noe found that some of the reasons given by late enlistees, conscripts, and substitutes for avoiding or delaying service included being too young to enlist, having wives and small children to care for, or having farms to run or businesses to manage. William had none of these excuses. His diary reveals almost nothing on the subject, but it is possible to speculate on one cause for his hesitation based upon a few diary entries and an event that took place just after the war's conclusion.

William likely wanted to stay in Richmond and out of the army because he was in love. Miss Florence Smith was his object, and William took every opportunity to be near her after he was in the army. Just months after the war's conclusion, on December 13, 1865, William and Florence were married, despite the fact that their city was economically devastated, he was unemployed, and both of their families were financially ruined. It must have been love; little else can explain either his reluctance to join up or the couple's rush to wed before it was sensible to do so.

Once William did join the ranks of the Confederates, we must ask—given his initial reluctance—what kept him in service? The diary itself reveals the answer, addressed at length in chapter 7.

***

Private Charles P. Young remembered the day he and William joined the Confederate cause:

> On Friday, March 14, 1862, there assembled at the wholesale warehouse of Messrs. Crenshaw & Co., on the Basin bank, between Tenth and Eleventh streets, Richmond, Va., one of the jolliest, most rollicking, fun-loving crowd of youngsters, between the ages of 16 and 25, that were ever thrown together haphazard, composed of clerks, book-keepers, salesmen, compositors, with a small sprinkling of solid business men, from Richmond, reinforced with as sturdy-looking a lot of farmer boys from the counties of Orange, Louisa, Spotsylvania and Culpeper as one generally comes across.[5]

What a happy lot! *Except,* these recollections were penned by an old man for a Civil War historical journal forty years after the war ended.

Peter Carmichael, in his 1990 work, *The Purcell, Crenshaw and Letcher Artillery*, has provided an excellent resource to mine for a more comprehensive understanding of the men who mustered with Crenshaw's Battery on that day in March. Based on his research, we can glean an idea of who these men were and how much William had in common with them. Excluding the farmers and farm laborers, the most common profession among the group of occupations is printer (or worker in the printing trade) in the city of Richmond (nine in total). Following that, there are clerks (seven), skilled craftsmen and machinists (six), and merchants (six), followed by a salesman, a physician, a druggist, a dentist, and a student. These were reasonably well-educated, skilled young men, most of whom worked in downtown Richmond. Nine of them shared William's profession. They were his neighbors, coworkers, and friends.

What was convenient for William Ellis Jones and his peers working on Shockoe Hill was that William Graves Crenshaw (one of Richmond's wealthiest and most successful merchants and a man with whom Thomas Norcliffe Jones and William B. Jones had financial ties) entered the fray, obligating his own resources to finance, equip, and man an artillery unit comprising young men from Richmond's merchant and trade classes. A generation of young men who had come into the skilled trades in Richmond together were organized as a military unit. They would remain together, barring illness, injury, or death, until the bitter end.

In March 1862, Richmond was on war footing and on edge. Soldiers from all over the Confederacy poured into town, filling its hotels, spilling onto the streets, making the new fairgrounds and the various army camps around the city look like home base for the occupation force it actually was. The whole character of Richmond changed. Upon becoming the capital city of the Confederacy, it was transformed into a fortress, encircled and invaded by an ever-growing army of green recruits and their arms. Instead of speculating about rumors (a preoccupation in that town since the Nat Turner uprising in 1831), the city dealt with true crime: home invasions, petty theft, prostitution, stabbings, and murders all committed on once-tranquil residential streets. Secession and the Confederate army brought perdition to Richmond.[6]

William's Civil War diary reveals a conflicted character if one examines its author through the lens of the time and his position as a rank soldier, when to express clear opposition to the direction and leadership of the Confederate army was regarded as an act of insubordination. To discern William's truest feelings, we must consider his actions, his interactions, and his relationships with the people who stood to gain the most by a Confederate victory. We also need to consider what he chose to record in his diary over those nine short months of 1862, as well as what he left out.

As example, the following is the first substantive entry William wrote.

> Saturday, May 3, 1862
> . . . nothing transpired of an exciting nature except the hanging of a spy by the name of Webster on Tuesday 29th of April.

The Richmond papers carried detailed accounts of the event.[7] The diary continues:

> Never in my life did I ever see men so eager to witness a performance of any kind as they were to see this man launched into

eternity with all his sins upon his soul. It is a sad commentary
. . . that we would rather see such revolting sights than to go and
hear the Word of God from some devout minister.

Note that William capitalizes "Word of God." He is disturbed by his fellow Virginians' enjoyment of the exhibition—the suffering of a human being played out as something approaching entertainment. Contrary to the arch-Confederates who saw this performance as an act of religious obedience—carrying out God's will—William saw the act as shameful.[8]

"He was the first spy I ever saw hang and do not wish to see another," William states. Timothy Webster was the first spy hanged in the Confederacy. He would not be the last. Nor was his execution the last William would witness while in service to the Confederacy. There was more to come concerning how this war was conducted that William Ellis Jones would ultimately take issue with. Nevertheless, his loyalties to Virginia and the Confederacy remained steadfast, even while loyalty to his commanding officers wavered as his first year of service unfolded.

William B. Jones, Richmond merchant, mail agent, and alcohol and sugar supplier for the Confederate War Department. He became one of the wealthiest men in Richmond during the Civil War as a result of speculation and strategic stockpiling of scarce commodities. *Image courtesy of Virginia Lee Warden Minton.*

Civil War diarist William Ellis Jones. This photograph was captured early in the twentieth century, toward the end of his life. *Image courtesy of Virginia Lee Warden Minton.*

Robert Alonzo Brock, a lifelong friend of and longtime collaborator with William Ellis Jones, served as corresponding secretary of the Virginia Historical Society from 1875 through 1893, secretary to the Southern Historical Society from 1879 through 1883, and associate editor of the *Richmond Standard* and was a member of more than seventy historical and antiquarian societies worldwide. *L. Tyler*, Encyclopedia of Virginia Biography. PD-*US*.

Richmond, Virginia, looking west down Main Street from 19th Street, April 1865. It is possible one of Thomas Norcliffe Jones's warehouses appears in this image. This section of town was spared the evacuation fire and appeared very much the same in 1865 as it would have when William was a youngster in Richmond. *Library of Congress, https://www.loc.gov/item/cwp2003005708/PP/; photographer, John Reekie.*

The slums of Shockoe Valley, home to the enslaved, the free black population, and poor white citizens before and after the Civil War. The White House of the Confederacy, home of President Jefferson Davis, can be seen at the top of the hill (*center left*). Despite the vast chasm of status and wealth between Richmond's elite and the people who served them, this image demonstrates just how proximate the connections between the classes were. *Gustavas A. Weber, Society for the Betterment of Housing and Living Conditions in Richmond, Whittet & Shepperson, printers, Richmond, Virginia, 1913. PD-US.*

Found on the refuse-strewn field following the Battle of Gaines' Mill, the notebook William used to record his 1862 Civil War diary. *Images courtesy of Clements Library, University of Michigan.*

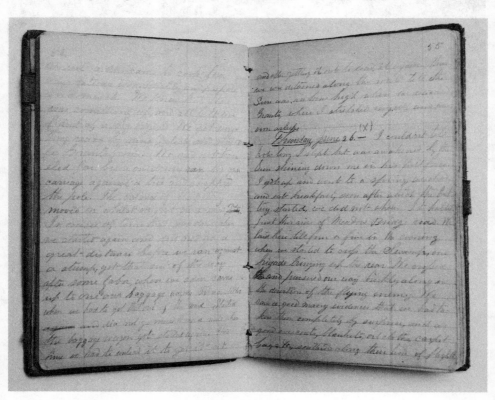

"Eastern View" as William first saw it in May 1862. Today "Prospect Hill" is preserved as part of the Fredericksburg and Spotsylvania National Military Park. *Image courtesy of Buddy Secor.*

Massaponax Church, a landmark and popular meeting location for both the Confederate and Union armies during the Civil War. This image, taken by Timothy O'Sullivan on May 21, 1864, following the battle of Spotsylvania Court House, shows Union soldiers and their horses occupying the church and grounds in advance of Grant's famous war council. This is the church just as William would have seen it when he wrote in May 1862 that his battery rushed to "march against the enemy, as they were coming down the telegraph road." *Library of Congress, Prints and Photographs Division, Civil War Photographs, reproduction number LC-DIG-cwpb-01190.*

Hawkwood plantation house as it appeared in the 1980s following a fire that nearly gutted it. The grand Tuscan-style house would have offered a more exotic prospect to William when his battery camped there and the men were treated to its owner's hospitality in July 1862. *Library of Congress, Prints and Photographs Division, Civil War Photographs, reproduction number HABS VA,55-GORD.V,9–15.*

Mayhurst. On Friday, August 8, 1862, William wrote, "There are many handsome private residences, but none so fine as Jno. Willis' country residence situated where we encamped last night." Just south of Orange Courthouse, Virginia, Mayhurst, built in 1852, is as stunning today as it was more than 150 years ago. *Author's photograph.*

Hawfield plantation house, "Capt. Crenshaw's farm." Hawfield plantation was acquired in 1847 by Mr. Jonathan Graves for his daughter, Fanny Elizabeth, the wife
of William Graves Crenshaw, captain of Crenshaw's Battery. The battery remained
encamped at Hawfield for several days. On August 19, William wrote dispassionately
about the execution and burial of two of his fellow soldiers, condemned for desertion.
Scott, History of Orange County, Virginia. *PD-US*.

Bollman Truss bridge. On Saturday, September 6, 1862, William wrote that his battery was "encamped on the banks of the Monacy [that is, Monocacy] river, where the Baltimore and Ohio R.R. crosses." On the next day, he noted that "we made three attempts to blow up the bridge across the river but failed. It is a splendid structure called the iron lattice bridge but it must be knocked to pieces some (*way*) or other." Shown here is a Bollman Truss bridge on the Baltimore & Ohio Railroad, spanning Little Patuxent River in Howard County, Maryland. It is very similar to the bridge over the Monocacy River described in the diary. *Library of Congress, Prints and Photographs Division, Civil War Photographs, reproduction number HAER MD,14-SAV,1–13.*

Bolivar Heights, Harpers Ferry. On Monday, September 15, 1862, following the
Battle of Harpers Ferry, William wrote that "after firing ten or fifteen minutes, they
raised the flag and surrendered. We captured about ten thousand troops; fifty or sixty
pieces of heavy and light artillery, seventy tons of ammunition, some commissary
stores and a splendid lot of horses, altogether the greatest achievement of the war.
Harper's Ferry bears the marks of the war from its present aspect, must have been a
sweet place to live in the summer." This view of Harpers Ferry, captured from atop
Bolivar Heights, is likely just as William would have seen it, following the battle.
*Library of Congress, Prints and Photographs Division, Civil War Photographs, reproduction
numbers LC-D43-T01-1754-L-B and LC-D43-T01-1754-R-B; panorama created from two
separate images.*

Tedium of camp life. Throughout his diary, William recorded life in camp on those long days between battles when the battery wasn't on the march. He and his comrades occupied themselves with laundry and bathing, playing cards, reading, and writing. This 1861 photograph, captured by the firm of E. & H. T. Anthony, shows members of the Boston Light Artillery in camp surrounded by drying laundry as they write letters, read the newspaper, and, apparently, sew. *Library of Congress, Prints and Photographs Division, Civil War Photographs, reproduction number LC-DIG-stereo-1s02987.*

Fredericksburg, pontoon bridges. On December 11, 1862, the first day of the Battle of Fredericksburg, William wrote that "the Yankee's were shelling the town and laying down pontoon bridges, in which they were quite successful." This view is likely similar to the one William witnessed, on that day and the days following, from his battery's position on Prospect Hill overlooking the Rappahannock. The photograph was taken from the Union side of the Rappahannock, looking across the valley toward Prospect Hill (approximately). A handwritten note below this 1862 image reads, "Pontoon bridges at 'Franklin's crossing' 2½ miles below Fredericksburg, Va. . . . Bridges were laid here in Dec. 1862." *Library of Congress, Prints and Photographs Division, Civil War Photographs, reproduction number LC–DIG–ppmsca-31500.*

Mulberry Place plantation house. Pegram's Battalion overwintered at Mulberry Place from late December 1862 through the spring of 1863. The grand Federal-style dwelling was constructed in 1827 by Jourdan Woolfolk to house his growing family and to express his social, political, and financial status. Situated near Bowling Green, Virginia, Mulberry Place was an ideal location for the artillery battalion to encamp, as it was strategically located on the railroad and important overland transportation routes, with ready access to a nearby telegraph office and mail drop. *Author's photograph.*

Confederate winter quarters. This ramshackle assortment of lean-tos and log cabins (captured in Centreville, Virginia, in 1862), with stick-and-daub chimneys and no convenient access to clean water or sanitation, vividly illustrates the living conditions similarly endured by rank-and-file members of Pegram's Battalion during months-long winter camping at Mulberry Place. *Photographer, George N. Bernard; Library of Congress, Prints and Photographs Division, Civil War Photographs, reproduction number LC-DIG-cwpb-03888.*

Spotsylvania Court House. On the morning of May 10, 1864, Crenshaw's Battery found itself positioned just outside the courthouse in Spotsylvania, Virginia, facing Federal troops in advance of the Battle of Spotsylvania Court House. That morning, while readying his guns for the coming battle, William was struck in the foot by a sharpshooter's bullet, ending his career with Crenshaw's Battery. The image above likely represents a view of the courthouse as William last saw it, prior to his evacuation with thousands of other casualties of that bloody, ferocious, and now legendary battle. *Library of Congress, Prints and Photographs Division, Civil War Photographs, reproduction number LC-DIG-ppmsca-35111.*

Richmond in ruins. The evacuation fire, which preceded the surrender of the city to Union forces on April 3, 1865, destroyed more than twenty blocks, more than a thousand homes and businesses, and almost all the food and provisions remaining in town. The fire, the surrender, and the rapid occupation of the city by Union soldiers stunned the city's residents, who were already wearied by wartime privation and isolation enforced by the Union's siege of the city. *Library of Congress, Prints and Photographs Division, Civil War Photographs, reproduction number LC-DIG-ppmsca-33070.*

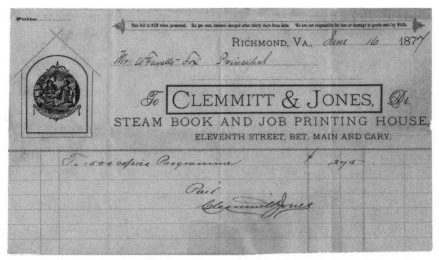

Clemmitt & Jones invoice for goods. After the war, William rejoined his old friend William Clemmitt at the printing company and, in 1869, was made a partner in the firm. The first book to bear the company's new imprint "Gary, Clemmitt & Jones" was Robert Alonzo Brock's *Register of the Confederate Dead, Interred in Hollywood Cemetery, Richmond, Virginia*. In 1871 William Clemmitt and William Ellis Jones bought out George Gary's share of the firm, renaming the firm "Clemmitt & Jones, Steam Book and Job Printing House," as shown here. In 1878 William bought out his old master and business partner, launching the new imprint "William Ellis Jones, Steam Book and Job Press," often simply rendered as "Wlm. Ellis Jones, Richmond, Virginia." *Original document in author's possession.*

6. ❈ The Civil War Diary of William Ellis Jones, of Richmond, Virginia

Twenty-three-year-old William Ellis Jones voluntarily enlisted as a private in Crenshaw's Battery. In time the battery would be incorporated into Pegram's Battalion, part of the Third Corps, Army of Northern Virginia, under the command of Confederate general Robert E. Lee.

William mustered into service on March 14, 1862, with 139[1] other men. He served continuously until being wounded at the Battle of Spotsylvania Court House, May 10, 1864. Following his injury, he was retired to the invalid corps on February 1, 1865, where he served as a clerk in the Post Quartermaster's Office until the fall of Richmond on April 3, 1865.[2] Charles P. Young, Thomas Ellett, and Robert Alonzo Brock, in their "History of the Crenshaw Battery," describe the origins of the company:

> The company was christened "The *Crenshaw* Battery," in honor of its first captain (William Graves Crenshaw). His gallant bearing on the field of battle subsequently, and his noble generosity to the company, always, proved that the name was fitly chosen. *Captain Crenshaw* equipped the battery with handsome uniforms, overcoats, blankets, shoes, underclothing, and everything necessary for its comfort, at his own expense, and advanced the money necessary for the purchase of horses and guns to the Confederate government, thereby getting into the field much earlier than would have been the case under ordinary circumstances.[3]

The journal reproduced on the following pages is William Ellis Jones's account of the first ten months of his service, from initial muster in Richmond through ten important battles, including Seven Pines, the raid at Manassas Junction, Second Manassas, Harpers Ferry, Antietam, and Fredericksburg. The journal closes at the establishment of winter quarters on December 31, 1862, in the woods south of the Chickahominy River near Bowling Green, Virginia, at Mulberry Place, the ancestral home of the Woolfolk family of colonial Virginia fame.

No effort has been made to edit or redact any part of the diary. The text that follows is an exact transcription of the original; the few errors that the haste of camp life allowed to creep in have been retained. Considering the conditions under which the manuscript was written, it is remarkably free of grammatical error. For the transcription, I have taken the liberty of showing obvious misspellings in *italic*. In the rare instance when a word has been omitted that can be filled in by taking context into account, the word has been included inside parentheses (*and in italic*). Words handwritten in the original manuscript that are illegible are shown as (*illegible*) in the transcription. Where words appear <u>underlined</u>, this is how they appeared in the original. The only other editorial liberties taken have been to add editorial notes where more information may be necessary in order to understand or fully appreciate the referenced diary entry and to break the diary into sections conforming to what we now understand as military movements, campaigns, or strategically important battles. While the author was often unaware of these distinctions in troop movements or his commander's plans, this organization of events may prove useful to the reader. All diary entries appear in the order in which they were recorded.

Part 1

FIRST MUSTER AT RICHMOND THROUGH
MANEUVERS AROUND FREDERICKSBURG, VIRGINIA
MARCH 14–MAY 23, 1862

This portion of the diary offers an excellent introduction to William Ellis Jones's personality, his dry and often irreverent sense of humor, and his ability to make friends easily. Excepting one dark entry (May 3, 1862, describing the execution of Union spy Timothy Webster), most of the material included in this section provides a lighthearted glimpse into the absurdities of camp life, from adrenaline-inducing false alarms to poorly choreographed parade routines performed by green soldiers. There is a good deal of information in this section shedding light on how the local inhabitants received the army and welcomed individual soldiers to the neighborhood.

Not counting the battery's early training in Richmond, from March 14 through May 23 the men traveled on foot just over eighty-six miles, a tiny fraction of the total ground covered during the whole of 1862. At this early

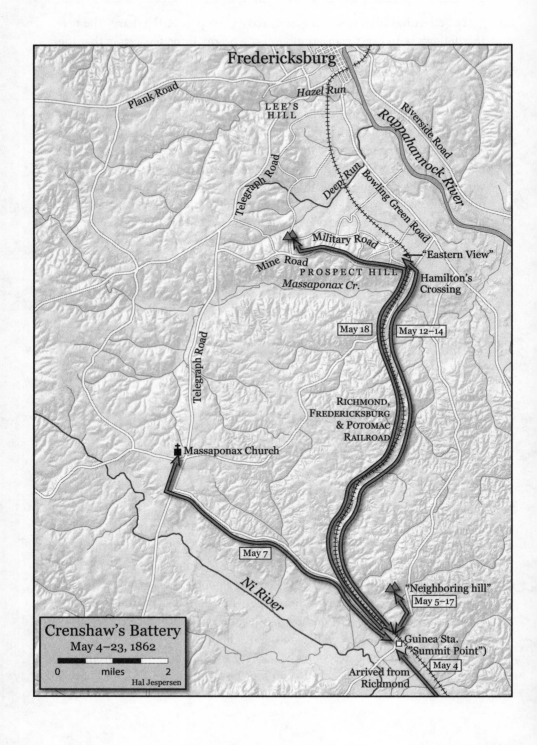

Fredericksburg

Plank Road

Hazel Run

LEE'S
HILL

Telegraph Road

Deep Run

Bowling Green Road

Riverside Road

Rappahannock River

Military Road

"Eastern View"

Mine Road

PROSPECT HILL

Massaponax Cr.

Hamilton's
Crossing

May 18

May 12–14

Telegraph Road

RICHMOND,
FREDERICKSBURG
& POTOMAC
RAILROAD

✝ Massaponax Church

Ni River

May 7

"Neighboring hill"
May 5–17

Guinea Sta.
("Summit Point")

May 4

Arrived from
Richmond

Crenshaw's Battery
May 4–23, 1862

0   miles   2

Hal Jespersen

stage hardships were few, there was plenty to eat, and the work was comparatively light. It is worth noting that several geographic locations mentioned in this first section recur numerous times throughout the remainder of the journal as the battery became more purposefully engaged in the war. Also worth noting are William's first references to poetry and myth, which were recurring elements punctuating his daily prose.

Friday, March 14, 1862
Crenshaw's Battery was this day mustered into service on the basin bank in Richmond, VA., and I as one of its members. We remained in rendezvous there till Tuesday following.

The battery's initial armament consisted of six guns, including; two ten-pound Parrott guns, two twelve-pound brass Howitzers, and two six-pound brass guns.[1]

Tuesday, March 18, 1862
Nothing doing, except squad drill, of special interest, when we were marched to Camp Lee[2] for instruction in drill. I expect it was amusing to a spectator to witness our first attempt at tent pitching, for it took us about four hours to get all the tents in right trim; but *perserverance* and patience will accomplish any difficult task. Then came our first effort at cooking, which was accomplished in tolerable style, after a little emphasizing of the English language for (*illegible*). Thus we were initiated into camp life.

Wednesday, March 19–May 3, 1862[3]
From this date until May 3 nothing transpired of an exciting nature except the hanging of a spy by the name of Webster on Tuesday 29th of April,[4] when we were ordered out of the Fair Grounds,[5] as all the rest of the companies were, to keep the citizens from round the enclosure and jumping on the fence. All sorts and grades of knives were brought into requisition, so as to cut holes in the fence through which we might witness the hanging, and those who were not fortunate enough to have one knocked knot holes out with anything they could get. Never in my life did I ever see men so eager to witness a performance of any kind as they were to see this man launched into eternity with all his sins upon his soul. It is a sad commentary upon poor human nature that we would rather see such revolting sights than to go and hear the Word

of God from some devout minister. Between the hours of eleven and twelve he was carried to the scaffold and in a few minutes the rope was adjusted and the trap door fell, when the rope broke. Never do I wish to witness another such sight, for the heart turned sick and a faintness came over all the body. He was immediately supported to the scaffold and ere he was conscious he was dangling between heaven and earth. He remained there about twenty minutes, when he was cut down and consigned to mother earth. He was the first spy I ever saw hang and do not wish to see another.

President Davis came out to see the camp several times, which always created quite a stir among the boys, for they would line the route he took around the grounds and cheer after cheer would rend the air until he was out of sight. He certainly possesses the hearts of his countrymen and should exert all his power and talents to set them free and make them an independent and happy people.

Sunday, May 4, 1862

This was a busy day for us, for we had to pack up and join the army around Fredericksburg. It was no light task to load the cars with cannon, caissons, baggage wagons, etc., but with willing hearts and hands it was accomplished by twelve o'clock M., when the roll was called to mark all absentees so that they would be sent on afterwards; then came the farewell partings between relations and friends, the unbidden dropping of tears, and quickly shaking of hands, for the heart was too full to speak, when "All Aboard" rang on the ears with a dismal and unwelcomed sound, that seemed to snap the chords of the heart asunder; then the rush for the cars, seats next to the windows eagerly jumped into, so as to obtain the "last lingering look behind" of old Richmond, my native City. "Toot, toot" sounded the engineer, when amidst waving of handkerchiefs and the cheers of the boys, the cars moved off. It is impossible to express the feeling that possessed me at that moment, nor will I attempt it. We moved along very slowly for fear of a collision, as there were several trains on the road. We reached Summit,[6] which is about six miles from Fredericksburg, about ten o'clock that night, when we had to unload the cars, which was a very perilous job indeed in the dark, for the rolling down the ordnance the least varying of the wheels would have been death to some of us, but I was truly glad to say that everything was taken off without the least casualty by three o'clock in the morning. Broke down would not be saying enough, we were perfectly exhausted with the labors of the day and night, and it was with no slight feeling of joy that we looked about or prepared places where we could rest our wearied bodies, and obtain a little of "Nature's restorer, balmy sleep."[7] Two comrades and myself placed some planks under one of the baggage wagons, where we laid down with the firm conviction that a soldier's life was a "hard road to travel."[8]

Monday, May 5, 1862
Was awakened this morning by the rain dripping from the side of the wagon and spattering in my face. Laid thus ruminating upon the vicissitudes of life, while I noticed a party eating breakfast, when all at once a *knawing* appetite was engendered and I immediately joined the party and set to work to destroy as much of the victuals as a small person could eat at one meal, after which I regained my wonted cheerfulness. As soon as it stopped raining we pitched tents on a neighboring hill, which was a healthy and pleasant place. We devoted the balance of the day to making the tents as comfortable as possible, as the ground was wet and sobby.

Tuesday, May 6, 1862
We were ordered to be prepared to be reviewed at eleven o'clock by Brig. Gen. *Grigg*,[9] to whose brigade we were consigned. Of course there was some fixing done so as to present a fine appearance, and a good deal of curiosity was excited in the hearts of those uninitiated as to the manner of doing it, and what sort of a general was to command us. At the appointed hour we were on the ground, and everything would have passed off in fine style but for a few balky horses, which caused some confusion in several manoeuvres. I was well pleased with the appearance of the general, for his manner was affable, and nothing like haughtiness about him. After the review we were drilled about an hour, when the artillery was parked and the company dismissed. In the evening felt unwell, had a very bad headache, took a couple of pills.

Wednesday, May 7, 1862
Spent a disagreeable night, but felt much better only a little weak. Had two drills in the *manuel* of the piece[10] in the morning. After dinner[11] our instructor was showing us how to mount and dismount the cannon,

when the Long Roll was heard in the infantry camp, and presently a courier came dashing up with orders to prepare instantly for a march against the enemy, as they were coming down the telegraph road.[12] The bugle sounded the alarm, and the men ordered to pack their knapsacks as soon as possible. All was confusion and hubbub, for a considerable excitement prevailed for a short while, but it soon subsided as the boys began cracking jokes as if going on a frolic. Everything being ready, away we go preceded by two regiments of infantry and followed by another. It was a rather warm afternoon and after a march of about four or five miles, was brought to a halt at *Massapomax* Church[13] much fatigued. The boys, as they marched, began to be a little more anxious, but none that I saw seemed to flinch in the least. After staying there about an hour an order came for us to return to camp, (It was a false alarm) which we had no objections to, and was done with alacrity, so as to enable us to reach camp by sundown. Of course, after reaching the camp, everyone felt himself a little raised in his estimation, and soon all had made themselves "veterans," except our bugler, for an ugly rumor got afloat detrimental to his courage, which was that he had use for a laundress upon his arrival at camp. The truth of it I do not vouch for.

Thursday, May 8, 1862
Had two drills in the *manuel* of the piece in the morning and a battery drill in the afternoon. Nothing of interest transpired except the usual routine of camp life.

Friday, May 9, 1862
On sick list; nothing serious though. Company had two drills in the morning and a battery drill in the afternoon. Some of our men were detailed to burn charcoal; went over to see them make the kiln, there met a comrade; to him I made a proposition to go to a farm house not so far off to see what we could buy, to which he acceded when we started and soon arrived at the place. We were too late to buy anything, but was promised some butter and milk next morning. Had a pleasant chat with Mrs. Bullock, the wife of the owner of the farm, and got a glimpse of her two daughters which only increased our desire to become further acquainted.

It is possible that William was previously, if indirectly, acquainted with the Bullock family. Given nineteenth-century conventions, and especially at this early stage of the war, it seems unlikely that a young man with manners would have invited himself to a go visit a farm where he had no business. The Confederate army had not yet reached the stage where soldiers were required to forage for food. Some prior introduction or shared acquaintance may have been made, especially given that he received an invitation to return. Remember, William was one of thousands of soldiers in the area. Had every soldier been welcomed as he was, the farm would have been quickly overrun.

Saturday, May 10, 1862

Got up bright and early; fixed up in the best style, and was soon on our way to Mr. Bullock's. We met him this morning and a pleasant old Virginian he is. He informed us that he had five sons in the army,[14] and that he felt interested in the welfare of soldiers. After chatting awhile the breakfast bell rang, to which he invited us when we accepted and sat down to an excellent breakfast, to which we did ample justice. It passed off pleasantly in conversation with the ladies and gentlemen, and will be remembered for many a day. After it was over she filled three canteens with milk and would take no pay, and would only receive fifty cents for the butter. She was to let us have more butter on the following Monday. Company had its usual drills.

Sunday, May 11, 1862

On guard today. Had guard mounting[15] for the first time, which proved a perfect farce in the bungling way it was done, for it convulsed all with laughter, from the Captain down to the negro cooks. Had inspection at nine o'clock, which was tedious, but also diverting at the way our orderly gave commands; one was "Take open order" which nearly upset the gravity of the privates, and became quite a jest with the boys from the way it was passed between one another. About three o'clock the Long Roll was beat and the bugle sent out its shrill alarms, couriers were seen riding furiously along the roads, and in a few minutes the different camps were busy with their preparations for meeting the foe. After getting the battery in marching order, the Captain received orders to remain so until further commands.

Monday, May 12, 1862

At three o'clock this morning we were aroused from our slumbers by the alarm call from the bugle, when everybody was busy packing their knapsacks and cooking their breakfast. Just as "Gray-eyed Morn smiled at frowning Night"[16] we started towards Fredericksburg, and as old Sol rose from his watery bed in the East, throwing a golden sheen over as fair a scene as I ever witnessed, causing the dew drops to glitter and sparkle with a brilliancy unsurpassed, we took up our position on "Eastern View" in mask. "Eastern View" was a high hill from which place you had an extensive and varied view towards the East,[17] overlooking as lovely a tract of lowland as one would wish to see, hemmed in on the South by a succession of hills, and on the North by the Rappahannock River. It was here I saw a Yankee encampment, and it was with no feeling of love that I beheld it. Skirmishers were thrown out from our brigade, who went within half a mile of Fredericksburg, but failed to meet or draw out any of the infamous Yanks. Orders then came for us to return to camp which we reached about middle of the day, rather fatigued by our jaunt. We were excused from battery drill in the evening, which I was very glad of, for I did not feel like trotting around in the old field for a couple of hours.

Tuesday, May 13, 1862

Had two drills in the morning and a battery drill in the evening. Everything was quiet and all went to bed with the expectation of a good night's rest.

Wednesday, May 14, 1862

We were doomed to disappointment. At three o'clock in the morning we were again aroused by the alarm call of the bugle, and the command to "Fall In" fell on our ears with anything but a welcome sound. We received orders to prepare to march by five o'clock, and by maledictions on the Yanks and the war, we set about to meet the hirelings of Old Abe. At the hour we took up the line of the march and were soon in our former position on Eastern View. Whilst patiently waiting for the enemy to attack, it commenced raining which added nothing to the comfort of our position but enhanced our impatience at the tardiness of the Hessians. We were in the humour just then either to fight or return for camp. After waiting several hours in the drenching rain, we received orders to go back, which we did at double quick, and not at all in love with war. After spending a miserable epithet at the Yankee's, we turned in and were soon wrapped in deep slumber.

". . . we set about to meet the hirelings of Old Abe."—William's language is in keeping with the Confederate propaganda he had been exposed to. To gin up enough emotional commitment to get men to risk their lives, it was necessary to demonize the enemy. This has been a fact of war since ancient times and it continues today. One of the accusations leveled against Union soldiers was that they served only for the benefit of regular rations and a paycheck. These "money grubbing" soldiers were without a cause to fight for, according to white Southern newspaper editors and politicians. The term "hirelings and mercenaries" was used by Confederate vice president Alexander Stephens to describe Union soldiers. "Hessians" was another favorite employed by newspapers, likening the Union soldier to the German mercenaries hired by King George to fight against the Continental army during the American revolution.[18]

Thursday, May 15, 1862

This is my twenty-fourth birthday. "Tempus fugit,"[19] and it is as miserable a day as one could wish, the rain coming down pit-a-pat on the tent and the heavens presenting a woeful and cheerless aspect. Seeing my comrade in arms, we agreed to go over to Mr. Bullock's. We met several ladies on this visit and had a very agreeable and pleasant conversation with them; indeed the time passed so pleasantly that ere we were aware of it the dinner bell rang and were thus put in for a good dinner, which we were not particularly adverse to; thus I was enabled to have a good dinner on birthday, which was a windfall, I must say. It is needless to say that the table groaned with the good things of life, and that when I was through the weight on it was considerably lessened. After dinner spent an hour or two in conversation, bidding them a reluctant adieu, wended our way back to camp, knowing that there was one family that could appreciate and be kind to the poor private. On reaching quarters the boys wanted to know where we had been, and after being told they got off some pleasantries at our expense, one was, that we did not go to see the Bullocks but the "*Heiffers.*" No drills today on account of the weather.

Friday, May 16, 1862

This was a day of rest, the ground being too wet and soft for a drill. Everyone killing time the best way he could. When there is no drilling it is the most indolent and careless life imaginable.

Saturday, May 17, 1862

The usual drills were had. All quiet at the different camps, not a note of war was heard. Went to the cars[20] saw a cousin from Richmond,[21] learned that the Yanks were very close to that city and that their gunboats were beaten back in an attempt to run the blockades. Received a letter from a dear friend which cheered me very much, and also a box containing a jug filled with the extract of rye, which had an enlivening influence on the mess.

The only known cousin William had in Richmond was William B. Jones, who held the contract with the Confederate War Department as mail carrier between Fredericksburg and Brunswick County, Virginia, among other business interests tied to the Confederate government. His business would have required significant travel on behalf of the Confederates, for whom he was a supplier of foodstuffs and other essentials. It follows that William B. Jones, who was also a large supplier of alcohol to the Confederate army, would be the man to provide William with the "extract of rye." This is the first of several mentions of alcoholic drink appearing in the diary.

Sunday, May 18, 1862

The sun rose in cloudless splendor, proclaiming a beautiful and lovely day. Had inspection at nine o'clock, which was the most tedious affair I have ever had to undergo. The officers got into a dispute about the mode of going through with it, thus keeping us in the hot sun an hour longer than was necessary. Having nothing to do, a party of us started out for a ramble and to get some milk, which we drank with the greatest gusto. Some of the boys then proposed to stop at Mrs. Bullock's wishing to see those ladies I had given glowing account of, to which I assented. We met Mr. Bullock who greeted us in the old Virginia style. After spending a short time in conversation he invited us to dinner, which we accepted and sat down to a fine country dinner, to which we did ample justice. After dinner we adjourned to the hall, where we were pleasantly engaged in conversation, when a major came in quest of South Carolina soldiers who informed us that our battery had orders to change quarters. We immediately took our leave, after hastily bidding the family adieu, and hurried over to the camp. The boys on the way expressed themselves highly pleased at the manner we were entertained. We found the whole camp busily engaged in striking and rolling up the tents, loading the wagons, etc., and that we had been crossed on the roll book. Nothing daunted, we packed our knapsacks and fixed our other tricks, placed them in the wagon, filled our canteens with water and were ready for the march. The command "March" was soon given and the battery moved off. We soon arrived at the new camp ground, which was about half a mile to the West of the Eastern View. By dark we had our tents pitched and things fixed tolerably well, when we turned in and went to sleep without rocking.

Monday, May 19, 1862
Excused from drill today so that we might be enabled to get everything straight around camp. Company was called together soon after breakfast, when myself and others who had also been crossed, were called to the front and ordered to build a dam across a small stream to water the horses in. After wasting two hours and lots of fun, we finished the dam, thus expunged the foul "X" against us. The balance of the day was spent in ditching around our tent, putting up a table to eat on and laziness.

Tuesday, May 20, 1862
Had two drills in the *manuel* of the piece and battery drill in the evening. The day went by without any excitement of any kind.

Wednesday, May 21, 1862
The usual drills took place, and by the balance of the day was spent as the day before. On guard today.

Thursday, May 22, 1862
Several of us went fishing and had fine sport part of the time, bringing back with us a good dish of fish, which furnished our table with a delicacy unknown to it before. Had the usual drills. At tattoo[22] the captain read the infamous proclamation of General Butler in regard to the ladies of New Orleans, which aroused the choler and indignation of every member of the company; also an order carrying out one of the articles of war about swearing, with the following penalties: The

commissioned officers a penalty of one dollar for each offence, non-offence, and for the privates second offence an additional fine of twenty four hours confinement on bread and water. The men were put out, but of the opinion that it would not work. Nous verrons!²³

"Several of us went fishing . . ."—Throughout the diary William references creative foraging habits, from buying milk, butter, and eggs from local farmers to this mention of fishing in a nearby stream to supplement the meager army rations of hardtack and (if fortunate) dried pork or beef. Lack of fresh food was the principal complaint of soldiers during the Civil War. Accessing fresh food, regardless of how an individual soldier came to acquire it, was a form of self-care—taking personal responsibility for his own well-being, outside army regulations—that often made the difference between remaining healthy and surviving or succumbing to fatigue or disease.²⁴

". . . the infamous proclamation of General Butler in regard to the ladies of New Orleans . . ."—Union general Benjamin Franklin Butler was a controversial figure on the Union side of the Civil War. A lawyer by profession, he was given command of Fort Monroe in eastern Virginia upon the outbreak of the war, where he originated the concept of the slave as "contraband" (depriving Southern slaveholders of the benefit of slave labor in support of the Confederate cause, whether peaceful or otherwise.) In 1862, Butler was made overseer of the Union-occupied city of New Orleans. His "infamous" order read as follows: "As the officers and soldiers of the United States have been subject to repeated insults from the women (calling themselves ladies) of New Orleans, in return for the most scrupulous non-interference and courtesy on our part, it is ordered that hereafter when any female shall, by word, gesture, or movement, insult or show contempt for any officer or soldier of the United States, she shall be regarded and held liable to be treated as a woman of the town plying her avocation."

This proclamation was published first in newspapers in and around New Orleans, and later throughout the south. A firestorm of indignant protest followed, and Butler was forced to withdraw the letter and apologize to the ladies of that city.²⁵

Friday, May 23, 1862
Had our usual drills. The day was passed in indolence, when not on duty, and discussing the probability of the Yanks getting into Richmond. The Captain²⁶ and Second *Lieutanant*²⁷ were fined nine dollars, the former two and the latter seven.

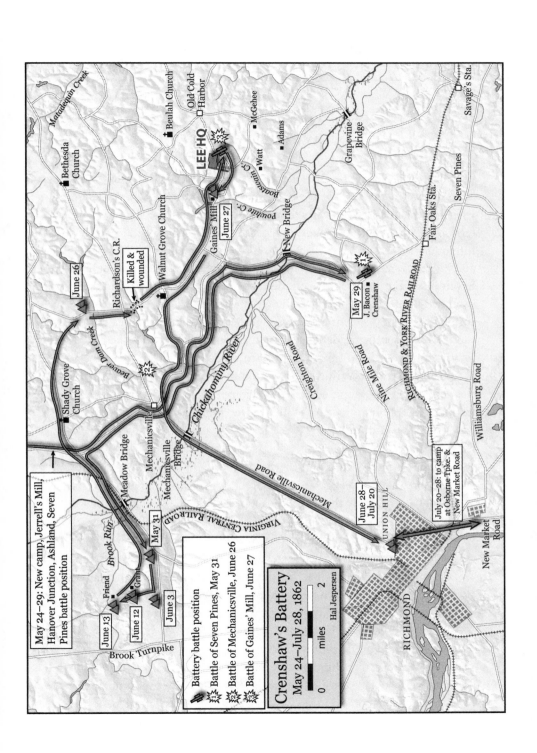

Crenshaw's Battery
May 24–July 28, 1862

May 24–29: New camp, Jerrell's Mill, Hanover Junction, Ashland, Seven Pines battle position

Battery battle position

💥1 Battle of Seven Pines, May 31

💥2 Battle of Mechanicsville, June 26

💥3 Battle of Gaines' Mill, June 27

Hal Jespersen

0   miles   2

June 28–July 20: to camp at Osborne Tpke. & New Market Road

LEE HQ

💥3

June 27

Gaines' Mill

June 26

Killed & wounded

Richardson's C.R.

Walnut Grove Church

New Bridge

June 28–July 20

Poindexter's Ho.

Boatswain C.

Watt

Adams

McGehee

Old Cold Harbor

Beulah Church

Bethesda Church

Matadequin Creek

Grapevine Bridge

Fair Oaks Sta.

Seven Pines

Savage's Sta.

RICHMOND & YORK RIVER RAILROAD

Williamsburg Road

Nine Mile Road

Creighton Road

💥1 May 29

J. Bacon Crenshaw

💥2

Shady Grove Church

Beaver Dam Creek

Chickahominy River

Mechanicsville

Mechanicsville Bridge

Meadow Bridge

May 31

Brook Run

Friend

Grant

June 13

June 12

June 3

VIRGINIA CENTRAL RAILROAD

Mechanicsville Road

UNION HILL

New Market Road

RICHMOND

Brook Turnpike

Part 2

THE PENINSULA CAMPAIGN
MAY 24–JULY 28, 1862

O ver the course of a 106-mile-long march, this portion of the diary introduces us to the first real taste of a soldier's experience of the Civil War. Beginning with homesickness and a desire to see friends and family, to slogging through terrible weather on worse roads, to martial punishment issued in response to infractions against military discipline, and recurring bouts of illness, William and his fellow soldiers engaged in their first violent conflicts throughout the Seven Days' Battles, losing comrades and seeing hundreds of men dead and wounded for the first time in their lives. These early experiences were bracing, turning the attitude of our previously lighthearted young artillerist toward the shadows of resentment, defiance, and apparent indifference as he attempted to quietly, manfully process what he witnessed and participated in.

Tensions between William and his commanding officers escalated during the Peninsula Campaign, while his opinion of them—expressed candidly in his journal—plummetted. As William describes this period himself, this is "the first dark chapter."

Saturday, May 24, 1862
After breakfast orders came to cook four days rations and prepare for a march. Accordingly the wheels were greased, harness looked over and everything put in order. Meanwhile a cold, drizzly rain set in, which rendered everything uncomfortable. Speculation was rife where we were going, some thought to the West, some to Richmond, but all remained ignorant till sundown, when the company was mustered and the captain read the orders, which was for us to join the army around Richmond and fight for the glorious old capital of the Commonwealth and the Confederate States, which sent a thrill of joy through my heart, for all places I would prefer fighting for, and on, it is around my native city. Just as old Sol sank behind the Western hills we started, leaving elegant campfires to delude the foe. The roads were in horrible condition, which rendered the locomotion slow indeed and decidedly laborious to the men. After toiling all night till near the sunrise we reached *Jarrett's*

Mill[1] in Caroline County and about eight or nine miles from where we started; here we hauled to feed and rest.

Sunday, May 25, 1862

After resting two or three hours at the Mill we resumed our march and proceeded much more swiftly than we did the night preceding. No accident of any kind occurred during the day. On coming to a stream (a few of us crossed it above where the road tapped it) we met several ladies, two of them rather good looking. Our chagrin can be imagined, not expressed, when we found out that by crossing above we missed the chance for a close and good look at them, for we had not seen a lady for a good many days, and it was refreshing to look at them, but we consoled ourselves with getting as near the waters edge as possible and straining our pupils while the horses were watered. We bivouacked about six miles from Hanover Junction[2] at twilight.

Monday, May 26, 1862

At sunrise we were awakened, to pack knapsacks and put everything in order to resume the march when the order was given. Several of us went to a neighboring house to get breakfast. The bill of fare was corn cake, fried ham, butter and coffee (I should have said slop) for which we were charged <u>fifty cents</u>, truly a modest sum to ask a soldier for such <u>luxuries</u>. On reaching camp we found everything nearly in readiness to take up the line of the march, which we did soon after. We reached Hanover Junction about twelve o'clock when the infantry took the cars. Whilst waiting here for orders I got into a doze on top of a caisson, when one of the boys awakened me and said that two ladies wished to see me at the cars. I doubted him at first, for I knew no one hereabouts, and said it must be some other Jones in the company, but he said no, for they repeated my middle name, when, at that moment it struck me that some of my acquaintance were spending a few weeks in that neighborhood. I started and on reaching there was not disappointed in finding them the self-same friends. The meeting gave me great pleasure indeed, and I was loathe to part with them. They were endeavoring to get to Richmond, but could not on account of soldiers occupying all the cars. We spent half an hour or so in pleasant conversation, which cheered me considerably, when they took their departure for home. Soon after reaching the company we started and reached the Slashes of Hanover[3] about six o'clock, where we were stopped by baggage wagons in advance which had gotten stalled. Here was a pretty pass, near night, clouds threatening rain every moment and some miles from the place where we were ordered to camp. Well, we had to wait patiently for them to move ahead, and just as twilight set in we moved off and did not get more than a hundred yards when we again came to a halt. Captain got mad, men swore and everything in the battery was in a bad humor. We had a turnout in the woods, got ahead of some of the stalled wagons, and pushed over as bad a road as ever existed until eleven o'clock, when we again came to a stand still by some of the wagons camping in the road, thus blocking our way. Our mess turned in and made a fire on the side of the road out of fence rails when the owner came up and commenced talking about his fence rails and a new gate of his that had been knocked down. Sergeant Strother[4] soon sent him off with a flea in his ear.[5] It commenced raining, which added nothing to the sweetness of our tempers or the comfort of our position; but nevertheless I laid down and soon fell asleep. I don't know how long I slept but was soon awakened by the sergeant who said the captain got the wagons out of the way and had ordered the battery to march on, determined to get to camp that night. Well, off we start, the rain coming down in torrents, and before going a hundred yards, shish we go in a mud hole and came to a dead halt. "Double on the wheels men," and down we jump in the mud and water, and tug and push, but to no purpose. "Bring along your lead horses," (*illegible*) "be quick about it," now they are hitched, the men doubling on the wheels, "Now all together," and away it goes out of the mud holes. Thus it has been all night. We start again and go a short distance when the same scene is repeated. We proceeded in this way for about a mile when we came to an extra deep mud hole and we halted till daylight. I laid back on the caisson and went to sleep but was awakened by water running down my back. Got up and stood under a tree with some others; went fast asleep standing up, a thing I never did before in my life, was again awakened by punching someone in the back with my nodding head; determined to lay down spread my old cloth and was soon in the land of Somnus.[6] Some of the boys obtained several canteens of the extract of corn on the route, the consequence was that two of them had to be strapped on the caissons to keep them from falling off at nightfall.

Tuesday, May 27, 1862

I was roused from my watery bed soon after daylight with the cry that the battery was about to move on. After floundering through seas of mud we reached camp in about an hour. I need not say we were truly glad, although the rain continued to pour down. Two or three others and myself stretched the *taupaulin* which protected us from the rain and then partook of a hot breakfast which cheered us considerably. Lit my old pipe, smoked all my troubles away, and then stretched myself on some rails and snatched a little repose. After dinner heard heavy firing to the North of us. Many were the conjectures as to where it was, but all remained in ignorance. It commenced clearing off about twelve o'clock and by three the sun was shining brilliantly, when we were ordered to pitch tents, which consumed the balance of the evening in doing and fixing up things.

"After floundering through seas of mud . . ."—William's varying descriptions of the mud and miserable, wet conditions are not hyperbole. Mud was the most common complaint among soldiers who described eastern Virginia's terrain in 1862. "Camp Quicksand," "floating sea of mud," "cased with mud to the waist, at least," and "adhesive mud" are just a few of the ways other soldiers wrote of their muddy lives that spring and summer.[7]

Wednesday, May 28, 1862

Aroused just before day by the alarm of the bugle. Orders given to pack knapsacks, strike tents and get everything in marching order. About six we started toward Ashland. On the way we met several females who informed us that the fight occurred at Hanover Court House the previous evening and that our forces were compelled to retreat,[8] some of them in a shameful manner took to flight. We hurried on and after marching four or five miles halted. I do not know how long we stayed here but I stretched out in the shade of a tree and went to sleep. I had a long nap and was wakened by the sun shining on me, when I crossed the road where some of my companions were. The captain was conversing with Mr. Fox, near whose farm our camp was, who was giving an account of the battle. He drew off the plan and showed how our reinforcements would have got to them from our lines in an hour or so, and said he showed the same to General *Grigg* who was eager to go but could not as General *Fields*[9] was in command, who said the firing was way down river somewhere. Pretty soon orders came to go back to camp, which we lost no time in doing as the sun was very warm. As soon as we reached camp, a courier came up and said the Yankees were coming down another road, when we were ordered to remain in marching order. The forces were pushed forward and a line of battle formed, hospital fixed for the wounded, scouts thrown out, who proceeded down the road and came up with about forty scouts of the enemy, when they fired into them which they did not relish much for they "skedaddalled," ingloriously to their main army. About nightfall we started. After marching about three miles we bivouacked within a mile of the enemy. We built big fires, stretched the *taupaulin* on the ground, laid down and soon forgot the excitement and labors of the day in the arms of Morpheus.[10]

Thursday, May 29, 1862

Aroused at the light by the reveille. Breakfast was cooked hastily, and soon after sunlight we started to leave the camp. Felt unwell from dysentery, the soldier's bane, which commenced on me the day before. We soon found out that we were going to cross the Chickahominy and take position on the extreme left of General Johnston's army. After crossing the swamp we moved on till we came to J. Bacon Crenshaw's residence, where we encamped in an oak grove opposite. There I reported myself sick, for I felt very unwell. The boys pitched our tent and fixed up things round it, cooked supper and turned in for a good night's rest.

"*. . . we moved on till we came to J. Bacon Crenshaw's residence . . .*"—*The property mentioned here refers to a secondary plantation owned by J. Bacon Crenshaw, not his principal and much more famous residence, "Shrubbery Hill," located in Hanover County, north of the South Anna River.*[11] *John Bacon Crenshaw was a Quaker leader, born in Henrico County, Virginia, in 1820. (He was no relation to Captain William Graves Crenshaw, commanding officer of the Crenshaw Battery.) During the Civil War, Crenshaw worked to promote good relations between the Society of Friends and the Confederacy. He petitioned the government to respect the denomination's pacifism while providing aid to both Union prisoners in Richmond and to Confederate wounded. After the war he attempted to promote better opportunities for African Americans. J. Bacon Crenshaw died on May 10, 1889, and is buried at Shrubbery Hill.*[12]

Interestingly and probably not coincidentally, the grandson of our Civil War diarist, also named William Ellis Jones, left several books in his library with poems and notes handwritten on the inside cover and end papers, each bearing the inscription "At Shrubbery Hill." It seems likely that William Ellis Jones (diarist) was familiar with J. Bacon Crenshaw and visited his home after the war, perhaps taking his grandson with him. The Crenshaw residence is located not far from where William Ellis Jones (diarist) built his home, "Summerfield."

Friday, May 30, 1862
Feel a great deal worse. Physician came to see me, prescribed brandy and laudanum, and to rest myself as much as possible.[13] The boys had no drilling to do, as there was no field contiguous upon which we could have a battery drill. Wrote home.

This is an important, albeit brief entry that's indicative of William's concern for his own physical well-being and his determination to care for himself. On May 29, he wrote that he "felt unwell from dysentery, the soldier's bane . . . ," which had come on him the day before. On the third day of his illness, he "wrote home." It is a well-documented fact that dysentery was among the single most common causes of serious illness and death in the ranks. We lack records for the numbers of victims in the Confederate ranks; however, the Union army records 1.3 million cases of dysentery resulting in 35,000 deaths. These numbers are likely underreported, and it has been suggested that Confederate soldiers suffered from this ailment at a higher incidence than their Union counterparts.[14] William was aware of the danger to him. When he "wrote home," it is doubtless he was writing home for help in battling this ailment.

Saturday, May 31, 1862[15]
Felt about the same as I did yesterday, only a little weaker. Heard heavy firing on the right wing of the army. Battery ordered to go to the swamp. Went with them when I should not, but could not help it for expected a fight. We were halted about a mile this side of the bridge that spans the Chickahominy.[16] While here a courier came up; from him we learned that about thirty thousand Yanks had crossed the Swamp the evening before and that our forces attacked them and had driven them about two miles back and taken their camp. This was joyful news. The courier had come with orders for *Stewart's*[17] flying artillery.

Presently orders came for us to move forward, when we took the place occupied by them. We had not been there long when we were ordered back to camp, which we reached just after dark.

Sunday, June 1, 1862
Awoke this morning feeling worse. The dysentery had turned into diarrhea which weakened me considerably. Orderly Scott[18] gave me a cup of milk which strengthened me a little. The doctor came around in the morning and gave me three pills and a bottle of misture.[19] The battery was ordered to go on picket. They took the same position they had left yesterday. When they were gone it was lonesome indeed, the merry laugh, the good natured jest was not heard, familiar faces were missed, and the camp seemed like "some banquet hall deserted,"[20] but there were several of my companions left on the sick list, and we made the day pass as agreeably as we could.

Monday, June 2, 1862
During the night we had a most terrific thunderstorm, the rain coming down in torrents, bursting through the tent and rendering our position uncomfortable. Feel much better. Father came to see me today and brought tea, sugar, etc. in the nourishing, and a bottle of brandy in the stimulating line.

I was very glad to see him and his visit cheered me considerably. I took the brandy and misture together which seemed to have a good effect on me.

While it's reasonable to assume that Thomas Norcliffe Jones would have had little difficulty obtaining a pass to leave Richmond (due to his business associations and political connections), doing so at this time shows some bravery, considering both the Union and Confederate armies were quickly building toward an imminent confrontation. The fact that Jones appeared in camp just three days following his son's letter indicates he was equally aware of the risks of dysentery and willing to go to a good deal of trouble to aid his son.

Tuesday, June 3, 1862
Feel much better and much stronger. The tea and brandy bringing me right up. Orders came to move the camp, when everything was packed up by those who were well and the negro cooks. We reached our new

camp ground late in the afternoon,[21] which was within two miles of the bridge. We had hardly got our tent pitched before it commenced raining. Night soon set in and we laid down to rest, with the prospect of ducking before morning.

Wednesday, June 4, 1862

Awoke this morning by a commotion amongst my messmates, arising from water in the tent. I was congratulating my escape from it, when raising my knapsack I found a perfect stream had been running under my head. The rain continued to fall, with the prospect of doing so all day, which put none of us in a good humor as there was no immediate chance of us getting breakfast. The day was spent in the tents and as comfortably as possible under the circumstances. Some of the boys ran the blockade to Richmond.[22]

Thursday, June 5, 1862

The weather still continues cloudy and rainy. Mayo, one of the blockaders, was strapped on one of the guns today. Knowles, *Gooseby*, Mallory and Burroughs,[23] blockaders came back today. The captain went to the city this morning owing to which act they were not punished today. Some little excitement this evening by two of the companies getting into a fight, but they were parted before any damage was done.

". . . was strapped on one of the guns . . ."—In this form of martial punishment, the victim was tied in crucifixion pose to the wheels of the cannon's caisson and left for hours to be observed (and ideally, ridiculed) by his fellow soldiers and passersby. In hot weather, in full sun, this could cause extreme discomfort or even become life-threatening, as the steel wheels heated up, burning the skin, as well as putting the victim at risk of heat stroke or severe sunburn.

Friday, June 6, 1862

Rose this morning feeling much better, in fact nearly well of the dysentery. After breakfast some of the baggage wagons were going to Richmond and fool like me, jumped into one of them and ran the blockade. I spent a good time in Richmond with the boys. We went to see General Hospital to see the wounded of the Battle of Seven Pines; found an acquaintance there from Alabama, he was wounded only slightly. He informed me that Jno. McCarthy,[24] another Montgomery Alabama[25] friend, was killed, which made me very sorrowful indeed, for he was a man who all could honor and trust. He had just been promoted to a captaincy. It is hard indeed for us to lose our dearest friends in a struggle that could have been averted but for fanatical, yeah, satanical beings in the north. Had a walk after supper, met a couple of lady friends with whom I had a pleasant chat. One of the boys procured a bottle of brandy which we used up.

". . . fanatical, yeah, satanical beings in the north."—This is the first intense demonization of the enemy we hear from William. Confederates were moved by the injury, death, and hardships put upon themselves, family, and friends to embrace the propaganda of wholesale dehumanization of all Northerners (not just soldiers). For deeper insight into the propaganda of dehumanization created and disseminated by white Southerners, see George C. Rable's Damn Yankees!

Saturday, June 7, 1862
Started back to camp about ten o'clock accompanied by a friend. We were fortunate enough to ride most of the way back. Just before we reached camp overtook a working party of our boys, who were caught running the blockade, when they informed me that I was caught. Soon after reaching camp a thunderstorm came up which lasted an hour or two. I was informed that the blockaders who came back on Thursday were punished by being tied together in front of the captain's tent. At five o'clock Ferneyhough, Allen, Snead, Colquitt, Burgess and myself, were strapped on the guns where we remained until ten o'clock at night.[26] It is needless for me to say that I was never so mortified in my life. As soon as we were relieved we sought our respective couches to drown our feelings in sleep. Truly every sweet has its bitter. This was the first dark chapter in our battery.

Sunday, June 8, 1862
After breakfast were again called before the captain's tent. There was one additional one this morning, W. E. Jones,[27] a name-sake of mine. We were ordered to strike all the private's tents including the hospital tent. After this was done and everything made ready to change quarters, we were ordered to take an ax a piece and go ahead of the battery to clear the new camp ground of undergrowth, in which operation I

raised a considerable blister on my right hand. We were then ordered to pitch the hospital tent, and just as we finished the task the captain came down and let out his hypocritical cant, much to my disgust and wound up by making us promise not to run the blockade any more, or he would continue the punishment until he thought proper to cease, pusillanimous tyrant. Went to dress parade of the 14th regiment, S.C., had lots of fun.

". . . pusillanimous tyrant . . ."—According to the 1988 Compact Edition of the Oxford English Dictionary, this is a tyrant "lacking in courage and strength of mind; faint-hearted, mean-spirited, cowardly." It's worthwhile to note that a statement such as this one, made in writing, would have been viewed by William's command as a stroke of disrespect toward a superior officer, an offense that was taken seriously and punished. This statement is a short step away from calling Captain Crenshaw a coward, one of the harshest insults one could conjure in this era. It is also interesting that William spelled this word perfectly, indicating he had some measure of repetitive experience using it and writing it. What is even more telling is that despite Captain Crenshaw's "cant," William was permitted to attend the dress parade of the 14th Regiment and indulge himself in "lots of fun."

Monday, June 9, 1862

I forgot to state that Jones was strapped to the gun[28] on yesterday after the camp was put in order and kept there until nine or ten o'clock. The captain would have taken him off but he would not promise not to run the blockade any more. He was strapped to the gun again this morning early, and was taken down after giving the required promise about eleven o'clock. The day was passed in idleness, there being no drills.

Tuesday, June 10, 1862

On guard today. And a miserable day it is, the rain falling almost ceaselessly. After standing my first two hours, Sergeant Newman[29] asked me to ride his horse to water which I did. Soon after getting back I commenced to feel very badly indeed, and late in the evening I had the dumb agues[30] most beautifully. I stood out my second hour and then reported myself sick to the sergeant, and laid down in my tent with a splitting headache. About nine o'clock the doctor came around and prescribed quinine[31] which I took and turned over to sleep.

Wednesday, June 11, 1862

I awoke this morning without a headache and very little fever. During the morning the doctor came around, prescribing *epicac* and calomel merged into blue mass, the first to be taken immediately and the latter just before going to bed. The *epicac* did no good for I only threw that up and nothing else. On going to bed I took the pill, feeling very badly indeed.

"Blue mass," also referred to as "blue pill," was a common remedy in the nineteenth century, purported to cure everything from parasites to fever. Pharmacists and physicians often compounded remedies themselves, based upon their own experimentation. Blue mass[32] gets its unique name from either blue dye or blue chalk (used as emulsifier) in a variety of preparations. The primary ingredient in blue mass was mercury in elemental or compound form (frequently as mercury chloride, commonly called "calomel").

Today we know that mercury is toxic, and ingestion of mercury can be fatal. A standard nineteenth-century dose of two or three blue mass pills in preparation represented ingestion of more than one hundred times the safe daily limits for mercury set forth by Environmental Protection Agency guidelines. Symptoms of elemental mercury poisoning include tremors, memory loss, intestinal tract pain, insomnia, and mood swings.[33]

Thursday, June 12, 1862

The medicine did not have the desired effect. I am very much weak with fever and a soreness in my abdomen which is almost excruciating. Late in the morning the captain received orders to go on picket, when another scene of bustle and confusion ensued in putting the camp in moving order. About five o'clock the sick were put in baggage wagons and carried along. I never experienced such a ride in my life before, for at every little jostle it seems as if a dull knife was being driven through my stomach. We arrived at Mr. Grant's farm just before night, where I dragged myself to a barn and laid down to rest.

Friday, June 13, 1862

Feel much worse this morning. Captain came to see the sick. I asked him to send for a doctor, which he abruptly replied to by saying "He couldn't get a doctor." I spoke of the pain it gave me to ride in the wagon, when like a brute he replied by saying that I could walk to Richmond and back when I was sick before. I told him that I neither walked there nor back, but rode. He turned on his heel and left. It was all the consolation I got. The Battery was soon on the road again. We reached Dr. Friend's farm[34] about six o'clock in the evening, which is near the New Bridge on the Chickahominy Swamp. As the Doctor's family has moved to the city, we made a hospital out of his parlor. Before going to bed I took fifteen grains of calomel,[35] to see if that would not help me.

Saturday, June 14, 1862
Feel much better this morning, the calomel acting with talismanic effect on my liver.[36] I took a dose of salts soon after getting up, which had its desired effect. I lounged about all day, killing time the best way I could. During the day the Yanks would favor some of our batteries with a shell or two, which would arouse us from a state of lethargy.

"I took a dose of salts soon after getting up . . ."—See the diary entry of Wednesday, June 11, 1862. Hopefully this "dose" was not mercury-laced. Mercury (II) salts are usually more toxic than their mercury (I) counterparts because their solubility in water is greater; thus, they are more readily absorbed by the gastrointestinal tract.[37]

Sunday, June 15, 1862
I may truly say I am a convalescent. I feel very well, only the medicine making me quite weak, which will render it necessary for me to keep from duty for several days to recruit my usual strength. In the afternoon we had a severe thunderstorm, bringing on a very cold rain, rendering a little fire comfortable. This was a quiet day along the lines.

Another symptom of mercury poisoning is muscle weakness.[38]

Monday, June 16, 1862
Our battery is now divided into three sections, one on Dr. Friend's farm and the other two behind two masked batteries[39] about a half mile from the first. The Yanks have a splendid battery about a mile and a half off in an open field. There is no telling how far they can throw their shells for they throw them whenever they please. Pretty quiet today. They have a water battery[40] about a thousand yards from our masked batteries; they showed themselves today. The day was spent looking around and trying to catch glimpses of the Hessians.[41]

Tuesday, June 17, 1862

Dabney's Battery,[42] composed of Long Tom[43] taken at *Mannassas* and a heavy piece taken at Portsmouth Navy Yard, arrived this morning and will be put in battery tonight. They are intended to reply to the heavy battery of the enemy in the field. There was a pretty brisk artillery duel this evening between this battery and others of theirs, and one of ours. One of their shells wounded five of our infantry. Could not tell whether we inflicted any injury or not on them.

Wednesday, June 18, 1862

The sergeant of my detachment, who was also on the sick list, and myself went over to our piece, which was in one of the masked batteries to report for duty, but I felt so bad after walking in the hot sun that I thought I would not report until next morning. The captain came over in the evening at roll-call, and because I had not reported kicked up a shinny, and said I should stay up at the house or report for duty. I explained how it was, but I might as well talk to a barbarian, for he seemed to possess neither sympathy nor the finer feelings of humanity. Some of the boys wanted me to go back, and not report for two weeks, but I thought it would be better to stay, as it would relieve me of his presence a good deal, as he stayed up at the house mostly.

Thursday, June 19, 1862

Reported for duty this morning. The morning passed off very quietly, nothing to disturb our *equinamity*. About five in the evening the water battery opened up on one of ours, which was behind an *embrasured* fort and could not be hurt much. It opened and after firing about twenty or thirty shots silenced the water battery, making the Yanks skedaddle from every quarter but to no purpose. On guard tonight.

Friday, June 20, 1862

It was agreed that all our batteries should open on the enemy this morning; Long Tom was to open the ball. Our two masked batteries were not to open until the water battery fired. The other batteries had fired some time and we began to think we would not have a shot, when a white smoke arose from behind the brushes where the battery was and a shell came whizzing over. We opened with great vigor, some shots having a telling effect on the enemy, for they did not fire but once more, when they skedaddled most ingloriously. After firing some ten shots from our piece we were ordered to cease firing. Meanwhile Long Tom and Laughing Charlie,[44] as it is dubbed, drove the heavy battery of the enemy from the open field, and placed the deuce with a wagon train about two miles off. While looking around we saw some of their wagons about a mile off, when we wheeling our piece around, put in a ten second shell, blazed away, which accelerated their movements amazingly. Presently a number of horsemen came in view when we saluted them and it was truly laughable to see them put whip and spur to hide their carcasses behind a skirt of wood. This was our last shot on that day. The other batteries continued off and on all day. We moved our piece, which is rifled, to Dr. Friend's farm, after we were through firing, which pleased me as it was a better position.

Saturday, June 21, 1862
On guard today. Nothing transpired of any note. It was a very quiet day on both sides.

Sunday, June 22, 1862
Had inspection as soon as we came off guard, after which a long batch of rules and regulations from General Hill[45] were (*read*) to us. After they were read we were dismissed, when Billy Burgess[46] and myself went down to the woods back of the house and shot off his pistol. We had hardly done so when we were arrested by a corporal and two privates and carried before General Pender[47] who was visiting his pickets. He asked us didn't we know better than be shooting about there. We told him no. He sent us to the captain under the same escort, with the remark that he would take the next in hand himself. I had some fun in quizzing the guard. Told them I felt honored in having such a good looking body guard, (they were as ugly as they make them). The captain was gone away, and they made the report to Lt. Hobson,[48] who said alright. That was the last I heard of it. All quiet again today.

Monday, June 23, 1862[49]
We had several shots at a party building a fort, in conjunction with Long Tom and Laughing Charlie, in the old field I mentioned before. I suppose it was done to try the range of our rifle-pieces, which was very satisfactory indeed, as we threw shell away over the working party.

I don't think we inflicted much damage although we threw one shell which exploded in the midst of them. The balance of the day passed off quietly.

Tuesday, June 24, 1862
On guard today. There is an unusual silence along their lines in front of us, which betokens no good to us. We were undisturbed by a single shot during the entire day.

Wednesday, June 25, 1862
Came off guard at eight o'clock. Soon after coming off the Yanks opened up on us. I went down to the battery from the house to see the fun. While there two shots came over the battery and fell fifty yards in the rear, exploding and making a hole in the earth big enough to bury a man. I went to the house to get dinner and just as I passed in the yard around the house a shell came over my head and killed two of our horses. The shell broke the back of one and entered the other, exploding while in him. I don't think I ever saw such a sight before in all my life. His heart, liver, lights and entrails were completely blown out of him, and for five yards the ground was covered with small particles of flesh and blood. Captain Dabney,[50] came up soon after from the city, and swore like a trooper at his battery not replying. They told him orders had been issued not to return fire unless on a body of troops. He sent over to know if General *Grigg* intended to let the Yanks kill all the horses and they not return the fire. His reply was, if he could do any damage, to give them hell. He opened fire and we were under a terrific shelling all afternoon, but without further damage. Just before sunset orders came to cook four days rations immediately and prepare for a march. We knew there was something up; and all felt confident of a big fight. We got everything ready by nine o'clock and started for Grant's farm. We had not traveled far before our driver ran the gun-carriage against a tree and snapped the pole. The balance of the battery moved on whilst we put in a new one. In course of time that was done when we started again and did not go a great distance before we ran against a stump, got that out of the way after some labor, when we soon came up to one of the baggage wagons that was stalled, when we had to get that out of the mud. Started and did not go farther than a mile when

the baggage wagon got stalled again. This time we had to unload it to get it out and after getting it out, load it again. Thus we were detailed along the route till the sun was an hour high, when we reached Grant's, where I stretched myself and was soon asleep.

Thursday, June 26, 1862

I couldn't tell how long I slept but was awakened by the sun shining down on me in his full force. I got up and went to a spring, washed and ate breakfast, soon after which the battery started, we did not (*know*) where. It halted just this side of Meadow Bridge road. We stayed here until four or five in the evening, when we started to cross the Swamp, our brigade bringing up the rear. We crossed and pursued our way briskly along the direction of the flying enemy. We saw a good many evidences that we had taken them completely by surprise, such as good over coats, blankets, oilcloths, carpet bags, etc., scattered along their line of flight. They kept up their flight till they crossed the Mechanicsville Turnpike and gained their fortifications. Here they made a desperate stand and resisted successfully all our attempts to carry them. The cannonading was the most terrific I ever heard for about two hours. Purcell Battery[51] won an enviable fame. They had thirty killed and wounded. We were in the reserve *corp*, and therefore were not actively engaged, but were under a fearful fire from some of their batteries which sent shell and round shot in a too dangerously close proximity to make us in the least comfortable. The fight raged till nine o'clock when with mutual consent, it ceased, and all laid down on their arms to begin the bloody work again in the morning. We laid down with the firm conviction that on the morrow some of us would fall, and answer no more to our names when the roll was called. It was a sad and melancholy conviction, but there was none so sanguine as to think all of us would come out of the conflict in safety.

During the first of the Seven Days' Battles, at the Battle of Mechanicsville, the Confederates endured substantial losses. Nevertheless, the pitch of the fight rattled Union major general George B. McClellan. Confederate losses (1,400 out of almost 10,000 engaged) were severe compared to Union losses (361 out of about 8,000 engaged); nevertheless, McClellan gave up his base, retreating to put distance between his army and Lee's.[52]

Friday, June 27, 1862

Was awakened just before sunrise. The battle had already begun. After feeding and watering the horses, we took a bit ourselves. We had hardly got through and filled our canteens with fresh water, before we were ordered forward. Just as we got to Mechanicsville Turnpike we were halted. We waited here until the last of General Longstreet's[53] division passed. In the meantime our forces in front had flanked the fortifications of the enemy and caused them to evacuate and beat a rapid retreat. We were soon on the march again, when we passed in front and by these fortifications. They were built on both sides of the road about half way up the hill and were intended for infantry, whilst on top of the hill batteries could be placed which would command the road for a long distance and the hill opposite. In the bottom directly in front of the earthworks, was a strong, wide and deep stream, on both sides of which an *abattis* had been made of fallen trees. It was here that our troops failed to beat them back, and it is not to be wondered at, on yesterday. Many a brave soldier fell here. There were a great many killed and wounded lying on the edge of the public road winding in front of the works. They were lying in all shapes. I saw one that seemed to have been instantly killed in the act of kneeling to shoot, and I suppose the weight of his gun carried his body forward, for he was lying in the same position that a person would be in if he was to kneel down and let his head fall forward till it touched the ground with his face covered by his hands.

But we had only a moment or two for observation. Whilst there I gave a wounded soldier a drink of cool water, as I was leaving him he said we must give the Yanks the devil. We were again in motion. We came up to the Yankees camp where there were several piles of knapsacks; pillaging had already commenced and we helped those who were at it. I got a hat, this memorandum book in which I am writing, and several other articles of small value. We jogged along until one o'clock, when the infantry in front of us reached the open field just this side of Gaines Mill, when they had a skirmish with the enemy. The Maryland Battery, which was in front of us, took position on the left and sent them flying to the rear. When we reached the field the other side of Gaines Mill, we were halted and told to remain till orders came. We were not long there before an aide came up with orders to bring the battery up as soon as possible. "Cannoners Mount," was the command, and away we went in full gallop. We knew we would be in it in a few minutes, but there seemed to be no fear or slinking out. We did not go more than half a mile, when we were turned into a small field on the right, and just before us, through a wide gap in the woods, in an open field the Yanks could be seen in the battle line, whilst on our right in the woods it was alive with them behind strong breastworks. We opened on them in a minute and our fire was not returned for ten minutes, but when they did, how they rained shell, *shrapnell* and special case around us. Well, we were into the fight so quick, that I did not have time to get scared, and after you are in it you don't mind it a great deal, and the longer you stay in the less you care for their fire. We remained under their fire for half an hour before anyone was hurt. Benton Graves was the first to be carried off, wounded in the foot. Marion Knowles soon after followed him, wounded in the leg, and before we were ordered off, Daniel Lancaster mortally wounded. *Ryder*, severely, Sergeant Sidney Strother, mortally, and Robert Hines, killed instantly. Our detachment was not hurt, although several horses were killed. The death of Hines cast a gloom over all. I suppose we had been under fire some two hours or more when we were ordered off. We halted about a quarter of a mile from where we were. I had not much more than fixed my ammunition in the limber-chest, and refilled them, when we were ordered back. I ran all the way so as to keep up with my piece, and when I got there I was nearly out of breath. I had the honor of being the first cannoneer on the field. We were soon lumbering away again, playing sad havoc with the enemy's infantry. Their fire was terribly hot; words inadequate to describe it; you can imagine how terrific it was when eighteen heavy guns and a regiment of sharpshooters were firing at us. We remained under the fire until nearly sundown when we were ordered off, Johnson's battery taking our place. We came out this time with only three slightly wounded, Messrs. George W. Young, Thos. Mallory, and Corp. Wm. Allen. Corp. Allen fired four shots after he was wounded. The protecting hand of Providence is certainly over us for Johnson's battery did not remain over half an hour, when he lost sixteen or twenty wounded and one killed. I was speaking to an acquaintance of mine in the battery who is an Englishman, when he said it was the hottest place this side of —ell. Our loss during the evening was one killed and eight wounded amongst the men,[54] twenty-one horses killed and wounded, two gun carriages disabled, and the caisson to my detachment was so impaired that it was left on the field. Some of our boys lost their overcoats, blankets and jackets by the caisson being left. They were taken by our own soldiers. Even the body of Robert Hines was robbed. I had no idea that we possessed in our army so monstrous a villain as to rob our own dead. But it is too true. Soon after we left the field the enemy was routed from their strongholds, and a number of pieces captured. We fell to the rear about a mile, and the men were so tired and broken down, that everyone fell asleep almost as soon as he could make his couch on the bare earth and the heaven for his roof. There is no doubt many a prayer of thankfulness was uttered by those who came out unscathed ere they did go to sleep.

The second of the Seven Days' Battle, the Battle of Gaines' Mill followed the relatively inconclusive Battle of Mechanicsville. General Robert E. Lee renewed his previous days' assault against the right flank of the Union army, which remained isolated on the north side of the Chickahominy River. Around nightfall the Confederates launched a coordinated attack, breaking Union lines and driving the Union infantry back toward the Chickahominy River. The Federals retreated across the river during the night. While Lee failed to pursue the retreating Union army, his army's success at the Battle of Gaines' Mill preserved Richmond for the Confederacy. The defeat of Union forces convinced Union commander Major General George B. McClellan to abandon his advance on Richmond and beat a hasty retreat to the safety of his earlier encampment farther east, on the James River. See Burton, Extraordinary Circumstances: The Seven Days Battles.

Saturday, June 28, 1862
Awoke this morning feeling tolerably fresh. My right eye was a little swelled and a slight breaking-out on my left temple. After taking a good wash and eating breakfast, our battery was ordered forward to join the division. The captain sent word that he could only bring three pieces. General *Grigg* reply was "Bring them along, they are as good as six of the enemy's." We were soon hitched up and on our way to join the brigade. Soon after we reached it we were ordered by Major General Hill to go to Richmond and refit. Captain insisted with the wish of Gen. *Grigg* that we should be allowed to go with our brigade, but he said no, he had plenty of artillery, and that we deserved to go to the rear and go we should. When the captain told us we had elicited praise from both our generals, it done us more good than any else that could

be named. After taking a drink of old rye round at the commissary tent, we started for Richmond. We passed a large number of soldiers soon after starting going in *persuit* of the enemy. We reached Richmond about the hour of six in the evening and camped on Union Hill. The captain gave us permission to visit our relations in the city until next morning at ten o'clock. We brought the body of Robert Hines along to be buried with his relations. We heard that Sergeant Strother[55] was dead which sent a thrill of sorrow through our hearts, for he had endeared himself to all of his affable and gentlemanly bearing.

Sunday, June 29, 1862

Reached camp this morning just before time for roll call. From that time till dinner I was kept busy packing ammunition. At five o'clock we were mustered to attend the funeral of our departed comrade in arms, Sidney Strother. As we marched through the streets many asked the question if we were Yankees, judging us to be from our blue uniforms. We went to the residence of his father and (*as*) the services were over, escorted the body to Hollywood Cemetery and consigned to Mother Earth. The captain then gave us permission to go home, which I was very glad of, for it was a great deal nearer than camp, and I was completely broken down. After eating a hearty supper I retired to seek rest in balmy sleep.

Monday, June 30, 1862

My right eye was greatly swollen,[56] and the eruption had spread high up on my forehead. I determined to go see a doctor before reaching camp, therefore went to see Dr. Thomas[57] who told me I had become infected with poison oak and wrote the same to the captain asking a few days to be relieved. He very churlishly refused by saying that I must get a certificate from a regular army surgeon, knowing that there was none near. I did nothing all day for I immediately put myself on the sick list. I got a pass from Lieut. *Johnson*[58] to go home. I started for home with a considerable fever and was truly glad when I reached it, determined not to hurry myself back.

Tuesday, July 1, 1862

Reached camp about 12 o'clock feeling very badly indeed. I lounged about until six o'clock in the evening when I went home with a high fever. Went to see a lady friend and had an elegant time. Met an old friend there who I had not seen but once in six months. After leaving there, he accompanied me home staying all night.

Wednesday, July 2, 1862

Got up this morning feeling much worse than I had done yet. The rain was pouring down and I could not go to camp. Got father to go to Dr. Thomas and see if he could not come and see me. He came back with some medicine and said that Dr. told him I was to take it and must not leave the house. I did so. In the evening I thought I would burn up with fever. I don't recollect of having so hot a one before.

Thursday, July 3, 1862[59]

Feel much better this morning although the fever has not entirely gone. Father went to the camp to explain my absence, whilst there the battery started to join the brigade and I was left behind, the first time since I belonged to it, and it is my wish to be with it now, but cannot go through weakness. From this date until July 15 I remained in town. Nothing of an exciting nature transpired. Met E. A. Smith have not seen him before in three years. Those ladies I met at Hanover Junction arrived in the city Sunday, July 6. Spent a good many happy hours in the company of one of them during my stay. I left her very reluctantly indeed and if I did not wish the war would end, nobody ever did.

"Father went to the camp to explain my absence . . ."—This entry strongly implies that Thomas Norcliffe Jones and William Graves Crenshaw had a prior relationship and that William Ellis Jones's presence in the battery was at least partially a result of that relationship. Under no other circumstances could it be conceivable that a parent would go to an army camp, during wartime, to visit a soldier's commanding officer in order to make excuses for his son's absence. The only supportable idea excusing William's absence is that his father had a business or social relationship with Crenshaw. Since it is unlikely these two men moved in the same social circles, the presumption is that Thomas Norcliffe Jones (or William B. Jones) was useful to Crenshaw in his myriad business and political endeavors.

"Met E. A. Smith have not seen him before in three years."—William writes of meeting Edgar Alonza Smith, who, after completing a year of his voluntary enlistment following Virginia joining the Confederacy, returned to private life in Richmond. By March 1862, he was working in offices on Main Street in Richmond.[60] The lady whom

William "left . . . very reluctantly" refers to the then Miss Florence Smith, Edgar's sister, who would (almost immediately following the war) become Mrs. William Ellis Jones. This statement supports William's initial reluctance to join the Confederate army.

Tuesday, July 15, 1862
Started to camp this morning in company with W. W. Smith,[61] a comrade in arms. The day was extremely hot and it was late in the afternoon when we reached it. I was very sorry I came out, for the camp is in a miserable place and anything but healthy. Captain is sick, and Jas. *Ellet*, 1st Lieut.,[62] commands, and the men say he is playing a rough game, tying the boys on the guns by the wholesale.

Wednesday, July 16, 1862
Nothing of importance to relate today. We had a ration of whiskey, which put a smile of satisfaction upon the faces of all. The day was killed by the boys the best way they could.

Thursday, July 17, 1862
Had another ration of whiskey this morning. It is a pity we cannot get it every day; I think the health of the army would improve. *Goosby*[63] ran the blockade yesterday and came back today, when he was made to ride the gun, for two or three hours. Had severe thunderstorms this evening, the wind very nearly blowing the tent down.

Friday, July 18, 1862
There was a serious accident today. Mr. Loving[64] whilst going to the woods with his ax on his shoulder stumbled and fell, and by some means or other the ax fell across his left hand and cut off his forefinger and very nearly his middle one. The doctor took his finger off at the middle joint, but left the other. Life in camp, as it is now, is decidedly tedious and monotonous.

Saturday, July 19, 1862
Had a drill this morning in the manual of the piece which helped pass the morning off. Corporal Hackley[65] was broke of his office and placed on the gun. He was tied in a very severe manner and caused him a great deal of pain. He was punished thus for running the blockade to Rich'd. Fell in at five o'clock for drill but were excused as we had received orders

to change camp next morning at eight o'clock. We were pleased with this order. This is the second dark chapter.

Sunday, July 20, 1862

We were prepared at the prescribed time and after marching about half an hour reached our new campground which was the junction of Osborne and New Market roads. It was a large field covered with undergrowth but "nary" a tree to shield us from the sun. We had to go to work and clean a place for our camp, which was hot work, for the sun seemed to have power enough to boil an egg. We soon pitched our tents and by night had everything tolerable comfortable, or as much so as we could in that place.

". . . Osborne and New Market roads."—Today this location remains a place generally bereft of shade. There is a historical marker at the site informing passersby that this location is the place where the formal surrender of Richmond took place, two years and nine months after William Ellis Jones camped there with the Crenshaw Battery.

Monday, July 21, 1862

Nothing to do today but eat and sleep. Whilst splitting wood for to cook dinner I hit myself a severe blow on the shinbone just below the knee. As the ax was descending it came off the helm and the end of the helm came down with great force on the bone. I was unable to walk to the tent and had to call for help. I don't think I ever experienced such pain before in my life. I had to pass the balance of the day laying down, which was not at all to my liking.

Tuesday, July 22, 1862

My leg is much worse. Can't walk without a stick bearing my foot off the ground. Battery drill was resumed this morning. This is the first one since we left *Massopomax* Hill, near Fredericksburg. Nothing happened to change the monotony of camp life.

". . . since we left Massopomax Hill, near Fredericksburg."—Here, William referred to the location where the battery was stationed in May, which he previously called "Eastern View," now known as Prospect Hill. Brigadier General Joseph R. Anderson, in a May 17, 1862, note to General R. S. Ewell, refers to this location as "Camp on Massaponax Hill."[66]

Wednesday, July 23, 1862

My leg is a little better; I can bear a little more weight on it. Had battery drill again this morning. The day was passed in eating and sleeping.

Thursday, July 24, 1862

My leg is better. I can walk without a stick but with some pain. As the battery was on drill it received orders to join the brigade. Came back and everything put in marching order. We moved off just after dinner. I was left at the division hospital, as I was unfit for duty. It was the first time I was ever in one as an inmate, and it was with no very agreeable feelings that I entered the hotel for sick soldiers. I was put in a large tent, and to consider that as my castle, although I may have to receive some guests ere long. I went to the burial of two soldiers just at sunset. The first time I ever witnessed such a scene, and was not at all pleased at the unceremonious manner in which they were put under the ground. The doctor gave me some liniment to rub my leg with, which I applied vigorously before going to sleep.

Friday, July 25, 1862

My leg is much sorer than it was yesterday. I suppose I had to walk too much on it. The day was passed in indolence. I had to receive six guests this morning and had more coming, but I cried out that my "castle" was full to over flowing.

Saturday, July 26, 1862

My leg seems to be at a stand still, for it does not mend any. Dr. Powell examined it today, and said I had not (*illegible*) in the bone, as I thought, but had broke some of the muscles in my leg, which caused the acute pain in the calf when I walk. One of the patients in the third tent had a fit today. I never saw anyone have such a fit before in my life. He made a noise more like a cat than anything I ever heard, and as he got better he would call for his "Mammy" for a minute and then break out in horrid oaths. It was horrible to hear how he carried on.

Sunday, July 27, 1862

My leg felt a little stronger this morning. After breakfast I took a good wash and fixed up a little, when I thought I would walk across to the 40th regiment of Virginia volunteers to see an acquaintance and carried a strap he loaned me a week back. I spent a couple hours very agreeably in conversation, when I returned to my castle. In the afternoon Col. Walker's[67] orderly, when he told me he had orders for the company to cook rations for three days, and that the whole division had to join Jackson, I was glad of this and determined to go with the battery.

Monday, July 28, 1862
The battery passed just before dinner, when I jumped into the ambulance and went along with the battery. We encamped on Union Hill[68] for the night, so as to allow the men living in the city time to go and see their relations and friends and bid them goodbye. I got a pass till four and a half o'clock next morning. Saw my relations and bid them all goodbye. Went to see a lady friend,[69] who is quite favorable with me, and spent a couple (*hours*) in pleasant and agreeable conversation, when I took my leave very loathfully. Went home to snatch a few hours sleep.

Part 3

MARCH TO JOIN JACKSON AND
ON TO SECOND MANASSAS
JULY 29–SEPTEMBER 1, 1862

This portion of the journal demonstrates the pace and rhythm the war would demand from William and his fellow soldiers. Beginning with daily marches often exceeding twenty miles in length and sometimes approaching thirty, Robert E. Lee's Army of Northern Virginia, once united with Thomas J. "Stonewall" Jackson's division, was in a constant race to outwit, outmaneuver, and sometimes outrun the invading Union forces, which sought to overwhelm northern Virginia. William's prose is deeply descriptive throughout this section, as he shifts from literary allusions to starkly haunting depictions of battle and death, all balanced by his clear recognition of the bounty and beauty of Virginia's countryside.

This "second dark chapter," as William styles it, details executions and cholera in camp and grave concerns he harbors about the quality of his battery's leadership, all while he and his comrades fight desperately to survive the Battles of Cedar Mountain, Second Manassas, and Chantilly. All of this is juxtaposed against occasional respite on the lawns of some of the finest

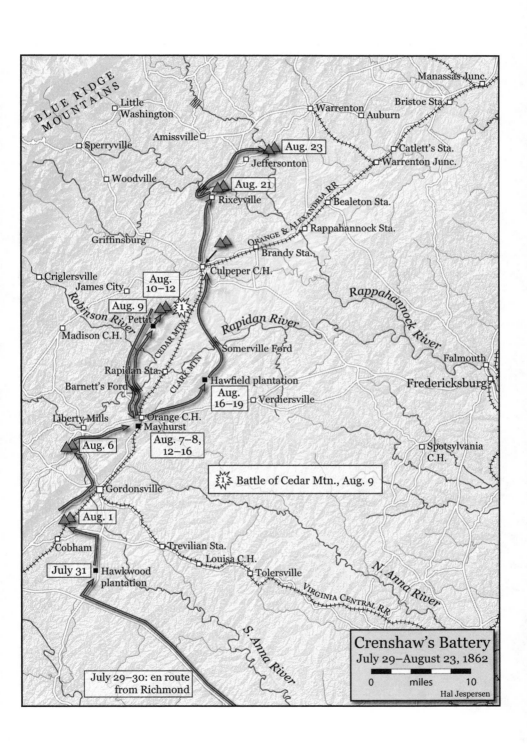

BLUE RIDGE MOUNTAINS

Little Washington

Sperryville

Amissville

Woodville

Warrenton
Auburn
Bristoe Sta.
Manassas Junc.

Catlett's Sta.
Warrenton Junc.

Jeffersonton
Aug. 23

Rixeyville
Aug. 21

Bealeton Sta.

Griffinsburg

ORANGE & ALEXANDRIA RR
Rappahannock Sta.

Brandy Sta.

Rappahannock River

Criglersville
James City

Aug. 10–12

Culpeper C.H.

Robinson River

Aug. 9
Pettit

Madison C.H.

Rapidan River

Somerville Ford

Falmouth

Fredericksburg

CEDAR MTN

CLARK MTN

Rapidan Sta.

Barnett's Ford

Hawfield plantation
Aug. 16–19
Verdiersville

Liberty Mills

Orange C.H.
Mayhurst

Aug. 7–8, 12–16

Aug. 6

Battle of Cedar Mtn., Aug. 9

Spotsylvania C.H.

Gordonsville

Aug. 1

Cobham

Trevilian Sta.

Louisa C.H.

N. Anna River

July 31
Hawkwood plantation

Tolersville

VIRGINIA CENTRAL RR

S. Anna River

July 29–30: en route from Richmond

Crenshaw's Battery
July 29–August 23, 1862

0   miles   10

Hal Jespersen

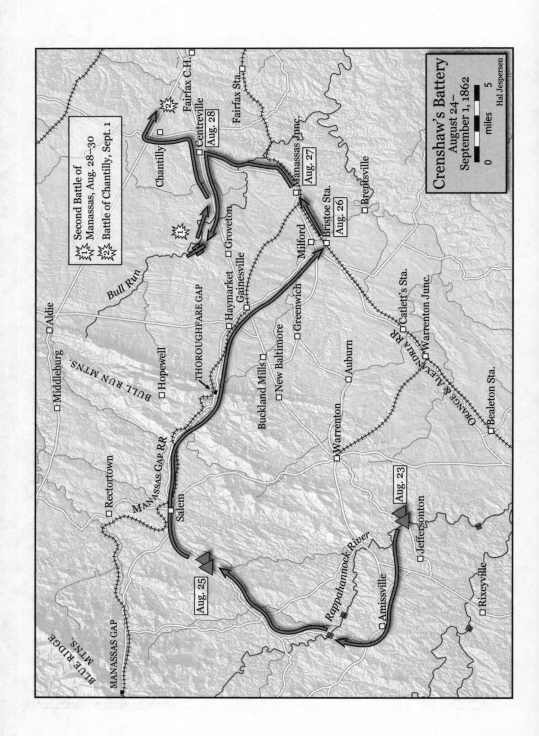

Crenshaw's Battery
August 24–
September 1, 1862

Hal Jespersen

0   miles   5

Second Battle of
Manassas, Aug. 28–30

Battle of Chantilly, Sept. 1

BLUE RIDGE
MTNS.

MANASSAS GAP

Rectortown

Middleburg

Aldie

Salem

MANASSAS GAP RR

Hopewell

BULL RUN MTNS.

THOROUGHFARE GAP

Bull Run

Chantilly

Fairfax C.H.

Centreville
Aug. 28

Fairfax Sta.

Haymarket

Groveton

Gainesville

Milford

Manassas Junc.
Aug. 27

Bristoe Sta.
Aug. 26

Brentsville

Buckland Mills

New Baltimore

Greenwich

Auburn

Catlett's Sta.

Warrenton Junc.

ORANGE & ALEXANDRIA RR

Bealeton Sta.

Warrenton

Aug. 23

Jeffersonton

Rappahannock River

Amissville

Rixeyville

Aug. 25

plantations in central Virginia. William also captures a close view of Jackson in a rare moment of the general's quiet contemplation.

The battery marched over 250 miles between July 29 and September 1, 1862.

Tuesday, July 29, 1862

Arrived at camp just in time for roll call. After hitching up we went to the corner of 17th and Main streets, to meet the other batteries of the division. They did not come up until about nine o'clock, when we passed through the city and took the James River road running into Goochland. The scenery along the route was very beautiful. Some of the farms done a person good to look at them, having such fine crops of corn and presenting a neat and interesting appearance. After traveling twenty miles we stopped to encamp for the night. At the roll call we were informed that we would be aroused at two in the morning so as to resume our march at daylight. Rather an unwelcome announcement, for I felt tired and unwell.

". . . 17th and Main streets . . ."—17th and Main Street, now 17th and East Main Street, is in the "Shockoe Bottom" neighborhood of Richmond. The modern location is about three blocks east of Richmond's historic "Tobacco Row" district and two blocks south of the old train station. This location would have placed the battery within easy sight of the slave market, which was the busiest enterprise in the "bottom" area of Richmond, and within blocks of where William spent his youth at William H. Clemmitt's printing concern.

Wednesday, July 30, 1862

Aroused at two, answered roll call, and not having any horses to attend to, went back to bed and took another nap. At good daylight we started when we did not go more than two miles when we came to a high hill, which delayed us at least two hours, during which the rain came down in torrents. Feeling quite weak and sick, and my leg paining me a great deal, I got in one of our baggage wagons and thus escaped the rain. After climbing the hill we traveled at a pretty good pace. We passed by Goochland Court House. It consists of a jail, court house, one or two residences, store and a bar-room, which was closed by Col. Walker till the batteries passed. It was opened as soon as they passed, when I thought if I could get a drink of good brandy it would do me good, therefore in I went; didn't have any brandy but whiskey was plentiful.

Asked the price, two fifty a quart. Took a drink and paid twenty-five cents for it, when it took the shine out of any villainous liquor I ever drank. If a man took three drinks of it, I believe it would make him steal.

After going about the same distance we did yesterday, we bivouacked for the night. The people all along the route vied with each other in doing kindness for the soldiers. One family sent the cooks to work and had a free table till the train passed. The country as a general thing was not as good as that we passed through yesterday, but yet the crops were very fair indeed.

Thursday, July 31, 1862

Started this morning in a drenching rain, which promised to last all day. I took some medicine which did me a great deal of good. It rained off and on all day, which kept us pretty close in the wagons with the cover drawn down, therefore excluding the country from my view. We stopped in sight of the "Southwestern Mountains," on Mr. Overton's farm who was very hospitable to our boys. We went to bed with the prospect of a good night's rest, as we were not to move until seven in the morning.

". . . Mr. Overton's farm . . ."—Despite being gutted by a fire in 1982, "Hawkwood" still stands today in Louisa County, Virginia. The grand and complicated house was designed in the style of a Tuscan villa by the well-known architect Alexander Jackson Davis for Richard Overton Morris in the early 1850s. The house is now owned by Preservation Virginia and is not accessible to the public.

Friday, August 1, 1862

We passed through the Green Springs neighborhood in Louisa County, and finer and prettier farms I never saw before in my life. Every farmer seemed to vie with each other in keeping the neatest farm. About one o'clock we came up with Jackson's division, which had retreated about six miles south of Gordonsville. His men had happy and cheerful countenances, and looked decidedly healthy. After being stopped on the road about two or three hours looking for a camp and watering the horses, we encamped about three miles east of the Southwestern mountains. These mountains are not very lofty but present a handsome spectacle. There is something about these marks of God's power that instills an awe, and suspends the breath at the first gaze, and inspiring you with the conviction that there is an over-ruling hand which guideth and controleth the world, despite the sneers of *Payne* and the ridicule of Voltaire and the teaching of the German philosophers. They speak with a still small voice to the heart that there is a God, and proclaim him beneficent to man, in bestowing upon him so bountifully the good things of nature. This is the gayest army I have seen yet. The men seem to have more life and spirit than any troops in service. They swear by Father Jackson, as they call him, and believe him to be the greatest general in the field. Their bands played lively airs till after ten o'clock, at the end of Maryland and Dixie,[1] the woods resounded with cheers of the men, showing that they have attentive listeners. On guard tonight.

Saturday, August 2, 1862

Went to see some friends in the 21st and 22nd regiments in Jackson's division. One I had not seen for some time and the meeting was very pleasant indeed. I spent an hour or two in conversation and took my leave, having left camp without permission. The day was excessively warm. The nights are cool and pleasant no matter how hot the days are, sometimes rendering a couple of blankets necessary. The day was passed, generally, by the men sleeping and lying about resting themselves after their long march.

Sunday, August 3, 1862

This is a lovely Sunday morning, the sun shining with great brilliancy, the birds caroling their sweetest songs, and the air, it seems, "a solemn stillness holds." Was visited by a couple of friends from the 21st Virginia regiment, whose company I had the pleasure of enjoying nearly all day. As luck would have it, we had a good dinner for camp life, to set out before them which they seemed to enjoy heartily. The evening was passed in jovial conversation, calling to mind good times we had in the past and dwelling on them with peculiar pleasure. We had several showers during the evening, and at night-fall it set in with the prospect of having a night's rain, which was not encouraging as the fly we had pitched had already commenced to leak. Learned today that we had been transposed from General *Grigg*'s to General Pender's[2] brigade, which caused a decided dissatisfaction with the officers and men. A rumour, also got afloat that the captain intended to resign and that he was going to put it to the men whether they wanted the company disbanded or not. It caused considerable discussion amongst the men, and a speech from our "Profitt"[3] who said if we voted to disband he would treat to whiskey when we got to Folersville, which elicited much applause. Disbanding, I soon found out, would be voted in toto.[4] No roll call on account of the weather.

"... 'a solemn stillness holds' . . ."—*This line is quoted from Thomas Gray's "Elegy, Written in a Country Churchyard." Gray is considered among the very best eighteenth-century English poets, and "Elegy" is his most successful poetical work.*

"Was visited by a couple of friends from the 21st Virginia regiment, whose company I had the pleasure of enjoying nearly all day."—Among these friends was almost certainly Private Robert Alonzo Brock, who enlisted with Company F, 21st Virginia Infantry, on April 21, 1861, at the age of twenty-two years. Brock was made corporal on April 22, 1862, and then detailed by General Robert E. Lee on June 12, 1862, for special service. In 1862 he was promoted to captain of infantry.

Also serving in Company F was Private James Caskie Cabell,[5] brother of Robert Gamble Cabell and father of James Branch Cabell. Many years after the war, James Branch Cabell, a Richmond author and genealogist of substantial fame, became friends with William Ellis Jones's eldest son F. Ellis Jones. Additionally, it is reported that William Ellis Jones and James Branch Cabell became friends late in Jones's life.[6] William Ellis Jones's firm published several of Cabell's genealogy books, including The Branch of Abingdon and Proceedings, 1783–1824: The Society of the Cincinnati in the State of Virginia. (See the list of materials published under the imprint of William Ellis Jones, available online at www.siupress.com/spiritsofbadmenlinks.)

". . . he was going to put it to the men whether they wanted the company disbanded or not."—This subject throws light on one of the most unusual features of the Confederate army. The original units were almost all volunteer organizations who selected their own officers. While it is true the passage of the Conscription Act made service a matter of compulsion, volunteer units still retained the right to disband as organizations if they chose. If they did so, the battery would be broken up and individual soldiers (now conscripts) would be assigned to other units.

Monday, August 4, 1862

Aroused this morning to roll call at two o'clock when we were informed that orders had been received to cook one day's rations by four o'clock and await further orders. As we had a cook I went back to bed to get a snooze as my eyes still felt heavy. Got up and ate breakfast and found nothing to carry along, as provisions had run short. The disbanding topic was on every tongue and nothing could be heard but "Are you going to vote for it?" "Yes, are you?" Which was generally answered in the affirmative. About ten o'clock the bugle sounded for the men to fall in, when all were required to be present. We knew something was out. The roll was called and the men counted, when 78 were found to be present.[7] The Captain then informed the men that he had been considering for sometime resigning his position as captain, and that he had determined to do so, for he thought he could do more good out than in the service. I was exactly of his mind. Jas. *Ellet*, 1st Lieut. then made a short speech, stating that since we had been mustered in the Conscript Act had been passed by Congress, which by promotion would make him captain, but that he would not take the position unless the men were willing to serve under him. He was not that kind of man. If we voted for disbanding he would send in our petition and do all he could to get it granted. He went on at a pretty strain but it did not do any good. Lieut. Johnston made a few remarks in which he said he stood exactly where Lieut. *Ellet* did and that we would be conscripts if we disbanded. Captain Crenshaw immediately said that if we could not be disbanded and *places* as were before to choose any company we wished, he would stay with us till the war ended, which remark was applauded by the men. Lieut. Thos. *Ellet* got up and said that he had nothing more to say than this, that what the company did would get his approval. The vote was taken, when 72 voted for, 3 declined to vote, on the fence, and 3 against disbanding. I don't think there were ever two more *cress*-fallen officers than *Ellet* and Johnston. They were grumbling and muttering all day. I think *Ellet* regrets placing himself on the platform as he did. If he had not shown such a tyrannical disposition when acting captain he would certainly have been made captain at the resignation of Captain Crenshaw. The boys were light-hearted all day, and no doubt went to bed only to dream of disbanding companies and crest-fallen officers.

Tuesday, August 5, 1862

The morning passed off as usual, the boys lying around in a lazy, listless manner. In the afternoon a portion of Jackson's division passed by us on their way to Gordonsville. I saw the well known Stonewall Brigade, and it was as fine a body of men as I ever looked upon. It was very warm, yet they walked along pertly, and the only desire they expressed was to get back to the Valley. They think that there is no spot on earth so supremely *blest* as their dearly loved Valley. No Mohammedan ever turned his steps with more loving devotion to Mecca than these troops cherish toward their lovely homes. They proved their devotion by the willingness with which they undergo hardships and pour out their hearts' blood in defence of it. A truly brave and patriotic people, and posterity will not soon forget them. Got orders to cook one day's rations just as night fall and to move at early dawn. Very bad piece of intelligence to me as I am on guard tonight, but am determined to get as much sleep as possible, for we may have a long march before us.

Wednesday, August 6, 1862

The camp was aroused at half past two this morning and everything was put in readiness to march by early dawn. But no orders came. Thus we laid about till half past three o'clock when orders came. Off we start, taking the road to Gordonsville. We soon reach this delectable village, situated at or near the base of the Southwestern mountains. Like all villages the houses are built on one street, the stores being at the head nearest the railroad. Some of the houses were very neat and handsome, bespeaking tasty inmates. I received a letter from a dear friend in Richmond just as soon as I reached the place, and I was so much taken up in the perusal of it, that I only took cursory glances. Saw a few pretty goodlooking damsels though, which would render a stop there of a week quite a pleasure if a fellow could bask in the sunlight of their smiles. We did not make any stop there, but kept in the "tenor of our ways," and were soon crossing the mountains. It is the first time I ever crossed and it was not a very pleasant journey as my leg has not ceased to hurt me. After crossing we were delayed an hour by the baggage train before us, and did not encamp till Old Sol gave up his sway to the milder rays of Cynthia.[8] We have a miserable camp and I hope we will make a short stay here. The scenery around here is decidedly mountainous and picturesque.

"... 'tenor of our ways' ..."—*This snip is from a sermon by the Reverend Matthew Henry titled "The Folly of Despising Our Own Ways," from The Miscellaneous Works of Rev. Matthew Henry, published in 1830 in London. The sermon is taken from Proverbs 19:16: "but he that despiseth his ways shall die."*

Thursday, August 7, 1862

Soon after roll call we were ordered to cook provisions to last till to-morrow night, which kept us pretty busy all morning. Those not thus engaged sought the cooling shade of a beautiful forest on a small mountain contiguous to our camp and passed the time in playing cards, (an *indispensible* sport it seems in camp life) and sleeping. At four o'clock the battery was put in marching order. Presently our old brigade came by heading our division. Our captain informed General Gregg we had been taken from him and put in Pender's brigade. He expressed great surprise and said it was the first he had heard of it and regretted very much that it was done. As the regiment passed a good many of them asked if "you'ins want going along with we'ins." These words are decidedly local and original with the South Carolinians. They soon passed and brigade after brigade followed till I could almost say their lines "stretched out to the crack of doom." We did not start till near about sunset and then it was up hill and down hill all the way, fatiguing the men very much. We reached the outer edge of Orange C.H. between 11 and 12 o'clock where we bivouacked for the night. It is needless to say that all went to sleep as soon as possible.

". . . 'stretched out to the crack of doom.'"—*The phrase "crack of doom" first appeared in Shakespeare's Macbeth, referencing a parade of kings who are shown to Macbeth by the prophesying witches in the play. This line also appears in a speech made by a Mr. Stanton, appearing on page 479 of the "Proceedings of the General Anti-Slavery Convention" from the British and Foreign Anti-Slavery Society, published in London in 1841. In this speech, Mr. Stanton uses the phrase to describe current U.S. foreign policy on institutionalized slavery—that is, the proposition that the United States, if left unchecked, would extend slavery universally throughout the hemisphere, spreading it to Mexico, South America, the Caribbean, and beyond.*[9]

Friday, August 8, 1862

Was aroused this morning by a comrade when I found Old Sol was bathing me in his morning smiles. Got up, took a bite or two and retired to the shade of the neighboring tree. Not long after we started and passed through the town and stopped on the northern edge. Orange C.H. is quite a pretty village about the size of Gordonsville. There are many handsome private residences, but none so fine as Jno. Willis' country residence situated where we encamped last night. Nearly all the citizens had left the place taking everything with them in the eating line and it was impossible to get dinner or supper for one-hundredth part that wanted it. About four o'clock we received orders to cook two days rations and park our artillery for the night. I then took a stroll into the place to look around and the closed stores and residences brought to mind Goldsmith's "Sweet Auburn, loveliest village of the plain" and therefore, a person could form no adequate opinion as to the character and hospitality of its people. Went back and was put on guard which was not agreeable to me, for we have a long day's march before us.

"*. . . none so fine as Jno. Willis' country residence . . .*"—*Mayhurst Mansion (now more commonly referred to simply as "Mayhurst"), built in 1859 for John and Lucy Willis, is a 9,200-square-foot Italianate-Victorian residence, distinguished by fanciful architecture and an oval-spiral staircase ascending four floors. Mayhurst is located just south of Orange, Virginia, and has recently operated as a bed and breakfast.*

"*. . . 'Sweet Auburn, loveliest village of the plain' . . .*"—*Oliver Goldsmith was an Anglo-Irish novelist, playwright, and poet, best known for his novel The Vicar of Wakefield. This line quoted by William is from Goldsmith's poem "The Deserted Village," written in response to an event Goldsmith witnessed in 1760. In rural Ireland an ancient village was destroyed; its houses, farms, and common lands were leveled to clear property for a wealthy man's estate and formal gardens. Goldsmith's poem expressed a fear that the closing of the common lands, subsequent depopulation and erasure of villages, and conversion of land from productive agriculture to ornamental landscape gardens would ruin the peasantry.*

Saturday, August 9, 1862

Started this morning before sunrise and all felt that we would have a fight before sunset. We traveled as fast as we could under a sun that must have been one hundred degrees in the shade. We crossed the Rapidan at Barnett's Ford where there was a pretty good skirmish last night[10] at twelve o'clock between 400 Yankee cavalry and some of our troops. A pretty daring dash for the Yanks. It is quite a novel sight to see a regiment crossing a stream. Such a pulling off of shoes and stockings, rolling up pants and the majority of them taking off their pants.

We had nothing of this to do for we rode on the caisson. We traveled on and saw a good many evidences of the outrages committed by the Hessians. There was one place which must have been a lovely spot before the war, but now a perfect waste. We crossed Robinson's River in the middle of the day,[11] a small stream which empties itself into the Rapidan and is the *boundry* line between Madison and Culpeper counties. We reached Mrs. Pettit's farm about four or five o'clock,[12] when the battle had commenced. We halted and were ordered to remain here until further orders. We could plainly hear the din at first but it gradually ceased till nothing but the sullen roar of artillery could be heard, and that died out by nightfall. We whipped the Yanks very badly after a sharp and bloody struggle and drove them back two miles. General *Wender,*[13] a gallant officer and commander of the Stonewall Brigade, was killed by a piece of a shell. His death was quite a misfortune to the country. The 21st and 23rd Virginia regiments done deeds of valor. At one time the 23rd was surrounded by the foe and had to cut their way out, which they did in gallant style. The Yanks fought with more bravery on this occasion than they have ever done, charging and receiving and giving bayonet thrusts, and in some incidences clubbing their muskets and tapping our brave boys on the cranium, but all this was met by Virginia lads with an ardor and coolness that they could not stand and therefore retired leaving the field and woods strewed with their killed and wounded. We took a great many prisoners. I saw a batch of two hundred and fifty amongst them were a great many officers. We also took *Brid.* Gen. Prince.[14] These prisoners seemed to be lively and very chatty. Some of them told awful big lies about their forces, saying that Pope[15] had four hundred thousand troops and that he would bring up two hundred and seventy one pieces of artillery during the night, all of which was believed. I got tired of listening to them and went over to where we were parked to get a little sleep, when a pretty severe thunderstorm commenced. I had not more than got there when orders came for us to report to Col. Walker about four miles down the road. Our boys were aroused and they soon put themselves in marching order. Soon after starting the cannonade ceased. We learned that Purcell battery was shelling the roads and that they were soon silenced, the enemy bringing three batteries up all bearing on them. Lieut. *Featherstone*[16] and a private were killed and eight wounded, also losing eight horses. Our march was anything but agreeable as we met ambulances filled with wounded all along the road, and as we approached the battlefield the groans of the wounded were pitiful to hear. A great many dead bodies were laying just on the edge of the road and their ghastly and bloody features were not pleasant to look upon in the moon's pale light. I don't think I ever shall forget that march. After getting to our stopping place we parked our pieces and immediately went to sleep. Although we were in good shelling range of their guns. There is one outrage I must not omit. Opposite to a mill at *Burnett's* Ford[17] lived two estimable ladies. Whilst the Yankee cavalry was leaving this ford this morning two infernal scoundrels took deliberate aim at them, whilst sitting in their door, and shot one of them just above the knee and the other in the foot. General Jackson took down as near as he could from some prisoners what company and regiment they belonged to. Hanging is too good for such miscreants. They ought to be covered with tar and set on fire.

This diary entry was penned on the day of the Battle of Cedar Mountain. While this battle raged, Confederates marched on Culpeper Courthouse to delay a Union advance into the area of Central Virginia. After taking a beating in the first part of the battle, the Confederates counterattacked and broke the Union lines, resulting in a Confederate victory. The Union counted casualties of 2,353. The Confederates counted 1,338 casualties. See Krick, Stonewall Jackson at Cedar Mountain.

"We traveled on and saw a good many evidences of the outrages committed by the Hessians."—As noted previously, many Confederates used terms like "hirelings" and "Hessians" to demonize their foe, associating Union soldiers with mere mercenaries who had no cause beyond a regular paycheck and rations. See Rable, Damn Yankees!

Sunday, August 10, 1862

Got up this morning before sunrise and with a couple comrades went back to the battle-field. About two hundred yards from our park lay three cavalry terribly mangled, one of them with his entrails on the ground. After walking about a half mile we reached the hottest part of the fighting ground and many a Yankee found a hospitable grave instead of niggers and a farm. I suppose there were three hundred dead on the part I visited, whilst I did not see three of ours. One thing I can say for them is that nearly everyone of them "fell with his face to the foe." Whilst in the woods a shell came whizzing past and burst beyond us, which made us hurry back to the company. As I was going back I picked up a testament, a book which I have wanted for some time. Soon after getting to the battery we were ordered to the rear half a mile. Here we found a brother with a couple of comrades burying a brother.

It was an affecting scene. As the grave was being filled with the loved ones lost to view forever on this earth, the brother's eyes were filled with tears and his form convulsed with grief. Rumors came that we were on the retreat and we were again moved which seemed to confirm them. Whilst stationed in park with a piece of woods out of sight of the Yanks, a stampede was caused by some cavalry. They started the wagon drivers and ambulances which came rushing down the road in headlong speed, they started a lot of sick and stragglers in a piece of wood, they started our boys, a good many of whom were asleep and two other batteries near us. Some of our boys, I must say to their shame, rushed out of the woods and passed their battery, when they were called to their senses by the officers. It came like a whirlwind and passed as quick. They came back and took their places at the piece, and when the Battery was ordered off it moved in good order. It stopped but a short while on a neighboring hill when it was sent further back. A heavy rain came up just as we got to the halting place, and I saved myself by getting in the ambulance. As soon as it was over we were again ordered off and it commenced raining as we started. Whew! What a rain it was! It came down in torrents and everybody was wet to the skin who had no oilcloth *overhauls*. We stopped pretty soon again and after the rain was over, built big fires and dried our clothes, cooked some fat bacon by holding it over the fire by a stick and ate it with some hard crackers and went to sleep, pretty well satisfied with our day's labor.

Monday, August 11, 1862

Awoke at sunrise, cooked a piece of fresh beef without salt and ate it with hard crackers. The enemy sent in a flag of truce to bury their dead, which was granted. General *Stewart*[18] went out to meet them, when he found they were advancing their troops under it. He informed them that they had to take down their flag of truce or stop the advance of their troops, he didn't care which. They stopped the advance of their troops and went to work burying their dead. At two o'clock (the time allowed them being up) they asked for more time, which was granted. I had a good look at Gen. Jackson today. I should never have taken him for the great Valley hero. He wore a faded uniform coat, pants and cape, somewhat round-shouldered and looks on the ground when he walks as if he has lost something; altogether he presents more the appearance of a well-to-do farmer than a military chieftain. He has an eye that sparkles with brilliancy and a brow that denotes a great thinker. You would pass him by in a crowd and never know him to be the pride of our people and the terror of the foe. Soon after sunset we were ordered to build fires to deceive the enemy, when the conviction flashed over everyone that we were going to retreat. At ten o'clock we started on our retreat, and had not gone more than a mile when we came to a standstill, and remained so for three hours, which time was occupied by our boys in sleep. We afterwards learned that this stoppage was caused by two brigades crossing Robinson's River on a foot trail. General Hill[19] rode up and gave the General in command particular fits for it, and they deserved it.

Tuesday, August 12, 1862

Morning found us on the road to Orange C.H. I forgot to mention a disgraceful thing that happened in yesterday's report. Two regiments broke and ran like sheep at the appearance of a few of our cavalry in the woods, yelling "Yanks, Yanks!" at the top of their voices. I tried to find out what two regiments they were but could not. After crossing the Rapidan we took position on one of the hills overlooking the ford. We had not more than unhitched and unharnessed the horses before orders came to fall back to Orange C.H. We drew two days provisions here, and it was a good thing we did, for we had been fasting since yesterday dinner-time and were hungry as wolves in wintertime. We encamped in the same spot we left before going out to meet the Yanks. The horses were unhitched and fed, we built fires and broiled our meat and before we could eat, orders came to move back to a mile and a half on the road to Gordonsville.

No one has an idea of the vexation these frequent moves cause troops unless he has been through the "mill." We hitched up and got to our stopping place just as a heavy rain commenced. "Shebangs" were put up in a hurry and all crawled under to get out of the rain; but the one I was under leaked pretty bad and consequently did not come out exactly dry. As soon as the rain was over, here came an order to move again, which was aggravating to the last degree; but there was no help for it and everything was put in marching order and as night set we started, the roads being in a horrible condition. We did not go over a mile when we bivouacked for the night and I was truly glad for I certainly was fatigued. And did not waste any time in going to sleep.

Wednesday, August 13, 1862

Awoke this morning feeling anything but well, having to rise during the night with the Summer complaint. Made as good breakfast as I could off of fat bacon and hard crackers. The privations that soldiers undergo should entitle them to be held in grateful remembrance by future posterity. In the middle of the night orders came again to move. We all thought they intended to march us to death, for it seems they intended to give us no rest. We were soon upon the road and, as luck would have it, did not go more than half a mile when we encamped in a cool pleasant place. We were pretty hungry but managed to buy some eggs and had a tolerable dinner. We lounged about till night making time pass as pleasantly as possible, when partaking of a scant supper, laid down to slumber and dreams of home and friends far away.

". . . Summer complaint."—This terminology described an acute condition of diarrhea, which usually occurred during the hot summer months. It is believed to have been caused by bacterial contamination of food and associated with poor hygiene, which would have been common for soldiers camping, preparing food, and disposing of human waste in close quarters. See Flannery, Civil War Pharmacy.

Thursday, August 14, 1862

I was troubled last night the same as I was the night before. Morse, a comrade, was taken sick yesterday evening, and we all thought it was a slight attack of colic or something of that sort, but we were mistaken, for it turned out to be the cholera, caused by imprudent eating of fruits and other things, and this morning whilst writing a letter in the same room, he breathed his last as calmly as an infant. Everyone was thunderstruck, and it was with light steps and suspended breath that they came in to look upon him who was yesterday as full of life as they and gave promise to live to a green old age, but now lies cold and motionless in the arms of death. He leaves a widow and three small children. Everything was done by the officers to save his life. The physician was with him to the end. Plank was provided and a nice coffin was made by some of the men, when he was put in it and the lid screwed down. He was then carried to the grave and Capt. Crenshaw read the Episcopal burial service and all that was earthly of Jno. F. Morse was consigned to mother dust, never more to rise till he shall take, I hope, his place in the great army of Jehovah. Gen. Jackson issued an order that no drilling should be done today and that it should be set aside for thanksgiving and prayer to God for the victory he gave us at "Cedar Run" and other *passed* victories, and the chaplains should preach at four o'clock. On guard tonight.

"Morse, a comrade . . ."—The soldier referenced here is Private John F. Moss. The confusion in last names may have to do with the idiosyncrasies of nineteenth-century Virginia dialects in combination with what may have been Irish, Scottish, or western English accents. Private Moss was born in Appomattox County and resided in Campbell County, working as a farmer prior to the war. He was transferred to Crenshaw's Battery on May 22, 1862.[20]

Friday, August 15, 1862
The morning passed off in idleness with nothing to stir up our sluggishness. In the afternoon we received orders to cook two days rations and be prepared to march at an early hour tomorrow morning. A North Carolinian belonging to our brigade made improper propositions to a young lady living in a house, in the yard to which we were encamped, this afternoon. Some little excitement arose, which aroused us from our lethargy. The mother of the lady made quite a fuss and had the scoundrel arrested and sent to Gen. Pender. What punishment he will inflict I do not know but I think he should be taught a lesson which will last him while he lives. Nothing else occurred of special note, and soon all hands were busy cooking our two days rations.

Saturday, August 16, 1862
We started this morning about eight o'clock and passed through Orange C.H., taking the road to "*Racoon* Ford,"[21] about fifteen miles distant. Nothing of interest during this march and about two hours before sundown we encamped on Capt. Crenshaw's farm, a beautiful tract of land containing 2200 acres. It was situated between mountains on one side and high hills on the other, forming a lovely valley. We were forbidden to have fires after nightfall, which led us to believe that we were near the enemy. I expect we will have a desperate and bloody fight before many days. May the Lord vouchsafe another victory to us and the Northern mind to peace—a peace that will bring joy and happiness in so many households on both sides of the contested lines. We had hailstorm in this section the other day and the atmosphere was decidedly cool after sunset, rendering blankets an indispensable article.

"*. . . we encamped on Capt. Crenshaw's farm . . .*"—*The property referred to in this entry is "Hawfield Plantation." In W. W. Scott's A History of Orange County Virginia, the plantation is described accordingly: "It was bought in 1847 by Mr. Jonathan Graves for his only daughter, Fanny Elizabeth, the wife of William G. Crenshaw, and since that time has continued in the Crenshaw family. The original house . . . was enlarged in 1881 to its present handsome proportions by Captain William G. Crenshaw. . . . It adorns a beautiful estate of more than three thousand acres . . ." (205).*

Sunday, August 17, 1862

Arose this morning after sunrise, the reason for which we had no roll call and the first thing I heard was that the horses had got into our bread and had eat all but four biscuits. Many were the maledictions uttered by our mess upon the horses and especially upon the man who left it in reach of them. As usual no one was guilty. Here was a pretty pass; all day before us and nothing to eat. I seized upon one of the biscuits and having brought some beef hash in a cup in my haversack, I made a tolerable breakfast. I finished a book called "The Expedition of Humphrey Clinker" and I don't know when I was more entertained and amused than with this book. The author was the second person ever who wrote a novel and it was of an old date, having been written in 1771. After finishing it I went up on one of the small mountains to look at the Yank's camp on the other side of the Rapidan.[22] On reaching the top I was greeted with a scene which well repaid my walk. At my feet lay a beautiful valley stretching for ten miles from me and brought to an abrupt end by the Blue Ridge Mountains, which seemed grand and sublime indeed, on this Sabbath morning, betokening the wondrous power of the Great Architect and Builder of the Universe. The camp among some spurs of the mountains could scarcely be discerned by the naked eye. There seemed to be some commotion among them and a moving of troops toward Fredericksburg. There is a beautiful blue mist that hangs around these mountains that brings forcibly to mind Campbell's oft quoted lines,

> "This distance that lends enchantment to the view,
> and robes the distant mountain in its azure hue,"[23]

And no doubt I would find upon closer acquaintance that much of the beauty and effect would vanish. There is no doubt but that I will have an opportunity before long of testing the truth of these lines.

William Ellis Jones makes numerous references throughout his diary to literature, poetry, song, and mythology. Despite the long marches and exhausting days, he seems to manage time for reading and writing, which illustrates something of his character. Tobias Smollett's The Expedition of Humphrey Clinker, published in 1771, is regarded as his finest work and a foundation piece of classic English literature. The novel provides a satirical picture of the social and political scene of eighteenth-century England, leaving no one unscathed. William's amusement with this novel provides some evidence that he sees comparisons within his own mannered society that are no less ridiculous. The compact, leather-bound volume William carried with him in 1862 has survived and is now part of the author's library.

Monday, August 18, 1862
Nothing of interest transpired today. I passed the day in reading "War Trail" by Capt. Reid,[24] a novel of poor merit but answered its purpose very well, for it kept time from hanging on my hands.

Tuesday, August 19, 1862
This morning passed off as dull as camp life could make it. In the afternoon I heard that some men were going to be shot for desertion and was curious enough to go and see the deed done. There were two in one division and one in another. Each of the divisions formed on three sides of the graves without arms. As soon as they were formed the prisoners were marched up to their graves, preceded by the band playing the dead march and their company without loaded muskets. The two in Jackson's division were shot first. After being tied in a kneeling position to a stake and blindfolded, the charges, pacifications, and decision of the Court *Marshall* were read out, followed by a prayer of great earnestness by a divine, when the officer commanding the squad gave the orders, "Attention! Ready! Aim! Fire!" One of them was killed instantly but the other poor fellow lived some minutes and in his death struggle raised his body up and fell over never more to move on this earth. The troops formed into sections and marched past the bodies, keeping step to some lively air. To look at this execution, in one sense it is a cold-blooded thing but when we reflect we come to the conclusion that it is necessary to keep the army together. The other execution was done in the same way.

When I got back, orders had come to cook two days rations and be prepared to march at early dawn. Concluded that General Lee had thrown down the pick and spade and taken up the sword in earnest, for he now commands the army in this region and it is no small one. Some of our boys commenced to saying after hearing that he was in command that we had better go about building winter quarters, wouldn't move till next fall. Slightly mistaken.

"*. . . I heard that some men were going to be shot for desertion and was curious enough to go and see the deed done.*"—*The dispassionate manner with which William describes witnessing these executions is remarkable when considered in contrast to his description of the execution of the Union spy Timothy Webster in the March 19–May 3, 1862, diary entry, which was loaded with condemnation of his fellow man and demonstrated a measured sympathy for the executed spy. This description seems detached and bland, indicating William has become inured to violence; he has become a "seasoned soldier."*

Regarding the crimes these executed soldiers were found guilty of, Kathryn Shively Meier writes with exceptional insight in Nature's Civil War about "strategic straggling" as a form of self-care that soldiers undertook to ensure that, when they were legitimately needed to perform their duties, they were healthy and strong enough to do so. She also observes that officers (and Jackson, in particular) viewed straggling—which diminished brigade ranks—as desertion. Toward the end of 1862, Jackson and other officers raised the stakes, instituting the death penalty for desertion. While the threat of being labeled a coward was bad enough, the idea of being executed was enough to motivate more men to remain with the ranks. The result of this draconian measure (for Confederate as well as Union forces, who undertook similar measures at about the same time) was that more men were present in the ranks at roll call but were less physically capable of performing their duties, as they were denied the ability to tend to their own well-being when the battles were not raging.[25]

Wednesday, August 20, 1862

Reveille was sounded at one o'clock, roll called and horses fed and harnessed, and as the East reflected the advances of coming day, we started taking the road to Somerville Ford, across the Rapidan River.[26] We crossed the river, after a toilsome march over some very high hills, about eight o'clock and took the road to Stevensburg to Culpeper.[27] We reached this antiquated looking place in the middle of the day and were greeted by the females with every demonstration of joy, chatting with the soldiers in perfect freedom. Whilst I jumped off the caisson to get some water and I had hardly got to the well before the battery moved off, when I ran up to get on the caisson, meeting J. Herndon at it,[28] when somehow or other I was pushed up against the rear wheel and my ankle and heel were bruised very badly indeed. If my boot had not given way, it is very probable my ankle would have been crushed and I would have been a cripple for life. I was placed in the ambulance and went along with the battery, I don't think I ever hated anything as badly in my life, for we expect to get into a fight pretty soon, and we needed everyone at the guns, as we are short of men. The cavalry had it this morning about two miles from the village but our boys made them skedaddle to the Rappahannock River, killing and wounding some and taking near one hundred prisoners. We encamped about nine miles from the river and after making supper off a cracker and a piece of fat bacon, and a very small piece at that, turned in to get a good night's rest.

Thursday, August 21, 1862
Awakened this morning by the preparation for the march. Gen. Jackson's Division passed and took the lead and we followed. After marching some six miles we came to a dead halt, for here we stood till late in the afternoon. All in front of us, along the river, cannonading was kept up pretty much all day. The Yankees have made a stand, it seems, on the other side of the river and are guarding the Fords with great vigilance and resisting all attempts of our troops to cross. Late in the afternoon we started and proceed about two miles, and stopped for the night in a forest not far from the road.

Friday, August 22, 1862
Started this morning for a Ford higher up the river.[29] We stopped in an open field to let some troops (*pass*) when looking across the river we could discern the Yankee's also pushing up. It looked a little like a running fight, and that the one which was the fleetest would gain the battle. We reached Hazel Run about one or two o'clock when we were told to sit with the rest of the ambulances till called for, when I should go with the captain's wagon. There was quite a severe fight on the other side of the Run, the Yankee's endeavoring, no doubt, to cut off Gen. Hill's wagon train. Just before sunset, after a portion of Whiting's[30] and Jackson's forces had crossed, the captain's wagon came up and we

crossed with them. We had no sooner than gained the other side when a severe thunderstorm came up and the rain fell in torrents. We stopped here thinking our Division was in the fight expecting the ambulance to be called for to bring off the dead; but after waiting sometime in the night we turned in to sleep.

Saturday, August 23, 1862

Awoke this morning by the wagoneers and the first thing I heard was Gen. Taliaferro[31] prohibiting them from making fires; as we were too near the enemy. Provisions gave out yesterday and had nothing to eat, and was hungry as the mischief. Logan, one of the officer's cooks, gave me a piece of bacon[32] and I have not had anything so sweet to me for a long time. Presently we heard our battery was several miles from there and that they were not in the fight. It was not long before we started on their trail. We went along without accident over a very rough road, until within a mile of Jeffersonton, when we had the misfortune to break the tongue off the ambulance. Here was a pretty go, far away from camp, nothing to eat and no one to fix the tongue. We managed to fix it so as to get to the town, where we found a wheelwright who put in a new tongue made out of a cedar sapling. We tried our best to get something to eat but could not, the people saying that the Yanks had taken nearly everything they had in the eating line. There was nothing prepossessing in the place and when we got the tongue in we shook the dust from our feet and left. We arrived at camp just as an artillery duel commenced between a portion of Ewell's[33] forces which crossed the river yesterday and the enemy. We were close to the river and a tolerable view of the affair. The rain on yesterday had caused the river to rise and rendered fording impossible, which put our forces across the river in a rather hazardous position. Our forces on this side commenced building a bridge and finished it just as the enemy commenced shelling. There was a great commotion among the infantry, firing off their guns and moving about, indicating an advance on our part and we retired pretty confident that we would cross during the night.

Sunday, August 24, 1862

Find myself exactly where I was last night. Instead of crossing over, our forces retired to this side, leaving them masters of the other. Our battery, being short range guns, was removed and put behind a small hill, while the other batteries commenced shelling with the Yanks, thus breaking the calm of the Sabbath morn with their unearthly shrieks. As usual we got in line of one of their batteries and was favored during the day with many of their shells, but doing no damage. I was sitting on the seat of the ambulance and saw a shell distinctly as it passed a few feet above the horse's heads. Just before sundown we left there and encamped for the night on the edge of "Jeffersonton" and cooked a day's rations.

Monday, August 25, 1862

Started this morning early for some Ford up the river and crossed in the middle of the day. It was a terrible descent and *accent*. In one place negroes had to push up the pieces the *accent* was so steep. After crossing we marched very rapidly and stopped within five miles of Salem.[34] We passed through the little town of Orleans in Fauquier and an antiquated looking place it is. The females waved their handkerchiefs and cheered us on our way and seemed very glad indeed to welcome the Dixie boys back again. We also passed through Amissville.

On this date and the day following, Jackson executed his encircling movement to get in the rear of Pope's army in advance of the Second Battle of Manassas.[35]

Tuesday, August 26, 1862

Made an early start on an empty stomach and passed through Salem in good breakfast time but nary a one I got, though some of the men did. This is quite a neat little place on the Manassas Gap R.R. and can boast of some female beauty, judging from the specimens seen. They exhibited the "Stars and Bars" and greeted us with cheering smiles during our passage through the place. We now found out that we were making for Manassas Junction to capture their supplies. We stopped in the middle of the day to eat and rest awhile. I made dinner off a cracker and an ear of corn roasted, washed down by a draught of execrable water. We started briskly on our way and just before we reached "Haymarket," another town about the size of Salem on the Railroad, we were overtaken by a carriage containing a young lady with rosy cheeks and dazzling eyes who, on seeing me stretched out in the ambulance expressed herself in the following sympathetic strain: "Ah me! Here is a poor sick fellow!" which caused a smile and an expression from Geo. A. the driver, which was anything but complimentary.[36] We passed by another place on the road in full gallop and did not stop till we had traveled several miles. We encamped at "Bristoe," a depot six miles from the Junction, where we destroyed considerable property for Uncle Sam, in the shape of cars, trucks, bridges, etc.

This entry notes the capture of Bristoe Station and the severing of the Union-controlled Orange and Alexandria Railroad by Confederate forces.[37]

Wednesday, August 27, 1862

Started early this morning for Manassas Junction where we had a sharp engagement in which our Battery participated,[38] doing good service from all I could learn. They were taken in charge by General *Stewart* who made them, to use the expression of Walter R., a noble boy,[39] "slosh round." He aimed some of the pieces himself. The Yanks were soon put to flight, leaving a large amount of stores of all sorts, seven pieces of artillery, tents, etc. I was left behind in the ambulance at the depot and the scene that ensued during the entire day beggars description. The soldiers fairly feasted on the good things of life and they deserved them for they had been fasting for a couple of days. In the afternoon Ewell's division had a fight with the Yanks at Bristoe Depot, keeping them at bay. We had quite a time looking for our camp, and after riding around asking everyone, we found out that it had been ordered to Centerville. J. H. Campbell was thrown from the caisson[40] whilst the battery was galloping into action and has his foot and hand bruised very badly. We found the captain's wagon and stopped with them to camp all night. Everything that we could not bring away at the depot was put in trim for burning and as night set in the torch was applied and a brilliant bonfire we had over our gallant dash at the enemy's rear. The comp(*any*) soon came back after our stopping, relieved us of our dilemma. We were then ordered to go to sleep for we would doubtless move away before morning, which was readily complied with by our worn out boys.

Thursday, August 28, 1862

We started towards Centerville this morning at 3 o'clock and arrived there sometime after daylight, stopping there long enough to get a good breakfast. This noted "burg" presents nothing attractive to the eye that I could discern as we passed through. It was very well fortified and considered by some almost impregnable.[41] We left it, taking the road to the northwest,[42] passing over a portion of the battleground of Manassas,[43] stopping after going about five miles. Just before sunset a portion of our troops had a severe fight with the enemy, driving them back almost two miles. Two of our brigades in the dark fired into each other doing more damage to us than the enemy. We bivouacked about nine o'clock confident that we would have a hard fight tomorrow and I have determined to pitch in.

Friday, August 29, 1862

Skirmishing commenced early this morning. We were put in a commanding position on a slight rise in an open field and had to keep a bright lookout for Yanks. We had not been long there before a column of them were seen making their way through a corn field about a hundred yards off,[44] when we opened on them a very destructive fire, saving Ge. Gregg's brigade from a hard fight, for they skedaddled ingloriously. We were under a hot fire from one of their batteries, shells bursting and scattering their fragments all around us but doing no damage to either the men or horses. We were pretty quiet after this, in front of us, till the afternoon, but on the right of us heavy skirmishing was going on pretty much all day, when heavy firing commenced with the infantry in the woods to the front of us. A battery commenced a flanking fire on some of our infantry, when ours and two others opened and soon silenced it. The fighting got to be earnest now and the *Minnie* balls flew all around us, we were so close to the infantry. We charged with canister but had no occasion to use it at that point. A colonel came up and showed us a point where we could throw a case shot in the midst of them, which we took, and the piece I was with had scarcely shot three shots when the axle tree gave way and it was ordered to the rear, where we put our gun on a Yankee howitzer carriage and returned to company about nine o'clock, ready to pitch into them the next morning. After I left, the boys tell me our forces (Branch's Brigade) were driven out[45] or retired from the woods to a grove a short distance in the field, where they formed a line and came out and pitched into the Yankees with a vim and vigor unequaled, driving them back with great slaughter. They say it was the grandest sight they ever witnessed and would not have missed it for a great deal. I regretted very much not being present but I could not help it. The enemy was driven back five times. It seems it was the intention of our generals not to advance but to maintain our position, which we did, against all of their assaults. During the morning we had a good view of some sharpshooters picking off the Yanks. They dropped some of them, for a Yankee battery shot canister and one round shot at them but did no good, for just as soon as one showed himself, he had an ounce of lead in. A Yank came out of a piece of woods in an opening on a horse and had hardly showed himself before he and his horse were both drawn down. It seems he was not hurt for he got up and ran like a scared hare. It was a capital shot and was witnessed by a good many. I laid down truly thankful that I had come safe.

Friday, August 29, 1862, was the Crenshaw Battery's first day at the Second Battle of Manassas, fought August 28–30, 1862, on the same ground as the First Battle of Manassas. Rather than a single battle, this event encompassed a series of conflicts occurring over several days.

History records Second Manassas as a Confederate victory, with 10,000 Union casualties out of 62,000 on the field, versus 8,300 Confederate casualties out of 50,000 on the field. It was the bloodiest battle fought to date in the Civil War. Second Manassas was a physical as well as psychological blow to the Union, and it temporarily turned the course of the war toward the Confederate side.[46]

Saturday, August 30, 1862

Spent a disagreeable night having left my blankets in the ambulance and nothing to cover with. We took the same position we had yesterday early this morning. The Yanks attempted to come up on our left soon after getting in battery, when two of our batteries opened on them stopping their advance. We stood ready with canister to pour into them when they came out of the woods, but they did not come. Everything was quiet along our line during the entire morning except some slight skirmishing. About one o'clock I had a severe attack of cramp colic[47] and for two hours I was never in so much misery in all my life. The Captain sent off and got me some Jamaica Ginger[48] which relieved me. I was having another attack about three o'clock and was in the act taking a second dose when orders came to move our position about four hundred yards to the right, the battle having commenced on our right wing with great fierceness. I threw the dose away and jumped on the horse and drove rapidly down to the place, I acting as driver instead of cannoneer, not being able to walk much. We loaded with canister and had another charge ready to play havoc with them if they drove our troops out, but we had no occasion to use them for our brave boys made a stand at the edge of the woods and soon had them on the run. We were under a terrible fire of infantry. I was standing by my horse with my right hand on the pommel of the saddle when a ball struck the animal in the shoulder not more than three inches from my head. It was truly a narrow escape. The fighting soon passed to the right of us, the enemy giving way. It was the largest and soonest ended battle on this continent. The Yanks were completely routed and the slaughter of them was dreadful the battle of Manassas being nothing in comparison,[49] they tell me. We drove them completely across Bull Run, capturing nine batteries, and would have followed them but darkness set in which put an end to the chase. Although we did not fire a shot, we felt highly honored in being put in a position of so much vital importance, for we would have had, in conjunction with a Louisiana brigade, to beat them back, or the centre would have been gone. If they had been able to come through and been beaten back by us, we would have made a lasting name, but it doubtless would have been written in blood, for some of us would have fallen. I am very glad as it is, for none of us was hurt. I came very near being wounded in the leg just before we took our last position, a *Minnie* ball striking close to my heel, knocking dirt on my neck. We remained in battery until after dark, when we bivouacked there. After eating a hearty supper I laid down with a heart full of thankfulness to the great Jehovah for preserving my life through the dangers of the day. Gen. Ewell was wounded in the knee in the fight of day before yesterday. And had to lose his leg. I am truly sorry for he is a brave man and a good general.

Sunday, August 31, 1862

Awoke this morning with the rain falling gently in my face, when I took refuge in the ambulance and finished my nap. This morning brought to mind the day after the battle of Manassas[50] for it rained very hard all that day. We cooked a day's rations and about one o'clock took up the line of march—where to I don't know. There is much speculation but no knowledge of our destination. After traveling until something after dark we encamped within ten miles of Fairfax C.H., pretty tired and sleepy. This is the last day of our Summer Campaign and it went out with a blaze of glory to our arms. May the Fall campaign end likewise, is my sincere prayer.

Monday, September 1, 1862

As our brigade headed the column yesterday it had to bring up the rear today, therefore it was late in the morning before we started on the march. Old September has come in like a roaring lion, the wind blowing "Big guns" and will probably go out like a lamb. After creeping along till 3 or 4 o'clock we flushed a corps of Yanks under the command of Major-Gen. *Kearney*,[51] when we had a most desperate fight, the enemy having a very strong position. Soon after the fight commenced a terrible rain storm came up, and between the artillery of heaven and earth, the roar of musketry and the torrents that fell, I spent the most hideous evening of my life. The artillery, as usual was parked directly in the line of the enemy's fire and was favored with several shells in a very few minutes, which caused all the artillery to change quarters. As we were leaving a shell burst in the midst of one of the companies and strange to say, did no harm. The *Minnie* balls came pretty thick where we were but did no damage. All the artillery, just before dark, that was not in use was sent to the rear, we amongst them. We built big fires and dried ourselves as well as we could and laid down to sleep the best we could in the wet and rain. Maj. Gen. *Kearney* was killed and when the fight ended we were in possession of one wing of the battlefield and the enemy the other. I do not vouch for this, as I only heard it from a very unreliable source, some straggling infantry who said they were in the fight.

Monday, September 1, 1862, was the day of the Battle of Chantilly. Stonewall Jackson's corps attempted to cut off the retreat of the Union army but were attacked by two Union divisions. During the battle, both Union division commanders were killed, but the Union attack successfully halted Jackson's advance. Victory by either force remained inconclusive, yet the Confederates retained the tactical advantage as they held the field after the battle. Jackson's success neutralized any threat from Pope's army, clearing the way for Lee to advance his plans for the Maryland Campaign. Union casualties were 1,300 (out of only 6,000 remaining on the field), while Confederate losses amounted to 500 of 20,000 in service that day.[52]

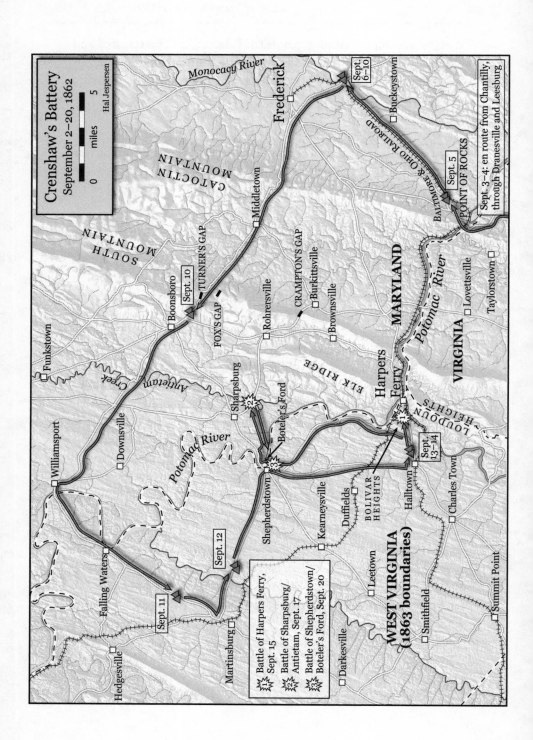

Crenshaw's Battery
September 2–20, 1862

Hal Jespersen

0   miles   5

Monocacy River

Frederick

CATOCTIN MOUNTAIN

SOUTH MOUNTAIN

Funkstown

Williamsport

Downsville

Antietam Creek

Boonsboro

Sept. 10

TURNER'S GAP

FOX'S GAP

Middletown

Sharpsburg

Potomac River

Boteler's Ford

Shepherdstown

Sept. 12

Sept. 11

Falling Waters

Hedgesville

Martinsburg

Darkesville

Leetown

Smithfield

Summit Point

Kearneysville

Duffields

BOLIVAR HEIGHTS

Halltown

Charles Town

WEST VIRGINIA
(1863 boundaries)

Rohrersville

CRAMPTON'S GAP

Burkittsville

Brownsville

ELK RIDGE

Harpers Ferry

MARYLAND

VIRGINIA

Potomac River

LOUDOUN HEIGHTS

Sept. 13–14

Lovettsville

Taylorstown

POINT OF ROCKS

BALTIMORE & OHIO RAILROAD

Sept. 5

Buckeystown

Sept. 6–10

Sept. 3–4: en route from Chantilly,
through Dranesville and Leesburg

Battle of Harpers Ferry,
Sept. 15

Battle of Sharpsburg/
Antietam, Sept. 17

Battle of Shepherdstown/
Boteler's Ford, Sept. 20

Part 4

ON TO MARYLAND, HARPERS FERRY, AND ANTIETAM
SEPTEMBER 2–20, 1862

With autumn setting in and shoe leather wearing thin, William found himself heading north and west rather than toward Richmond and home. In this portion of the journal it is revealed that even through the fog of war and the rhetoric so many young recruits believed just a few months earlier, they began to comprehend that this war was no short-lived adventure and the Union army was not going to just go home. Following the Confederate rout of Union forces at Harpers Ferry, then the Confederate retreat from the field following the carnage at Antietam, the Union army tenaciously kept coming with more and more men thrown into the chasm. Confederates fought on short rations, in bare feet, sacrificing friends along the way—friends and comrades they could ill afford to lose.

Tuesday, September 2, 1862
We have had a quiet day of it, the enemy falling back and our army taking a good position. Our loss on yesterday was very severe, but the enemy's was equally so. We received orders to cook three days rations and as we did not receive the flour till night, it was eleven o'clock before we laid down to sleep, and then with knowledge that we had to rise at two with the prospect of a heavy fight before you. The day was decidedly blustering and quite cold after dark.

Wednesday, September 3, 1862
Started this morning, taking the road to *Drainersville*.[1] It was as lovely a morning as I ever saw and everyone seemed in good spirits. The road was principally through fine oak and chestnut forests and passed over the battleground of *Drainersville*. The woods bore ample testimony to the toughness of the fight, for many of them were cut into. We passed through this village and encamped on the Leesburg turnpike. There are some very fine residences in this place but bear evidence of the presence of Yankees. There were some very pretty ladies who waved us a welcome with sweet smiles upon their faces.

Thursday, September 4, 1862

We passed over as rocky a pike as ever built and reached Leesburg about three in the evening, I met Dick Green, an old friend and Comrade-in-arms,[2] very unexpectedly here and had a pleasant confab as we passed through. Leesburg, from what little I saw, is a very pretty town. It is most built in brick and the streets paved and pretty clean. There was very little excitement and enthusiasm, owing no doubt to the strong Union settlement existing in the place. We encamped about two miles from the town.

Friday, September 5, 1862

Started this morning for "Maryland, my Maryland"[3] and after a tedious march crossed the noble Potomac at five o'clock and stood upon the shores of that downtrodden state. We traveled till eleven o'clock and then stopped for the night.

Saturday, September 6, 1862

Started before sunup and after traveling through a beautiful country for eight or ten miles, encamped on the banks of the *Monacy*[4] river, where the Baltimore and Ohio R.R. crosses.[5] There were two regiments of Yankees stationed at Frederick City three miles off, who getting wind of us, vamoosed, taking everything valuable with them. We drew three days rations of flour and beef and went to cooking in earnest, for we were hungry, our rations giving out yesterday.

Sunday, September 7, 1862

Rose this morning with the sun and after eating a hearty breakfast, went about washing my clothes, not having a change with me, for our knapsacks were left on the other side of Orange C.H., although it was the Lord's Day. I could not help it, for they were very dirty and I did not know when I would have another chance. We made three attempts to blow up the bridge across the river but failed. It is a splendid structure called the iron lattice bridge but it must be knocked to pieces some (*way*) or other. I understood that the old Legislature ousted by Hicks and the Federals intend meeting tomorrow in Frederick City, when they will be heard.

The bridge type William describes here was a Bollman Truss railroad bridge, the first successful all-metal bridge design to be adopted and consistently used on a railroad.

The design employs wrought–iron tension members and cast–iron compression members. Patented on January 6, 1852, by Wendel Bollman, it was an improvement over wooden structures, as the independent structural units lessened the possibility of structural failure. About one hundred of these bridges were built through 1873. The Baltimore & Ohio Railroad was a loyal client.[6]

Monday, September 8, 1862

There was nothing doing today. The bridge was blown up in the afternoon, which caused a little excitement. One man was killed and another wounded in blowing it up. The time was passed in lounging, killing time the best way we could.

The "Old Main Line" was the route of the first commercial railroad in the United States as it pushed west from Baltimore, Maryland, to the Ohio River. This bridge was a favorite target during the Civil War, and the Baltimore & Ohio Railroad had to rebuild it many times.[7]

Tuesday, September 9, 1862

The day was passed similarly to yesterday, nothing in the world like an excitement throughout.

Wednesday, September 10, 1862

Aroused this morning at one o'clock. One of the drivers being sick, I was detailed to drive. At three we started and passed through *Frederic City*.[8] It is quite a handsome inland town. All the stores were shut, according to the orders of Gen. Jackson. I don't think I ever saw so many ugly old women in all my life; the young ones were kept out of view for fear of fascinating some of the "rebels," I reckon. There was no excitement and the people seemed to be afraid to acknowledge that they had souls. During the morning we passed through Middletown, said to be quite a Union hold, having furnished 100 recruits to Lincoln's army. There was considerable life displayed, the ladies showing themselves without restraint, and laughed and chatted with our men. We passed over some mountains said to be a continuation of the Blue Ridge, and encamped for the night. There was a skirmish at *Boonesborough*[9] this morning between some of the Yankee cavalry and ours. It is said they tried to kill Gen. Jackson. We drew three days rations, and the best part of the night was consumed in cooking it. I think we are on our way to Pennsylvania, for we are on the turnpike leading to Hagerstown, which is only three or four miles from the line.

Thursday, September 11, 1862
Aroused early this morning. Passed through *Boonesborough*, which is quite a handsome little town. Like the other places we passed through, the stores were all closed. The people showed themselves more generally here than in any place I have seen. It commenced raining early and promises to be a wet day. Instead of keeping the Hagerstown road we turned off in the Williamsport pike and passed through this town just before sunset, crossing the Potomac and standing once more on Virginia soil. Williamsport is immediately on the Potomac and does not present as neat an appearance as the other places I have seen, in Maryland. We went into park about nine o'clock wearied in body; I was so much so that I laid down wet as I was and fell quickly to sleep.

Friday, September 12, 1862
Started early this morning for Martinsburg,[10] which place we reached about two o'clock. We captured a lot of corn commissary stores and military supplies. There is a great deal of Union sentiment in this town, much more than I expected. After drawing corn and crackers, we left the "burg" taking the road to Harper's Ferry. There were three regiments of Yanks who skedaddled to the Ferry when they heard of our coming. We took some of them prisoners who said they had not been in service but six weeks. We encamped about eighteen miles from the Ferry for the night.

Saturday, September 13, 1862
Started early this morning again and encamped within four miles of the Ferry. Firing was heard in the direction of the Ferry. Laid inactive all evening.

Sunday, September 14, 1862
Nothing doing till evening when we moved quarters and bivouacked near the enemy so as to open early in the morning.

Monday, September 15, 1862
Opened on the enemy early this morning. The enemy's fire was very warm for an hour or so, but did us no damage. There was a cessation of

fire when we were advanced a quarter of a mile nearer Bolivar Heights, and after firing ten or fifteen minutes, they raised the flag and surrendered. We captured about ten thousand troops; fifty or sixty pieces of heavy and light artillery, seventy tons of ammunition, some commissary stores and a splendid lot of horses, altogether the greatest achievement of the war. Harper's Ferry bears the marks of the war from its present aspect, must have been a sweet place to live in the summer. Capt. Crenshaw was detailed to get up the captured artillery, which kept us busy all day, and retired satisfied with our labor.

The Battle of Harpers Ferry, fought September 12–15, 1862, is considered by many historians to be one of the most striking Confederate army achievements of the Civil War. When General Robert E. Lee's army invaded Maryland, Major General Thomas J. "Stonewall" Jackson surrounded, bombarded, and then captured the Union garrison at Harper's Ferry, Virginia (now West Virginia), taking 12,700 Union prisoners, while only suffering 286 Confederate casualties. This surrender represented the largest capitulation of Union forces during the entire Civil War. The success of this event was important, as many on both sides of the battle lines saw Harper's Ferry as symbolic, it having been the location of John Brown's 1859 raid.[11]

Tuesday, September 16, 1862
We were hauled pretty much to the detriment of our shoe leather, which has become quite a serious affair with some of us, as we are nearly barefooted, and finally halted about nine o'clock at night, five miles from the Ferry. We stopped here to refit in horses. After making a hearty supper off vegetable soup, was detailed to unload our wagon with ammunition and load another to be sent to Gen. Longstreet in Maryland, as he was out, which job kept me out of my bed till midnight.

Wednesday, September 17, 1862
Started this morning for Maryland where Longstreet and the Yanks are having it merrily. Reached the scene of the battle about two hours before sundown and engaged the enemy on his left. McIntosh[12] lost three pieces just before we went in, but the enemy was driven back and the pieces recaptured. Our position was immediately on the left of the captured battery. The fire from the sharpshooters was severe indeed. Chas. Pemberton[13] was struck in the left side, producing a mortal wound. This was a terrible blow to all of us, for he had endeared

himself to everyone by his generous and affable conduct; Ed *Lynan*[14] and Jno. Gray[15] were also struck, but little damage done, the former coming back before we retired. The enemy was driven back with considerable slaughter but nightfall setting in we could not turn it into a rout. Chas. P. was carried to the nearest hospital and everything done to alleviate him of his pain and cure his wound, but the doctor shook his head and said it was useless, for the ball had gone in the direction of the heart. I stayed with him all night, to wait on him if he wished for anything. The 2nd howitzer was disabled by its recoil.

The Battle of Antietam, fought on September 17, 1862, near Sharpsburg, Maryland, was the first important battle in the American Civil War to take place on Union soil. Following the lengthy marches leading up to the Second Battle of Manassas and the Battle of Harpers Ferry, Lee's Army of Northern Virginia was exhausted and footsore, often shoeless, and gaunt with hunger. The Confederate ranks were devastated by stragglers, diminishing their numbers by a third to a half of the army's original size following the Peninsula Campaign. Antietam was recorded as the bloodiest single-day battle in American history up to that date, with casualties numbering 12,401 Union and 10,316 Confederate. Antietam was claimed as a Union victory due to the Confederates' retreat from the field. They had no other option, as they could not have continued the fight in their severely diminished condition. The result was enough of a public relations victory to give President Abraham Lincoln the confidence to announce his Emancipation Proclamation, which ultimately discouraged the British and French governments from recognizing the Confederacy as a nation. See Gary W. Gallagher, The Antietam Campaign, *and James M. McPherson,* Crossroads of Freedom.

Thursday, September 18, 1862

The battery was ordered back to the same position we had the previous evening and I was forced to leave my wounded friend against my wish, for we were shorthanded and the Captain had sent for me. Upon arriving at our position we could see the field where we were firing at black with the hated foe and was glad that Chas. was avenged. During the morning news came that he was dead. I could not realize the fact for none of us thought of his dying so soon. He seemed to be more cheerful than he was the night previous and I had entertained some hopes for his recovery, but alas, they were fruitless. This intelligence cast a heavy gloom upon all and many were the regrets expressed at his sudden and untimely end. We laid in line of battle all day, sharpshooters practising upon us without doing any damage. At dark we limbered up and crossed the Potomac, again standing on old Virginia shores. The entire army crossed during the night, I believe. We reached Shepherdstown after an *ardous* and rather perilous march along the banks of the river and encamped on the suburbs.

Friday, September 19, 1862

We moved our quarters about two miles further from town and cooked up three days rations. The day was pleasant and all appreciated the rest we enjoyed. There was considerable firing across the river, what damage done I did not learn. We retired to rest with the announcement that reveille would be sounded at half past three. It is needless to say I was not at all pleased.

Saturday, September 20, 1862

Learned this morning, after starting, that the Yanks had crossed the river during the night and captured some of our batteries. Our division was ordered to drive them back, which was done very easily, for the infernal scoundrels ran like dogs. We killed and wounded a good many, and captured several hundred prisoners. Just at sunset we started and traveled until a late hour in the night, and encamped in the road without unhitching.

A detachment of Union brigadier general Fitz-John Porter's V Corps, commanded by Brigadier General William Pendleton, pushed across the Potomac River at Boteler's Ford on September 19, 1862, attacking the Confederate rear. This assault resulted in the capture of four artillery guns. On the twentieth, Porter pushed portions of two divisions across the Potomac. Confederate general A. P. Hill's division responded by counterattacking, as many of the Federals were still crossing the river, nearly annihilating the 118th Pennsylvania, inflicting 269 casualties. Porter called off his pursuit, retreating back across the Potomac. On November 7, President Abraham Lincoln relieved Major General George McClellan of command (he had served in that capacity fewer than thirty days) because of his failure to pursue Lee's humbled army. Major General Ambrose E. Burnside rose to command the Union army.[16]

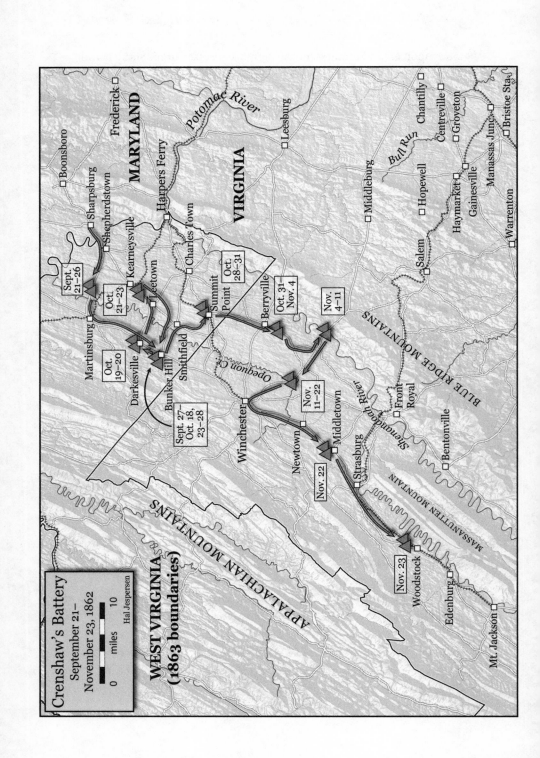

Crenshaw's Battery
September 21–
November 23, 1862

Hal Jespersen

miles
0   10

WEST VIRGINIA
(1863 boundaries)

APPALACHIAN MOUNTAINS

MARYLAND

Frederick

Boonsboro

Sharpsburg

Shepherdstown

Potomac River

Harpers Ferry

Kearneysville

Leetown

Charles Town

Leesburg

Bull Run

Chantilly

Centreville

Groveton

Bristoe Sta.

Manassas Junc.

VIRGINIA

Middleburg

Hopewell

Salem

Haymarket

Gainesville

Warrenton

Sept.
21–26

Oct.
21–23

Martinsburg

Oct.
19–20

Darkesville

Bunker Hill

Smithfield

Summit
Point

Oct.
28–31

Berryville

Oct. 31–
Nov. 4

Nov.
4–11

Opequon Cr.

Sept. 27–
Oct. 18,
23–28

Winchester

Newtown

Nov.
11–22

Middletown

Nov. 22

Strasburg

Shenandoah River

Front
Royal

Bentonville

BLUE RIDGE MOUNTAINS

MASSANUTTEN MOUNTAIN

Nov. 23

Woodstock

Edenburg

Mt. Jackson

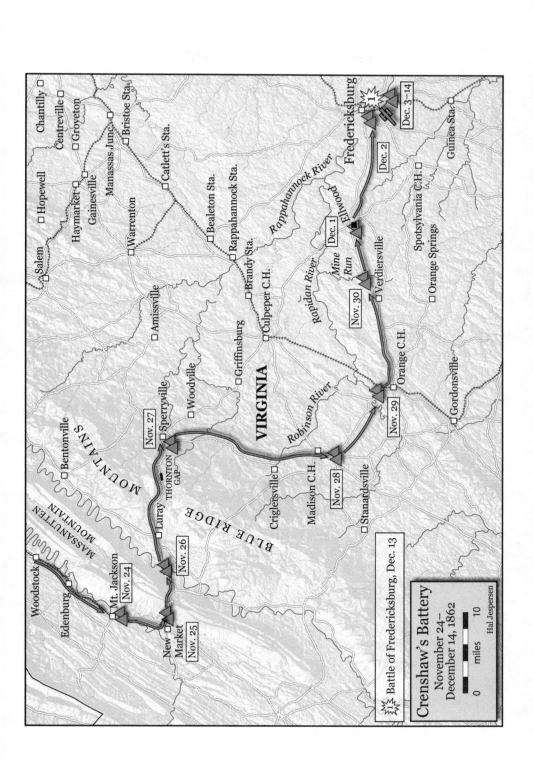

Chantilly
Centreville
Groveton
Bristoe Sta.
Haymarket
Gainesville
Manassas Junc.
Catlett's Sta.
Salem
Hopewell
Warrenton
Bealeton Sta.
Rappahannock Sta.
Brandy Sta.
Culpeper C.H.
Amissville
Griffinsburg
Woodville
Sperryville
Nov. 27
THORNTON GAP
Luray
Bentonville
Nov. 24
Mt. Jackson
Nov. 26
New Market
Nov. 25
Woodstock
Edenburg
MASSANUTTEN MOUNTAIN
MOUNTAINS
BLUE RIDGE
VIRGINIA
Criglersville
Madison C.H.
Nov. 28
Stanardsville
Robinson River
Orange C.H.
Nov. 29
Gordonsville
Rapidan River
Mine Run
Verdiersville
Nov. 30
Orange Springs
Spotsylvania C.H.
Guinea Sta.
Ellwood
Dec. 1
Rappahannock River
Fredericksburg
Dec. 2
1
Dec. 3–14

Battle of Fredericksburg, Dec. 13

Crenshaw's Battery
November 24–
December 14, 1862

0   miles   10

Hal Jespersen

Part 5
MEANDERING TOWARD FREDERICKSBURG
SEPTEMBER 21–DECEMBER 14, 1862

The cliché of war—long days of tedium punctuated by moments of sheer terror—is shown in its truest sense throughout this portion of William Ellis Jones's diary. As Lee struggled to rebuild his army, catching stragglers while allowing his veterans to rest and refuel, the men of the Crenshaw Battery received accolades from the Confederate command on their exemplary service, even as they languished in boredom under the shadow of mountains with winter storms bearing down upon them. Malnourished, often shoeless, with sleet falling on their heads, this tired army was called upon again in October to forgo the tease of a start on winter quarters and to march north and east to defend Fredericksburg.

Private W. H. Kitchens, a soldier with the 45th Georgia Regiment, Company F, recorded the grueling march in all its ugly detail: "Hundreds of soldiers barefooted; the snow and ice was three or four inches thick. You could track the men by their bloody feet, and I happened to be one of the barefoot boys."[1] Even Mother Nature seemed determined to punish both armies for what they wrought in the wake of their more than 235 mile march.

William Ellis Jones was not a superstitious young man, but many of his comrades were. The highly unusual appearance of the aurora borealis, which appeared in the southern skies when the guns fell silent following the Battle of Fredericksburg, was taken as an omen by some that the heavens were in an uproar over what had transpired on the ground.

Sunday, September 21, 1862
Started at day-break, and after getting within three miles of Martinsburg, halted and parked the artillery. Here we stayed until four o'clock, when we moved our camp about a mile from the *Opecquin*[2] River, drawing two days rations.

Monday, September 22, 1862
Cooked our two days (*rations*) after which the day was spent in idling about, resting ourselves after our laborious campaign.

Tuesday, September 23, 1862
The day was spent pretty much as yesterday, nothing occurring to disturb us in our laziness.

Wednesday, September 24, 1862
Our life is decidedly, at present, one of ease, nothing but the thought of home and friends makes it irksome. Nothing new occurred today.

Thursday, September 25, 1862
Everything passed off today with quietness and pleasure, for our knapsacks came to sight after being behind nearly two months. It put everyone in the very best of humor.

Friday, September 26, 1862
Received information that the camp would be moved today, but, owing to some cause, it was not done. At tattoo we were told that reveille would be sounded at four and that we must be ready by seven o'clock and a congratulatory order from Gen. Hill to the soldiers of the Light Division on their varied successes. Having a chance I will give it verbatim:

> Head Qrs. Light Division,
> Camp Branch, Sept. 24, 1862.
>
> Soldiers of the Light Division:
>
> You have done well and I am well pleased with you. You have fought in every battle from Mechanicsville to Shepherdstown, and no man can yet say that the Light Division has ever been broken. You held the left at Manassas against overwhelming numbers and saved the army; you saved the day at Sharpsburg and at Shepherdstown you were selected to face a storm of round shot, shell and grape, such as I have never before seen. I am proud to say to you that your services are appreciated by our General, and that you have a reputation in the army which it should be the object of every officer and private to sustain.
>
> (signed) A. P. Hill
> Major Gen.
> Official Signed—R. S. Wingates
> A.A.A.G

Saturday, September 27, 1862

Started this morning at the appointed hour, taking the Martinsburg Pike. After a most tedious march we encamped at Bunker Hill, ten miles from Winchester, about nine o'clock at night. The women, as we passed through Martinsburg indulged in some scurrilous remarks to our soldiers, snatching up their clothes and running in the house with the remark, "Don't touch me, you nasty trash." We would like to have a chance to shell that place.

"We would like to have a chance to shell that place."—This passing comment by William illustrates a clear turn in his character and characterization of his wartime experience. In his diary entry of March 19–May 3, 1862, William wrote that he was sickened at the sight of an execution and expressed shame at the crowd in Richmond who came out to see it as a matter of entertainment. After enduring the Second Battle of Manassas and the carnage at Sharpsburg, his expression had shifted toward vengeance and dehumanization of the opposing forces. In this entry, we see a soldier so invested in his mission that he states he would take pleasure in shelling civilians—women, no less—because they verbally insulted an invading army. The transition from a novice, relatively carefree young recruit into a hardened veteran is notable. For a thorough examination of the concept of vengeance during the Civil War, see Rable, Damn Yankees!, *95–117.*

Sunday, September 28, 1862

Went out foraging with two comrades today anticipating a glorious dinner. After walking several miles and getting within fifty yards of the house to which we were going, we were arrested by a guard sent out to take up all seen whether with pass or not. We were in for it and I was never so vexed in my life, but could not help it. They led us a merry dance from one headquarters to another until night, when they let us off.[3] I was both hungry and footsore when I reached camp and was greeted with jests and laughter by our comrades. Nothing doing in camp.

Monday, September 29, 1862

Tried my hand as a laundress and succeeded very well, quitting with knuckles skinned. Everything quiet in camp life.

Tuesday, September 30, 1862

Nothing exciting, the time spent in cooking and eating. I expect it is the calm before the storm.

Wednesday, October 1, 1862
All calm and quiet; nothing interesting occurred.

Thursday, October 2, 1862
Nothing for us to do now but cook and eat. Weather fine.

Friday, October 3, 1862
Orders came today to have two drills daily, morning and afternoon. The army is being put in a thorough state of drill and discipline, and is being augmented daily by stragglers and convalescents.

Saturday, October 4, 1862
Had drill morning and evening. At tattoo orders were read from Gen Lee, one being a congratulatory order, which I copy verbatim:

> Head Qrs. Army Northern Virginia
> General Orders No. 116 Oct. 2, 1862.
>
> In reviewing the achievements during the present campaign, the commanding general cannot withhold the expression of his admiration of the indomitable courage it has displayed in battle, and its cheerful endurance of privation and hardship on march.
>
> Since your great victories around Richmond, you have defeated the enemy at Cedar Mountain, expelled him from the Rappahannock, and, after a conflict of three days, utterly repulsed him on the plains of Manassas, and forced him to take shelter in the fortifications around his capital.
>
> Without halting for repose, you crossed the Potomac, stormed the heights of Harper's Ferry, made prisoners of more than eleven thousand men and captured upwards of seventy pieces of artillery, all their small arms and munitions of war.
>
> While one corps of the army was thus engaged, the other ensured its success by arresting at *Boonesborough* the combined armies of the enemy, advancing under their favorite general to the relief of their beleaguered comrades.
>
> On the fields of Sharpsburg, with less than one third his numbers, you resisted from daylight until dark the whole army of the enemy, and repulsed every attack along his entire front of more than four miles in extent.

The whole of the following day you stood prepared to resume the conflict on the same ground and retired next morning without molestation.

Two attempts subsequently made by the enemy to follow you across the river have resulted in his complete discomfiture, and being driven back with loss.

Achievements such as these demanded much valor and patriotism. History records few examples of greater fortitude and endurance than this army has exhibited, and I am commissioned by the President to thank you in the name of the Confederate States for the undying fame you have won for their arms.

Much as you have done, much more remains to be accomplished. The enemy again threatens us with invasion, and to your tried valor and patriotism, the country looks with confidence for deliverance and safety. Your past exploits give assurance that this confidence is not misplaced.

R. E. Lee
Gen. Comm'd'g

Sunday, October 5, 1862
Had inspection this morning at nine o'clock, which passed off without the tediousness attending some of our former ones. All is quiet.

Monday, October 6, 1862
Changed camp today; all the artillery is thrown together, forming a regiment. I am much pleased with the change, having plenty of shade.

The reorganization of the various artillery batteries under Major William "Willie" R. Johnson Pegram was instituted in order to allow the Army of Northern Virginia to concentrate its artillery fire without brigade and division officers working at cross-purposes with artillery officers.[4] It was around this time that William Graves Crenshaw resigned his commission and was detailed to civilian service abroad. Noting this adjustment in command, it is clear that when William wrote, "I am much pleased with the change, having plenty of shade," he was not referring to the change in camp location but rather to the change in his battery's command, and perhaps to an improved situation allowing him to blend in among many other artillerists rather than standing out to a commanding officer whom he neither liked or respected.

The following companies composed the newly formed battalion commanded by Major Pegram, with eight staff and field officers:

the Richmond "Purcell" Virginia Artillery, commanded by Captain
   Joseph McGraw
the Richmond "Crenshaw" Battery, commanded by Lieutenant
   James Ellett
the Fredericksburg Virginia Artillery, commanded by Captain
   Carter Braxton
the Richmond "Letcher" Virginia Artillery, commanded by Captain
   Greenlee Davidson
the South Carolina "Pee Dee" Artillery, commanded by Captain
   David Gregg McIntosh, with W. Gordon McCabe as adjutant[5]

Tuesday, October 7, 1862
Had a guest from Richmond, Mr. Elmore.[6] I was very glad to see him
indeed. Left this morning for home, kindly carrying letters for the boys.

Wednesday, October 8, 1862
The colonel formed a regimental guard this morning, when I was put
on it. This is something entirely new for artillery and caused the boys
to wonder what they would be at next.

Thursday, October 9, 1862
Came off guard this morning. Nothing unusual passed today. Just after
tattoo, orders came to harness the horses which caused a little excitement.

Friday, October 10, 1862
Commenced raining today, settling in quite cold towards night. Nothing that I have learned of a definite nature occurred to cause the excitement last evening.

Saturday, October 11, 1862
The weather continues cold and rainy. All quiet in camp.

Sunday, October 12, 1862
It seems that we are to have benefit of wet and cold weather as there are no
signs of the heavens clearing up. Quietness reigns throughout the camp.

Monday, October 13, 1862
On guard today, and a mean miserable day it is.

Tuesday, October 14, 1862
Came off duty at nine o'clock. I have been in service seven months today, and received not a red (*cent*) yet. Everything is quiet in camp.

Wednesday, October 15, 1862
We would hardly know what to do to kill time if it were not for the couple drills we have daily. The weather is better but continues coquettish.

Thursday, October 16, 1862
The day passed in quietness. A severe thunderstorm commenced, just at dark, rendering our shebang almost useless as the rain poured through its sluices. Just as I got in a doze the sergeants were assembled and orders were given them to have one day's rations cooked. After considerable growling and no little swearing, the men got up and cooked the rations in the rain by eleven o'clock, and went to sleep with the prospect of being aroused at any time.

Friday, October 17, 1862
Aroused at four o'clock and ordered to strike tents, pack knapsacks and load the wagons by six. The day was passed in the camp, no orders coming to march. At sunset orders came to cook another day's rations, which was done in quick time and the men laid down to rest their tired limbs, fearful of being called before morning.

Saturday, October 18, 1862
We were permitted to have a good night's rest on Mother Earth, not being waked until regular roll call. About three o'clock we started taking pike toward Martinsburg. We encamped in the edge of *Darksville*,[7] a small village six miles from Martinsburg, and ordered to cook a day's rations. Evening clear and cold, promising a frost.

Sunday, October 19, 1862
On guard today. Feeling unwell, having a fever. Stayed here all day. Cooked a day's rations, and was informed that reveille would be sounded at four and a half o'clock.

Monday, October 20, 1862
Reveille was sounded at half past four and everything put in marching order by six. About seven we took up our line of march, taking the Leetown road and after getting into the neighborhood of the Bo. & O. R.R. encamped. Had a very high fever. The boys had an exciting fox chase this morning. Caught him.

Tuesday, October 21, 1862
Nothing exciting occurred today. Doctor prescribed blue mas[8] and quinine[9] for me.

Wednesday, October 22, 1862
All quiet. Doctor did not come today. Had another high (*fever*) in the evening.

Thursday, October 23, 1862
Started this morning, and after a rapid march reached our old camp at Bunker Hill. I felt very unwell when I got there.

Friday, October 24, 1862
Got up stiff as a poker feeling a little better. The day passed in quietness.

Saturday, October 25, 1862
Nothing doing in camp. Towards night set in windy and cold, with a prospect of rain. Took big dose of quinine.

Sunday, October 26, 1862
A miserable day, windy rainy and cold. Feel better.

Monday, October 27, 1862
Reported for duty today. Cleared off but the wind remains high. Sunset clear and cold.

Tuesday, October 28, 1862
At roll call was informed that our camp would be left permanently and that the things must be packed up at once. Had a very heavy frost. Taking an eastern route we passed through Smithfield[10] where the youth and beauty, (very little of the latter) turned out to witness our

passage through their town. We encamped near Summit Point after dark, where we built large fires and bivouacked for the night.

Wednesday, October 29, 1862
Changed our camp after breakfast this morning, after which Idleness was the trump card.

Thursday, October 30, 1862
Had a drill in the *manuel* of the piece in the afternoon. The captain made himself decidedly *obstropulous* last night about (*illegible*) some corn. Informed at roll call that we would move in the morning at eight.

"Obstropulous" is an uncommon variation of the word "obstreperous," which according to the Compact Edition of the Oxford English Dictionary, 1988, is "characterized by a great noise or outcry, especially in opposition; clamorous, noisy; vociferous." The target of William's linguistic gymnastics in this entry was likely William Graves Crenshaw, as it is unlikely that Lieutenant James Ellett had taken command at this point.

Friday, October 31, 1862
Started at the appointed hour. Passed through Berryville, the county seat of Clarke, where we were cheered on our way by the sweet smiles of lovely women. Encamped about a mile and a half from the town.

Saturday, November 1, 1862
Everything quiet in camp, although the Yankees are not more than a thousand miles off,[11] if rumor tells the truth. Signal flags were flying pretty much all day, and they are generally a prelude to a fight. Nous verrons.[12]

Sunday, November 2, 1862
A beautiful Sabbath morn and as the church bells from the neighboring town invite all within its sound to the sacred precincts of the House of God, it carries us back to our homes, causing a homesickness that makes us truly melancholy. About twelve o'clock an order came to hitch immediately which was done and on the road to (*Harpers*) Ferry on the Shenandoah River in quick time. The Yankees had driven in our pickets and took possession of (*illegible*) Gap in the Blue Ridge.

After proceeding about a mile we were halted. We were here joined by several of our comrades who had gone to church at Berryville and were thus unceremoniously summoned from the House of God by the Yanks. About four o'clock we were ordered back to camp, which was joyously done for we did not like the idea of bivouacking, for the nights are decidedly frosty. This is the first day of excitement we have had for a month, and it put (*three words illegible*) in quick motion.

Monday, November 3, 1862

The morning passed off in quietness. I am on guard today and it is (*illegible*) cold, for old Boreas[13] is blowing his blasts neatly from the North. About four o'clock orders came to harness the horses and be in readiness at a moment's notice. We remained thus till seven o'clock, when the drivers were ordered to take off the harness and carry the horses to water. Also learned that the enemy endeavored to force the Ford but were repulsed by our artillery with a loss of eighty or ninety killed and wounded. At roll call were informed that we had to go on picket at eight o'clock in the morning. Mirabile dictu.[14]

Tuesday, November 4, 1862

Started at the appointed hour, and as we reached our position on a high hill, the scenery that was stretched out before us was *transcendantly* beautiful. A small mountain on the other side of the river presented the appearance of a huge bouquet, at which a nation (*illegible*) the autumnal frosts have tinted the leaves of the forest with all the hues of the rainbow, and amidst the variegated colors was interspersed an evergreen. Back of this mountain, right and left as far as the eye could reach, stretched the Blue Ridge Mountains in all their grandeur and majesty. All along the sides and summit the blue smoke that churls so gracefully above the tree-tops tells us that the enemy is there (*to*) mar all this scenery by "grim-visaged war"[15] with all its train of evils and horror. Heavy firing was heard all day, supposed to be at Ashby's Gap, several miles above us. The day passed off in quietness with us, not a Yank appearing.

Wednesday, November 5, 1862

We were relieved at ten o'clock and returned to camp pretty hungry, not having eaten breakfast yet. After the pangs of hunger had been satisfied, the day was passed in idleness.

Thursday, November 6, 1862
The day went by without anything exciting to disturb us. The weather is decidedly fickle, warm in the morning and by night turns very cold.

Friday, November 7, 1862
The Battery went on picket again this morning. I *staid* behind to take care of the mess things. Soon after they had gone it commenced to snowing in fine style. I was in a bad fix, the toes on my right foot being completely out of my boot. Pretty soon the Battery came back, leaving Purcell Battery there, as the Yankee's had evacuated the mountain. We captured 105 prisoners. It continued snowing all day. As I turned into my shebang for the night, it had comparatively ceased.

Saturday, November 8, 1862
When I arose I found it had ceased snowing and the prospect fine for clearing off. The day was passed in quietness. At roll call we were informed that we would move at 10 o'clock in the morning.

Sunday, November 9, 1862
Everything was put in marching order at the appointed hour. I got a pair of shoes to protect my feet from the frosts of winter this morning. In the afternoon we received orders that we would stay all night, which was received gladly, for the wind was blowing "big guns" and cold as the mischief.

Monday, November 10, 1862
On guard today. At tattoo received notice that we would move the next morning at eight o'clock.

Tuesday, November 11, 1862
At the appointed time we started, passing through Berryville, taking the Pike to Winchester. After getting within five miles of the latter place we encamped for the night.

Wednesday, November 12, 1862
Removed quarters this morning about a mile nearer Winchester. Col. Walker could not have picked a meaner camp if he had tried. Commenced raining before we had pitched tents.

Thursday, November 13, 1862
Received orders this morning to build stables, when we immediately pitched in by preparing the ground. This looks a little like wintering here.

Friday, November 14, 1862
The day was spent in shoveling dirt.

Saturday, November 15, 1862
On guard today and consequently relieved from working. The ground was finished this evening and Monday we will commence the erection of stables.

Sunday, November 16, 1862
All quiet in camp. The weather cloudy.

Monday, November 17, 1862
Raining and thus relieved from work.

Tuesday, November 18, 1862
The weather still continues rainy.

Wednesday, November 19, 1862
On guard today. Cleared off a little and the boys went to work on the stables.

Thursday, November 20, 1862
Received orders to cook two days rations and be prepared to march at six o'clock in the morning, which order was countermanded at dark.

Friday, November 21, 1862
Received orders to cook two days more rations and start in the morning at six. Speculation was rife as to where we were going and the general opinion was that we were going to leave the valley.

Saturday, November 22, 1862
Started this morning at the appointed hour, taking the Pike to Winchester. Passed through this town, which must have been a flourishing

place before the war, but the Yanks have nearly ruined it. The hills to the north of it have been splendidly fortified to resist any advance of our troops, but it was idle work. We passed through Kernstown, to the left of which Gen. Jackson fought the Yanks to keep them from cutting off the retreat of Gen. Johnston from Manassas. We passed, also, through Newtown,[16] which possesses some beauty, judging from the specimens I saw. After getting ten miles from Winchester, we stopped for the night.

Sunday, November 23, 1862
Was put on the rear guard to take up stragglers. It is a very cold morning and looks a little like snowing. We passed through Middletown and Strasburg, both neat little places. After leaving Winchester yesterday we took the Staunton Pike. After getting within a mile or two from Woodstock we encamped for the night. My feet are very sore from walking. About midnight the guard was awakened by some of David-son's men who had gone to Woodstock and got a plentiful supply of the "spirits of bad men made perfect," when they kicked up the devil of a row. They were arrested and we had to guard them all night. Very little sleep we got after that. Several of Pegram's and Johnston's men were also arrested.

". . . spirits of bad men made perfect . . ."—This euphemism for alcohol provides another fine example of William's wry sense of humor and his exquisite ability to turn a phrase. This one is a takeoff of a quote from Hebrews 12:23 (NIV)— ". . . the spirits of righteous men made perfect."

Monday, November 24, 1862
Was relieved this morning from the rear guard and got in the baggage wagon, not being able to walk. Col. Walker took two barrels of Apple Brandy in Woodstock and poured it on the ground. We passed through *Edinburg* and Mt. Jackson, all nice looking places. We encamped a mile from the latter place, in as pretty a spot of country as I have ever seen. Cooked a day's rations.

Tuesday, November 25, 1862
Resumed our march, and after traveling about eight miles encamped at the foot of the Massanutten Mountains. We went partly through

Newmarket, a thrifty little town, taking the Gordonsville road. Ate dinner there at a private house and was treated very cordially. After getting into camp had to cook two day's rations.

Wednesday, November 26, 1862
Made an early start and after an arduous and very cold march, camped in the Shenandoah Valley about four o'clock. We had a slight sprinkle of snow in the ascent. There was a beautiful view from the summit of the mountain but it was too cold to enjoy.

Thursday, November 27, 1862
Crossed the Blue Ridge Mountains and it was a much more toilsome march than the day previous. The ascent was seven and the descent eight miles. Cooked two days rations.

Friday, November 28, 1862
Passed through Madison C.H., quite a neat looking little place, and encamped four miles from it.

Saturday, November 29, 1862
Resumed the march this morning in a snowstorm, having quite a disagreeable time till it ceased, which it did about ten o'clock. On looking to the rear from a slight eminence we saw the Blue Ridge in snow, and it was a grand and pretty sight. We congratulated ourselves upon crossing as soon. Encamped about two miles from Orange C.H.

Sunday, November 30, 1862
Started at half past eight, passing through Orange C.H. which presented a much livelier appearance than it did when we were here before, taking the road to Fredericksburg. After a march of fifteen miles through a poor and uninteresting country, we encamped at Orange Springs.

Monday, December 1, 1862
Started at 6½ o'clock with a fine prospect for rain. We had a slight shower during the day. The country was less interesting than it was yesterday; encamped about fifteen miles from Fredericksburg.

Tuesday, December 2, 1862

Started at 6½ o'clock. During the march the comp(*any*) has given it two small flags, one of them my detachment, obtained. Nothing occurred of special note during the march. Encamped near the telegraph road,[17] not far from Fredericksburg.

Wednesday, December 3, 1862

Started this morning at eight o'clock and after a round-about march, encamped at our old camp which we left when we fell back to Richmond last May. It brought back recollections of pleasure, as we looked around and saw objects that were familiar to us. Off in front stands Eastern View where we first put our Battery in mask to await the coming of the hated foe; directly before us is this same old field where we trotted over learning the battery drill, which caused a great deal of grumbling, but which has been useful to us since. But then comes the sad thought that there are some who were with us then that are now absent, never again to join us on earth. Yes, many have gone. Some fell bravely at their post, fighting the invaders of their soil, whilst others by the insidious hand of disease. I hope they are in a better land than this. I hope we will stop here for several days to rest, for this is the *twelth* day we have been marching.

Thursday, December 4, 1862

Nothing doing in camp. The fellows are lounging about and enjoying the rest hugely.

Friday, December 5, 1862

All is quiet along our lines. Went to the railroad to see my cousin but it was not his day for bringing the mail. It commenced raining just as I started, which turned into hail and, just before night, snow which fell with great fierceness. There must have been great suffering amongst the infantry as they are but illy fixed for winter.

Saturday, December 6, 1862

The weather is clear and cold. Commenced the regimental guard again today. Nothing of interest occurred.

Sunday, December 7, 1862

On guard today and it is bitter cold.

Monday, December 8, 1862

Went to the cars and received a pair of gloves, two pairs of socks and some smoking tobacco which father sent me. They were very acceptable. My cousin, the mail agent, gave me a plug of tobacco also, which put me all right. I was glad to hear that all were well.

Tuesday, December 9, 1862

Both armies are quiet. Nothing unusual occurred in camp.

Wednesday, December 10, 1862

Went down to the cars this morning, and had to leave, there being a strong Provost Guard taking up all soldiers not having passes, without being able to see my cousin. Dick Walden[18] was taken up and Lt. Ellett had to come down to get him off. All quiet.

Thursday, December 11, 1862

Awakened this morning by heavy cannonading in the direction of Fredericksburg. We were kept in a state of preparation for leaving all day. Ordered to cook a day's rations. Learned that the Yankee's were shelling the town and laying down pontoon bridges, in which they were quite successful.

Thursday, December 11, 1862, was the first day of the Battle of Fredericksburg.[19]

Friday, December 12, 1862

Fredericksburg was evacuated today, after heavy skirmishing between Barksdale brigade and the advance of the enemy. Our forces fell back to a range of hills; upon them they await the onset of Lincoln's myrmidons.[20] We were not ordered out of camp. Cooked a day's rations. At tattoo we were informed that we would be aroused at twelve o'clock and take position at two.

Saturday, December 13, 1862

We were awakened at the appointed hour, when we learned that the second and third detachment would start at two, and the first and fourth at five o'clock, Lt. Jas. Ellett commanding the former and Lt. Thomas *Elliot*[21] the latter section. As Lt. Jas. Ellett started with his section he told the boys goodbye that would be in another part of the field. I was in Thomas *Elliot's* section, which moved out at the appointed time and took position on Eastern View, the very place last Spring a section of our battery took position to await the advance of the enemy. We were put here to watch a gorge to keep the Yanks from coming on us from Port Royal and turning our right flank. Soon after daylight the battle commenced and raged with a great fury till six o'clock. About ten o'clock Sergeant Robert *Ellott*[22] rode up and told his brother that Lt. Jas. Ellett was killed. It put a damper upon our feelings for we had begun to like him very much.[23] From our position we had a partial view of the battlefield and it was awfully grand.

Our section remained in action all day. About four o'clock they sent over for horses and men when we learned that John *Paine*[24] was killed, whose death was greatly regretted, for he was a noble boy. Corp. Mallory, Private *Douglas*, Pleasants, Burgess, Hart, Wheeler, Seeley, and Ruffin were wounded,[25] but none dangerously. Nearly every horse was killed or wounded in the section. The section was withdrawn just before sunset, and retired to camp. The result of the day's fighting was highly satisfactory and added another hue to our halo of glory. The enemy were repulsed at every point of attack with great slaughter, their loss being estimated at ten thousand killed and wounded. From all I can learn, our boys behaved with great gallantry under the heaviest shelling it has been province of any troops to stand. After getting to camp we cooked a day's rations and retired to rest willingly.

Our section was ordered out this morning, the other not being able to move on account of the horses. The day passed without a fight, the Yankee's being satisfied with yesterday's trial. They sent in a flag of truce to bury their dead in the afternoon, which I believe, was accepted. We returned to camp at twilight. Soon after arriving, we were greeted with the Aurora Borealis, which was grandly sublime.

Between December 11 and December 15, 1862, the Union Army of the Potomac, under the command of Major General Ambrose Burnside, hurled itself in multiple frontal assaults against well-positioned, deeply entrenched Confederate forces on Marye's Heights as well as on the high ground on the south side of the Rappahannock River at Prospect Hill.

By the conclusion of this event, the broken and demoralized Union forces suffered casualties at a level more than twice as heavy as those suffered by the Confederates, with almost 13,000 Union dead, wounded, or missing. The Confederate army lost approximately 4,500.[26]

As Frank O'Reilly points out at the conclusion of his definitive work on the battle, *The Fredericksburg Campaign*, the Battle of Fredericksburg was actually two distinct battles, fought miles distant from one another, with little communication or connection between them. Fredericksburg is best known for the carnage inflicted upon Burnside's soldiers at Marye's Heights and for the recklessness of the order behind that assault. The other battle, less well known, occurred at Prospect Hill (the place William called "Eastern View") between Jackson's troops and the Union's I Corps. Unlike the disparity of Union losses that occurred at Marye's Heights (8 Union dead for every 1 fallen Confederate), Jackson reported 4,000 lost at Prospect Hill, compared with the Union I Corps major general William B. Franklin's losses of 5,000. O'Reilly notes these numbers reflect the "savage closeness of the fighting," postulating that Prospect Hill should be considered the "decisive action on December 13," as opposed to events at Marye's Heights.

The resounding defeat of the Union forces at Fredericksburg struck a stunning blow to the morale of the Union army, from rank soldiers on the ground all the way to Washington, DC. Lincoln was embarrassed by the failure, while his critics were emboldened to further question and ridicule his leadership. Northern newspapers excoriated his interference in the Union command's strategic decision-making. At the same time, Fredericksburg solidified Robert E. Lee's standing in the Confederacy, while further establishing Jackson's reputation. The Confederate army's rank and file were buoyed by the uneven victory, believing the momentum could be sustained. Lee, who wrote General Longstreet following the battle that "victories like this will consume us," understood that losses on this scale were unsustainable. Nevertheless, he used the victory to psychological advantage throughout the winter and spring of 1863, harassing Union forces while simultaneously spreading his own army thin, further straining its resources and supply lines.[27]

Part 6
MARCH TO WINTER QUARTERS
DECEMBER 15–31, 1862

This portion of the diary offers a brief but revealing glimpse into the Civil War soldier's life. It includes bad weather, broken-down equipment, hungry men, and a hope to see home and family for Christmas, a hope that was to go wholly unfulfilled. The men of Crenshaw's Battery marched fewer than forty miles from Fredericksburg to their winter quarters camp and were finally paid for their service to the Confederacy for the first time since joining the army. When they finally settled in to their new accommodations, William made no mention of the grandeur of their establishment, only remarking that they were at "Mr. Woolfork's farm." In fact, the Woolfolk Plantation, "Mulberry Place," still stands among the finest houses in a state remarkable for its grand estates. In 1862 it was the seat of one of the wealthiest families of Old Virginia.

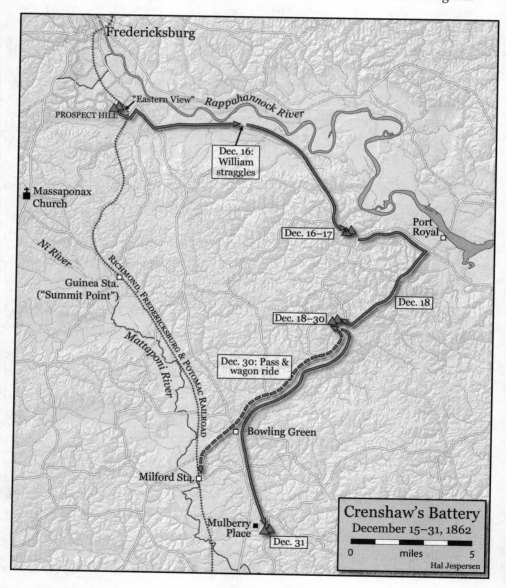

Crenshaw's Battery
December 15–31, 1862

0   miles   5

Hal Jespersen

Throughout the diary William managed to conjure many compliments for the great homes his battery visited, but here he said almost nothing, which raises the question, *What was the difference?* The difference, of course, was time spent. William had only a few days to consider each of the other fine plantation homes where his battery paused during the 1862 march. He had a full winter season—from December 31, 1862, until April 1863—to study Mulberry Place and its occupants, as well as observe the easy relations between the wealthy Woolfolk landowners and his battery's officers. He may have noted that he and the rank artillerists in Pegram's Battalion fared little better over the winter—in terms of provisions, warmth, and adequate accommodations—than many of Woolfolk's hundred-odd slaves.

For a young man already at odds with his commanding officers, the indifference shown to the well-being of the rank and file—while the officers dined nightly at Jourdan Woolfolk's table and were entertained throughout the season at an endless string of neighborhood parties—must have been galling. Whatever William's reaction, it was enough to cause him to lay down his pen and notebook for the balance of his part in the war.

Monday, December 15, 1862
Reveille was sounded at 3½ o'clock and moved out of camp at 5½ o'clock. The day again passed without the Yanks resuming the attack. Nothing occurred of special note. We returned at dark to camp, cooked a day's rations.

Tuesday, December 16, 1862
Soon after being aroused, the rain, fixed with a little hail, commenced descending with great violence, but it soon settled down into a steady fall. We started before light and had not gone over three hundred yards before one of the wheels of the gun carriage came off. Here was a pretty kettle of fish; but after a little hard swearing on all sides, we pitched in and put it on again. We reached our place without any more accidents. As soon as objects became distinct at any distance, our generals found out that the Yanks had recrossed the river, ignominiously leaving us masters of the field. Troops were hurried to Port Royal and we amongst them, only carrying one gun, the other being left behind, when the three pieces will be carried to Richmond and three heavy guns sent in their places. We trudged on after getting started (which was about three or four in the afternoon) and traveled

until late in the night. I got tired on the way and, with three or four comrades, encamped for the night. This is the first time any of our boys ever straggled, but it was owing to the fatigues they had undergone for the last three or four days.

Wednesday, December 17, 1862
Started at daylight and reached the battery at one o'clock, it being encamped about four miles from Port Royal. We left here about four o'clock, retracing our steps about four miles and encamped for the night.

Thursday, December 18, 1862
We left this camp at 9½ o'clock, carrying our knapsacks on our backs for the first time. After proceeding about four miles over as hilly a road as one can meet in a year's travel, we took up camp.

Friday, December 19, 1862
The day was spent in fixing ourselves up as comfortable as possible. Everything quiet along the lines. Our camp is ten miles from *Guinney's*[1] Depot and four from the river.

Saturday, December 20, 1862
The weather has been very cold for the last two days, rendering living in the woods anything but comfortable. The only talk in camp now is how to get home to spend Christmas, but all expect to be here and have a dull time. Nothing transpired of exciting note.

Sunday, December 21, 1862
Nothing doing, and time hangs heavily on our hands. Camp life is decidedly dull and monotonous and even a lazy man gets tired of it.

Monday, December 22, 1862
The officers have been working on payrolls and we expect to be paid off very soon. We have not been paid off since being in service.

Tuesday, December 23, 1862
The Yanks are perfectly satisfied with the drubbing they received, and are now quietly ensconced beyond the Rappahannock. I don't think they will trouble us this winter. I hope they will not.

Wednesday, December 24, 1862
We signed the pay roll today. Two detachments are going to the picket tomorrow. I, fortunately, was not detailed to go. Everything quiet in camp.

Thursday, December 25, 1862
Christmas Morn broke very threatening, but cleared off beautifully and warm. The boys started at seven o'clock to go on picket, after which the camp was dull and lonesome. During the morning we were called up and paid off until the 31st of October; $119.10, for clothes and wages. After dark the boys of ours and other batteries enjoyed themselves by having a battle with lighted port-fires, which presented a handsome pyrotechnic display.

Friday, December 26, 1862
Christmas has come and gone, and I sincerely hope I will never spend another in the army. The boys arrived in due time this morning from picket. Everything is quiet along the lines.

Saturday, December 27, 1862
The day passed off quietly, nothing occurring to mar the monotony of the life.

Sunday, December 28, 1862
The day was beautiful, and naught disturbed its serenity. We were ordered to cook a day's rations as we would probably move into winter quarters tomorrow.

Monday, December 29, 1862
Started this morning at eight o'clock, and after a march of about fifteen miles, encamped within two miles of Bowling Green. After getting into camp two comrades and myself went to this town to see what it was, and what we could buy. Went to the hotel and registered our names for supper, after which we endeavored to obtain a little of the "spirits of bad men made perfect" but without success. Bought some pies at fifty cents apiece, destitute of shortening in the crust and sugar in the pie. That man's soul is not larger than one thousandth part of a *knat's* eye.

About dusk we repaired to the hotel and waited as patiently as our appetites would allow us. Presently the bell rung, when twenty hungry soldiers made a rush for the table. Did you ever see a rush for the ticket box of the theater when it is open, every man fearful of not getting a good seat, if you have then you may form a <u>faint</u> idea of our rush. We finally got seated, and such a destruction of edibles I have never seen before. In less time than fifteen minutes we cleared the dishes of everything eatable, myself winding up with the last biscuit. I don't know what the proprietor thought <u>for I didn't ask him</u>. I am quite confident that no other twenty men could have done the job in as neat and clean a manner in the same space of time. After leaving the hotel we knocked around a little and went back to camp, well pleased with our trip, with the exception that we did not get some of the extract of corn.

Tuesday, December 30, 1862

Got up this morning at Reveille and obtained permission to go to *Millford*[2] Depot, as I expected a box of eatables. Found out that the battalion would not move today, which was the thing I wanted. After a walk of about four or five miles reached the station, but was too late for the passenger train and had to wait for its return. In due time it arrived and obtained my box. Soon after it passed, it commenced raining, which did not please me in the least. I, however, had the good fortune to get into a wagon which was going to camp, which arrived there at nightfall.

Pitched into the good things, which was decidedly acceptable. Received orders to march at nine o'clock.

Wednesday, December 31, 1862

Started this morning at the appointed hour. Passed through Bowling Green taking the road to Richmond, and after traveling about five miles from the town, took up our winter quarters on Mr. *Woolfork's*[3] farm, in a place of oak woods. We pitched in and fixed ourselves as comfortable as possible. Thus we ended our march with the year.

7. ❀ A Strange and Severe Life

After more than one thousand miles of marching from one end of Virginia to the other, crossing the Shenandoah Mountains into what is now West Virginia, slogging over the Potomac into Maryland and then back again, after enduring numerous brutally instructive battles along the circuitous route, sacrificing countless comrades to violence and disease, and surviving gnawing hunger and unrelenting exhaustion, on December 31, 1862, William Ellis Jones and his fellow artillerists were at last granted the opportunity to cease moving.

The place chosen as the artillery's winter quarters reflected the battalion officers' requirements and comfort more than that of the soldiers who served under them. Mulberry Place was the home of Jourdan Woolfolk, his wife, Elizabeth, and several of their children and grandchildren. The grand, Federal-style house was constructed in 1827 by Woolfolk for his growing family and as an expression of his social, political, and financial status.[1]

Mulberry Place, where no fewer than four generations of the Woolfolk family were born and reared into authentic Old Virginia aristocracy, was more than just a grand old house. It was more than just a working plantation with three thousand acres under cultivation and over one hundred slaves underpinning its operations. In 1863 Mulberry Place was the communications and overland transportation epicenter from the Tidewater region of Virginia to Richmond. The railroad and telegraph lines from Petersburg and Richmond to Fredericksburg and Washington lay within a mile of the stately manor house.[2] The Richmond-Fredericksburg Turnpike ran through the Woolfolk property, as did the stagecoach roads east into the Virginia peninsula. From their winter quarters at Mulberry Place the artillery command of Lee's army had access to communications from the far-flung reaches of the Confederate infantry and cavalry. Should the Union make a move along the James River toward Richmond or attempt another assault against Fredericksburg, the blunt force of the artillery could be brought to bear either by rail or by road within a single day's movement from its strategic position.[3]

In the fall and winter of 1862, a reorganization of the command and deployment structure of the Confederate artillery was proposed and implemented.

After a reshuffling of responsibilities and promotions given to senior officers, William "Willie" R. J. Pegram, who previously commanded Purcell's Artillery, was made major over the unified battalion, which included the Virginia batteries of Purcell, Letcher, Crenshaw, and Fredericksburg, as well as the South Carolina "Pee Dee" Artillery. Pegram's commanding officer was newly promoted Colonel Reuben Lindsey Walker, who reported directly to Brigadier General A. P. Hill, commander of the Third Corps of the Army of Northern Virginia.[4]

By the end of the 1862 campaign Willie Pegram had earned a substantial reputation for gallantry and bravery in battle. A rising favorite of both Robert E. Lee and A. P. Hill, Pegram was most distinguished for his diminutive stature, crippling nearsightedness, and his dogmatic devotion to God and the Confederacy, two entities he saw as uniquely intertwined and divinely aligned.[5] Newly minted Major Pegram fully comprehended the strategic importance of his battalion's placement. In a letter to his sister Jennie, penned on January 8, 1863, Pegram wrote, "There seems to be no probability of my getting a furlough. . . . Active operations may be resumed at any time."[6]

While Pegram and his officers certainly understood why the batteries were placed near Bowling Green, attached to the Woolfolks' all-important transportation and communications hub, it is less likely the battalion's soldiers appreciated the site selected as their home through the long and bitterly cold months of winter. Unlike the officers, who were frequent guests at the big house and who likely maintained indoor quarters, the rank and file were banished to a distant woodland on the edge of a swamp.[7] There, in the first weeks of January as snow fell, the footsore, exhausted, and malnourished artillerists hastily constructed log huts and lean-tos for themselves and their animals. The ruins of these crude mud and wood fortifications are still in evidence today in the woods at the edge of the swamp.[8] When contrasted against the timeless survival of the main house at Mulberry Place, these structures bear a sobering testament to the hardships the rank and file endured. From their rough, waterlogged locale a thousand yards distant from the grand house at the center of Jourdan Woolfolk's empire, the soldiers could observe—but not partake in—the daily routine of plantation life.

Like all the beautiful old homes William Ellis Jones encountered during the 1862 march, Mulberry Place was a working plantation—a town unto itself—overwhelmingly populated by slaves whose forebears built it, whose parents expanded it, and whose children were born and were destined to die on it, working in its fields the whole of their lives, their bodies buried in unmarked graves on the edge of the creeping black swamp. During those long months of winter when there were no battles, few drills, and nothing to do except observe, William saw his battalion officers welcomed into the big house for entertainment and generous meals, while he and his fellow soldiers gnawed on stale hardtack. He witnessed slaves chopping firewood and hauling it into the warm house, while outside in thrown-together huts of raw logs and pine board, he and his comrades shivered and plotted how to run the blockade to Richmond to see their families. He saw the Woolfolk family, finely dressed, plump and sated, conspicuously confident of their position as hosts to Pegram's Battalion. Daily the family and their guests moved through idle indulgences, organizing supper parties, neighborhood visitations, and late-night engagements for regal Confederate officers and elegant Caroline County families.[9]

The rooms of the old plantation buzzed with activity that winter. Finely dressed aristocrats drank their fill of locally produced wine until laughter echoed from the interior out into the damp cold where a thousand troops huddled around failing campfires. Meanwhile, Woolfolk slaves shuffled through never-ending chores, their rations perhaps even more meager than those of the hungry soldiers. The Woolfolk family and Mulberry Place represented everything William and his fellow enlisted men fought for, died for, or survived throughout the grueling campaign of 1862, whether they recognized it or not.

Following the withering fire during the Battles of Seven Days, Cedar Mountain, Second Manassas, Harper's Ferry, Antietam, and Fredericksburg, after the grueling march through hail and snowstorms over the Blue Ridge Mountains, after hunger and shared exhaustion, the men of Pegram's Battalion knew one another better than their own families knew them. Together they endured the brutality of mass murder—received and given—and together the survivors got through it, more or less intact. As Private W. H. Kitchens recorded in his wartime memoirs, "There is a fellow feeling among . . . soldiers that only death can erase. They learned to love each other on account of the hardships and suffering, fought, bled, and died for."[10]

William fought for Sidney Strother, who was mortally wounded at Gaines' Mill. He fought for Marion Knowles and for Charles Pemberton, at whose deathbed he sat vigil. He fought for R. H. Mallory, Thomas Catlett, Horace Holland, John Payne, and John Moss.[11] He fought for the three soldiers he saw executed on the grounds at Hawfield Plantation in August 1862. And he fought for James Broderick, a private in Letcher's artillery who was condemned to death and executed by firing squad at Mulberry Place on February 20, 1863.[12]

William fought for his fellow soldiers because they were the only people in the world who understood what it was to face fear and face death and still press on. They were the only men in the world who would risk themselves to preserve him. Everything else was just rhetoric, posturing, and politics. Behind the guns of Crenshaw's Battery, politics became irrelevant. The only thing that mattered was survival. William chose to survive.

After breaking winter quarters at Mulberry Place, the Crenshaw Battery, and William with it, went on to the Battle of Chancellorsville in May 1863. There, front and center, they endured one of the hottest artillery engagements of the war. Acting alone, Crenshaw's Battery reportedly drove the Union guns from their positions without any infantry support whatsoever. It was a miraculous artillery victory that Charles P. Young wrote "did not occur on any other field during the war."[13]

In July 1863 they were back on the long march through Maryland and Pennsylvania. At the catastrophic Battle of Gettysburg, according to Young, they "led to the front and fired the first artillery shot in the battle."[14] After Gettysburg, in the battery's first major defeat, they retreated with the Union army trailing their rear, threatening complete annihilation. Nevertheless, they pressed on, engaging the Union again at Gaines's Crossroads, Shepherdstown, Bristoe Station, and Mine Run. After wintering over in the Green Springs neighborhood of Louisa County, the 1864 campaign commenced with the horrific Battle of the Wilderness, followed by an early May engagement at Spotsylvania Court House. The Crenshaw Battery played a prominent role in that brutal, two-week-long encounter.[15] Despite confusing orders and withering fire from the enemy that decimated men, horses, and guns, some members of Crenshaw's Battery still maintained their humor in the early days of the assault.

On May 10, 1864, two days into the battle, while disengaged and awaiting orders under hot artillery fire, Crenshaw's gunners lay prone beneath their cannons for cover. One team of men discovered a box of half-eaten crackers on the ground. According to Charles P. Young and Captain Thomas Ellett, a hungry artillerist began munching the crackers, then passed the box to his companions in the dirt. A few yards away another gun team saw the men eating. One hungry man called out, "Pitch me a cracker!"

At that precise moment a Union shell impacted between the two guns, exploding with a terrible report, showering the men on both sides with cordite, rock, and dirt.

"There's a cracker," cried the man holding the box. "Catch that!"

All the men in the battery within earshot erupted into gut-busting laughter. Years later the story was recalled by members of the battery and for half a century following was passed down as evidence of their coolness and acerbic wit in the face of utter annihilation.[16]

That same morning of May 10, 1864, near the courthouse where Crenshaw's Battery lay positioned behind hastily constructed earthworks,[17] William Ellis Jones stood by one of the horses to steady her as his gun was unlimbered for battle. A Union sharpshooter took aim and fired.[18] The marksman missed, striking William with only a grazing shot to the foot, but the damage was immediately debilitating. Bleeding and hobbled by the shot, William was carried to the rear, his career with Crenshaw's Battery finally drawn to an inglorious conclusion.[19]

The Battle of Spotsylvania Court House is now the stuff of legend among students of the American Civil War. It was one of the bloodiest single battles of the war up to that date, with more than 30,000 casualties (18,399 Union[20] and 12,687 Confederate[21]). It was one of the longest lasting battles of the entire Civil War and the only one that did not pause for darkness or inclement weather. It was possibly the most brutal, large-scale battle ever fought in the war, with hand-to-hand combat persisting for nearly twenty-four hours inside the "bloody angle" before reinforcements could route the Union assault.

Spotsylvania and Wilderness historian Gordon C. Rhea wrote the following about this event, "The slaughter raged so intensely for so long and involved such close and sustained contact that several otherwise articulate chroniclers fumbled for words to convey its enormity. 'Nothing can describe the confusion, the savage blood-curling yells, the murderous faces, the awful curses, and the grisly horror of the melee,' a veteran remarked. 'Of all the battles I took part in, Bloody Angle at Spotsylvania exceeded all the rest in stubbornness, ferocity, and in carnage.' Another referred to the fight as a 'seething, bubbling, roaring hell of hate and murder.'"[22]

After the battle, dead lay unburied by the thousands across recently plowed fields. Thousands more wounded crowded into makeshift hospitals in churches, warehouses, and private homes from Fredericksburg to Richmond. Fredericksburg became a city of hospitals in the days and weeks following this debacle. Union casualties occupied every church and vacant building in the city, with walking wounded spilling into the streets like battered vagrants. Volunteers from all over the Union flowed into town to care for the sick and injured. Their presence and the presence of so many needy soldiers unsettled the city's permanent residents, who were already deeply war-fatigued, first by the Union shelling on May 3, 1863, and then by the military occupation that followed Fredericksburg's capitulation to Federal forces.[23]

Sometime before May 22, William was evacuated to a nearby hospital or perhaps was even on his way to Richmond.[24] Before he left Spotsylvania, he already had a good grasp of the horror endured by his fellow soldiers. It is probable that like so many others who were there on the field through this engagement, and so many who have studied this battle since, William realized that tens of thousands of Union and Confederate men were brutally thrown together—and pointlessly sacrificed—for a few small acres of earth in the middle of nowhere, earth that neither Grant nor Lee needed to protect and that both quickly abandoned as soon as it was expedient to do so.[25]

The minor wound William received at Spotsylvania paled in comparison to his manifest rage at the catastrophic losses his comrades suffered—the tragedy of all those needlessly shattered lives, the utter futility of this battle, the catastrophic pointlessness of the entire war. William returned to Richmond, but his broken heart remained with his friends on the road south to Petersburg.

A few weeks after this battle closed, an anonymous member of William Pegram's artillery battalion penned an editorial to the *Richmond Whig*.[26] (See appendix.) The author opens with a florid preamble stating that since no one has recognized the accomplishments and sacrifices of the rank and file members of Pegram's Battalion, he is forced to publish an "honorable mention" of the battalion's accomplishments in the "journal of the day" and become the "herald of their own deeds." His very next thought communicates that the people of Richmond ought to be suspicious of the glorified reputations of the battalion's command, insinuating that the officers' concern for Richmond's sons is not as it has been advertised, and a more careful parent would consider the soldiers' well-being more thoughtfully.

The author methodically lists the full names and rank of every officer in each of the batteries, excepting one: William Graves Crenshaw is listed only as "Capt. ——Crenshaw," as if the name itself is so odious he cannot bring himself to spell out the words. Later in the lengthy editorial, the anonymous author complains bitterly, "I will not mention name by name the battles of this army. Col. Pegram's Battalion has never (*missed one*).[27] Not for one moment has been accorded to us the respite which is the need for good service. We have never been in reserve. Though we have five battalions in our Corps and . . . three divisions, the day of our relief has not yet come."

The author goes on to question whether this fact is due to the self-serving, glory-seeking attitudes of the battalion's colonel and general, or whether it is due to the recklessness and ill-conceived ambitions of the junior officers. He states, "That we have known neither respite or repose can be attested by . . . the crows; the vales, from Malvern Hill to Gettysburg . . . made yet sadder than the Wilderness; . . . loneliness."

The author of this missive offered up Colonel William Pegram's insatiable hunger for glory as explanation for the battalion's heroic record. He follows by suggesting that the people of Richmond have failed to honor the service of the rank soldier, instead venerating vainglorious and reckless officers who sacrificed too many men in pursuit of self-serving ambitions. He returns to the deeds of his comrades, pointing out "how our men have striven and how they have suffered; how . . . they have gone to the conflict, and how . . . they have borne the sacrifices and disciplines of a strange and severe life; and how they have borne this for years."

This letter offers damning criticism of William Pegram's leadership, as well as a conspicuous affront to the motivations and integrity of every officer in the battalion command. While there were many well-educated men in the ranks of Pegram's Battalion, there were probably few bold enough or irreverent enough to write such an open letter who also had opportunity to do it. William Ellis Jones was conveniently convalescing when this letter was penned and posted to the *Richmond Whig*—the newspaper that gave William H. Clemmitt his professional start and to which Clemmitt and everyone associated with his printing concern retained an intimate affiliation.

It is probable that Pegram had the connections in town to quickly discover the identity of the author. It is equally likely there would have been repercussions for the soldier who wrote this very public and critical letter. If William was indeed the author of this missive, it is unknown whether he suffered consequences. What is known is that while his wound turned out to be superficial and his recovery swift and complete, he was officially declared "unfit for duty" by a board of surgeons for the balance of the war. It is entirely possible William's father, or his well-connected cousin William B. Jones pulled strings to get him out of combat and out of the ongoing feud with his commanding officers. William Ellis Jones was reassigned into the "invalid corps" in February 1865. He was attached to the Post Quartermaster's Office in Richmond as a clerk, where he served until the fall of Richmond in April 1865.

* * *

Even a cursory study of the 1862 diary reveals that from the very beginning of his service, William had a difficult relationship with the officers in command of his battery.[28] His earliest service is demonstrative of a less than enthusiastic soldier. He laid out a great deal, claiming illness in camp while enjoying a variety of entertainments at home. While on sick leave in Richmond with a case of poison oak, he brazenly defied his commanding officer's order to return to camp. He ran the blockade to carouse about Richmond and then complained he was too ill to march. He was hostile to his commanders, ignoring their orders, and in his journal was sarcastic and cynically harsh in his recorded judgments against them.

If William went into the service of the Confederacy reluctantly, he emerged from his wartime experience more certain of the cost of the war. Despite all this, while the battles raged, he remained on the field, fighting for the survival of the men beside him.

It is likely that William realized over the course of his winter at Mulberry Place and the brutality of the warfare that defined 1863 and 1864 that the Confederacy was doomed and whatever came after would require a resilience the magnitude of which he was only just beginning to comprehend. Whatever he thought, however he felt, the only thing that can be known for certain is that what came after, both personally and for the shattered Confederacy, would test every assumption William Ellis Jones ever held true, forcing him headlong into a reality that even he could have scarcely imagined.

8. Bad Men Made Perfect

If Thomas Norcliffe Jones's political and financial connections provided his son, William Ellis Jones, with a degree of cover between March 1862 and June 1864 (when that scathing letter was anonymously written to the *Richmond Whig*), then any confidence in continued protection was unceremoniously removed by October 1864. The following one-line announcement appeared in the *Richmond Daily Dispatch* on October 13, 1864: "Died. In Halifax, Nova Scotia, on the 3d of September, ultimo, of yellow fever, contracted in Bermuda, THOMAS JONES, a merchant of this city, aged forty-six years, leaving a wife and five children."

Leaving aside that the announcement contained an error—Thomas Norcliffe Jones was actually sixty-four years old in 1864—the fact that William's father did die that year under these curious circumstances is beyond doubt. What has so far been impossible to ascertain is the identity of Thomas's second wife, where their marriage took place, who the five surviving children were, and where this second family resided between 1859 (when Thomas allegedly remarried) and the time of his death in 1864.

To date, no record of this marriage taking place in Richmond has been found, and no indication that Thomas maintained any residence in the city other than his warehouse at 8 Main Street has been discovered. The last will and testament Thomas left has vanished from the public record, even though its wishes were publicly carried out by the Henrico County sheriff, H. K. Ellyson, working under the authority of the surviving "Mrs. Jones" through an unnamed attorney.[1]

By late 1864, William Ellis Jones was living in Richmond working at the Post Quartermaster's Office. As a resident of Richmond, he would have seen firsthand the deprivations under which the city's citizens suffered. War laid Richmond bare. There was not enough food, not enough money, not even enough firewood or coal to keep warm through some of the bitterest winters recorded in Virginia history. Richmond was a besieged city, its citizens on the brink of starvation, holding on to a shadow of a last hope for salvation, praying for a miracle that would return the city to its former dignity.

When Thomas Norcliffe Jones died, it is unlikely many in Richmond took immediate notice. Over the weeks and months that followed, when the various warehouse properties and manufacturing facilities owned or co-owned by him were opened and their contents exposed, it may be assumed that the hungry people of Richmond were both astonished and disgusted by what was revealed behind the locked doors and brick walls of Jones's low-profile establishments. Among the variety of goods advertised from just one of the warehouses were coffee, manufactured tobacco, cognac, almonds, syrup, and "a large number of hogsheads of LEAF TOBACCO . . . for the manufacture of 'Negro Head' and for foreign shipment." The ad continued, "This sale is worthy of the attention of the trade, and will be continued from day to day till all is sold."[2] There was so much leaf tobacco to be disposed of that it was impossible to find a buyer willing or able to purchase the lot. Leaf tobacco, as anyone living in that place and time readily understood, represented *real* money in the bank, not worthless Confederate notes.

The contents of Thomas Norcliffe Jones's Cary Street warehouse remained undisclosed in the local papers. What *is* disclosed in subsequent ads placed in the *Richmond Daily Dispatch* throughout January and February 1865 is that Thomas had an interest in a tobacco factory and a whiskey distillery, both of which had to be liquidated in order to settle his estate. Curiously, no liquor other than the cognac mentioned above was advertised for sale, despite the fact that he was manufacturing it throughout the war. How it was disposed of (or to whom) remains a mystery.

Beyond the questions this information raises, one rises above the rest: What was Thomas Norcliffe Jones doing in Bermuda in 1864? The South was under a complete Union naval blockade. At this late stage in the war, nearly all regular commerce between the Confederate states and the outside world had ceased except that which could slip through the dangerous and thoroughly patrolled Union stranglehold. It is unlikely the question posed can be satisfactorily answered. What is reasonable to venture is that for Thomas to risk his life traveling to Bermuda and back via Nova Scotia, whatever he was doing must have been extremely lucrative.

A few things are known for certain. William was not named as the executor of his father's estate in Richmond, and he does not appear to have been a beneficiary in any substantial measure. Finally, and very strange indeed, is that Thomas Norcliffe Jones's gravestone at Shockoe Cemetery is inscribed with a death date of 1867 (with no month and no day). By contrast, the stone for William's mother, Margaret Jones, clearly shows her date of death as June 1,

1859. Why the difference? And why is the date of death inscribed on Thomas's stone off by three years? It can be conjectured that due to the naval blockade, it was impossible to bring Thomas's remains back to Richmond in 1864. Perhaps he was interred in Nova Scotia and remained there until the conclusion of the war, when his son was able to muster the resources to have his father's remains returned to Richmond and laid to rest in the Shockoe Cemetery plot that held his first wife, Margaret, and daughter, Mary. This is only conjecture and is only one of the many mysteries lingering around the life and death of Thomas Norcliffe Jones.

Perhaps the most intriguing mystery of all lies in the meticulously recorded family history assembled by the grandson of the Civil War diarist (also named William Ellis Jones), which has served as primary source material and one of the major inspirations for this book. This document includes almost no detailed information about Thomas Norcliffe Jones. The manuscript contains extensive histories on Thomas Norcliffe Jones's brothers, his father, and even his grandfather, great-uncle, uncles, and cousins, but not even so much as a certain date of birth is recorded for the man who settled the first of the Dolgellau, Wales, Joneses in the New World. His history, the facts of his life, and the scandal he created for his surviving son in Richmond were essentially wiped clean from the family record. It is as if the man was a shadow who hardly registered in the scheme of things and the surviving family members wanted no part in carrying his name into the future.

After Thomas Norcliffe Jones's death, his son William had only one blood relation remaining in Richmond—his second cousin William B. Jones, the blockade-runner and contractor for the Confederate War Department who supplied alcohol, sugar, and other commodities to the rebel army. It has already been established that William B. Jones may have suffered under a tarnished reputation due to his commercial interests and extravagant lifestyle while Richmond struggled through the war. Once Thomas died, it appears that all connection between the cousins was permanently severed. Prior to the war's end, William B. Jones was probably just another figure our Civil War veteran tried to distance himself from. As the Confederacy stumbled and eventually fell, the cast of William B. Jones's shadow was eventually revealed in all its contemptible darkness. This enigma of a man, as it turns out, played a leading role in the riots that preceded Richmond's destruction by fire in April 1865.[3]

Prior to the surrender, William Ellis Jones was a survivor of the Civil War, probably living in near-poverty, working at the Post Quartermaster's Office in Richmond, and praying for the war's end. With no family to fall back on and very little money, it seems likely that he turned to his friends for consolation and support. Those friends, cultivated since his boyhood, would have been his salvation in every possible sense of the word. By that spring, William and his small circle of lifelong friends, along with every resident of Richmond, were all severely tested.

The Evacuation, the Conflagration, and the Surrender

A great portion of the early Lost Cause mythology and succeeding white Southern sentiment was born out of events that occurred in Richmond in the days and hours preceding the surrender of the Confederacy. As Robert E. Lee's defensive lines around Petersburg crumbled, that city fell into Union possession, leaving Richmond completely exposed. On Sunday, April 2, 1865, General Lee telegraphed Confederate president Jefferson Davis with the following ominous communication: "I advise that all preparation be made for leaving Richmond tonight."[4] That morning and on through the early afternoon, rumors ran rampant through the Confederate capital, but it was not until four o'clock in the afternoon that the citizens of Richmond finally realized—to their absolute horror—their government was abandoning them in their darkest hour. The city slowly descended into chaos.

Officials of the Confederate government, along with military officers and prominent private citizens, piled themselves and all the possessions they could carry onto train cars, wagons, and packhorses and began evacuating the doomed city. The vaults of every bank in town were emptied of their specie. The Confederacy's remaining gold and silver was hauled to the depot under guard and sent west in advance of President Davis and his cabinet.

Richmond's town fathers, fearful of a repetition of the carnage that occurred in Columbia, South Carolina, when that city fell to the Union, ordered all the liquor warehoused in town immediately destroyed.[5] What followed was an hours-long bacchanal in which Confederate soldiers and the people of Richmond—black and white, free and enslaved, soldier and civilian— literally drank alcohol from the gutters as it was poured into the streets. People collected whiskey in hats, shoes, and tin cups, consuming it as quickly as they could before diving back in for refills. It did not take long before the spirits took effect.[6]

Straggling, intoxicated Confederate soldiers began smashing shop windows and looting on their way out of town. Jewelry stores and candy shops were equally savaged. Grocers were a favorite target, as were boot makers and haberdashers. Lawlessness ruled the streets. The mob vastly outnumbered any remaining civil force. Nonparticipants who remained in town fled to cellars (if they had them) or barricaded themselves behind bolted doors while the city boiled.[7]

As bad as this situation became while the evening wore on, when darkness fell things grew ever more ominous. Evacuating Confederate commanders left a skeleton force behind in Richmond to execute final orders before abandoning the city to the rapidly advancing Union army. Their orders: torch the warehouses containing the Confederate capital's wealth of cotton, food supplies, and tobacco stores, and torch the munitions depots containing tons of gunpowder, artillery shells, and ordnance.[8]

In hindsight these orders smack of reckless disregard for the well-being of the people of Richmond. Historians have studied the circumstances around them, and to this day debate lingers about precisely who gave the orders and why, given that Lee was already on the path to surrender and the president of the Confederacy was in flight for his very life. Nevertheless, the orders were given and obediently carried out. The warehouses and mills at Shockoe were fired first. Tobacco, cotton, and tons of milled flour exploded into an inferno. No one warned the residents of Richmond what was happening.

During the war years Richmond's citizens suffered under crushing scarcity. By 1864, even once-wealthy families were threadbare and on the verge of starvation. According to Virginius Dabney, during the war, unwilling to give up their prewar diversions, high-ranking families hosted "Starvation Balls," where no refreshments were served, no meals were offered, and no fine attire was required. In this way loyal Confederates kept up morale and maintained their sense of humor. When the best families in town had no coffee, no meat, and nothing more in their cupboards than wormy peas, no one believed there was much left in the warehouses to destroy. The residents of Richmond were horrified by what they saw when the storehouses were opened and set to the torch.[9]

"The most revolting revelation," wrote LaSalle Pickett, "was the amount of provisions, shoes and clothing which had been accumulated by the speculators who hovered like vultures over the scene of death and desolation. Taking advantage of their possession of money and lack of both patriotism and humanity, they had, by an early corner in the market and by successful blockade running, bought up all the available supplies with an eye to future gain, while our soldiers and women and children were absolutely in rags, barefoot and starving."[10]

The outraged mob turned on the city, beginning an hours-long free-for-all of indiscriminate looting. The only thing that kept the people of the city from wreaking even greater havoc was the bright glow of flames and roar of fire as a warm southern wind pushed the flames up Shockoe Hill and into the residential parts of the city.

Sometime during the early morning hours of Monday, April 3, someone fired the Confederate powder magazine. It went off like a bomb, rocking the whole of the city with the force of a magnificent earthquake. The explosion knocked down nearby buildings, shattering glass windows for a mile around. Bricks from the buildings' heavily reinforced walls rocketed through the sky like missiles, piercing roofs and walls, killing sleeping citizens in their beds. This explosion touched off more fires, and soon the whole of central Richmond rippled in flames. The home of William's boyhood friend Edgar Alonza Smith and his sister Florence sat adjacent to the powder magazine. When the explosion occurred, it leveled the house and everything in it. The Smith family was spared, but they were left homeless and financially ruined.[11]

The powder magazine explosions were heard thirty miles away. The fire was visible from the earthworks above Petersburg. But the drama wasn't over yet. Confederate admiral Raphael Semmes wrote, "The Tredegar Iron Works were on fire, and continual explosions of loaded shell stored there were taking place. . . . The population was in a great state of alarm."[12] On orders from the fleeing Confederate command, Admiral Semmes torched his fleet of iron-clad battle ships moored in the James to keep them from falling into Union hands.[13] In moments the warships' arsenals exploded with a ferocity that is scarcely imaginable. Windows were blown out for two miles in every direction, tombstones at Hollywood and Shockoe Cemeteries were overturned, and the doors of buildings all over Richmond were ripped from their frames.[14] Richmond, the gleaming gem of the Confederacy, the original City on a Hill, was rendered in a few short hours to an inferno.

William Ellis Jones watched his city burn. From where and with whom is anyone's guess. Of all the horrors and desperate situations William endured in his years as a soldier, his greatest horror would have been watching his beloved Richmond consume itself. In his mind he might have returned to that day in late May 1862 when he wrote that his regiment had been ordered "to join the army around Richmond and fight for the glorious old capital of the Commonwealth . . . for all places I would prefer fighting for, and on, it is around my native city." William watched as "the glorious old capital" was shattered—by order of the Confederate government—and then ruthlessly ransacked by its own people.

The Union cavalry crossed the James in the early hours, entering a still burning Richmond shortly after sunrise on Monday, April 3, 1865. Just a few blocks to the west, the last Confederate stragglers beat a hasty retreat out of town. By 7:15 a.m., the 4th Massachusetts Cavalry flag flew over the capitol building. Union general Godfrey Weitzel fired off a telegraph to General Ulysses S. Grant: "We took Richmond at 8:15 this morning. I captured many guns. The enemy left in great haste. The city is on fire in two places. Am making every effort to put it out. The people received us with enthusiastic expressions of joy."[15]

It is more likely that the white citizens of Richmond received the Union troops with a sense of trepidation and hope for relief rather than joy. Law and order was quickly restored while well-regulated Union soldiers organized bucket brigades and set up firebreaks to combat the flames. The wind shifted late in the morning as cloud cover set in. The fires were soon brought under control.[16]

More than twenty city blocks of Richmond were reduced to rubble. As many as a thousand buildings were destroyed, leaving their inmates without provision or shelter.[17] General Weitzel wrote, "The rebel capitol, fired by men placed in it to defend it, was saved from total destruction by soldiers of the United States, who had taken possession."[18] Within hours of entering Richmond, Union forces occupied every principal corner of the city.

Within days, word quickly spread through town that Confederate soldiers willing to resign their station and take the Oath of Allegiance to the Union would be pardoned and released to return home. If William responded to that call, he soon found himself at Libby Prison along with hundreds of other Confederate soldiers, awaiting his turn. Once administered and recorded, he would have been free to resume his prewar life.[19]

No longer a soldier, no longer employed by the Post Quartermaster's Office of the fallen Confederate government, William would have tramped through the rubble of his burned-out town toward the place that had once been his home away from home: William H. Clemmitt's printing concern. Once there he would have found nothing but scorched hanging walls and piles of cinder.[20] The iron printing presses where he plied his trade before the war were slumped into slag by the intense heat of the inferno. The building that once housed them was nothing more than a blackened shell.

It is impossible for most of us who have never been through a war to conceive what this thing wrought on the inhabitants of Richmond. Outsiders who visited the city in the days and weeks following the evacuation fire and surrender were shaken and humbled by what they saw. To those who were born and reared in Richmond—people like Robert Brock, Edgar Smith, William Clemmitt, and William Ellis Jones—the impact was stunning, catastrophic, and deeply traumatizing. The wartime blockades starved them and deprived them. Living inside the walls of a fortified city isolated them. Living in the midst of a war zone terrified them. But watching the city consume itself overnight almost broke them.

The only thing that saved Richmond and its people from crumbling was the imposition of a functioning government and civil society brought into the city with the Union army on the morning of April 3, 1865. The Union army brought food and organized a system of distribution. It provided tents to shelter the homeless and doctors for the sick and wounded and organized brigades of men to clear the rubble. It returned law and order to Richmond's unruly streets and neighborhoods. In time the Union repaired the bridges, docks, canals, and railroads, allowing Richmond to rejoin the community of the world beyond its breastworks and trenches. The army offered protection to any business owner, professional, tradesman, workingman, laborer, civil servant, or citizen—whether black or white—who was willing and able to step up and begin the process of cleaning up the mess and restarting the city's operations.

Among the first businesses to reopen in postwar Richmond were the newspapers. The ever-present, incredibly efficient *Richmond Whig* never missed a beat, publishing an elaborate account of the evacuation fire on April 4, 1865.[21] Following the newspapers, those few businesses spared the devastation of the evacuation fire opened their doors and began trading.

Shortly after law and order was restored to Richmond after Robert E. Lee surrendered his arms at Appomattox, capital flowed in from the North with a stern eye toward the obvious necessity of rebuilding the wrecked city. Easy loans were made to men with little more than their good name backing the notes.[22] Among the takers for such peculiar generosity were Richmond printers William H. Clemmitt and George A. Gary, former competitors who combined forces, mortgaging their still-standing homes to finance the retooling of a small printing operation, becoming the first printing and publishing company in Richmond to start up after the fall of the city.[23] The first employee William Clemmitt rehired was his old apprentice and prewar journeyman printer, William Ellis Jones.

The period following the end of the war was not as kind to William's cousin William B. Jones. While Abraham Lincoln and his successor, Andrew Johnson, offered pardons to the overwhelming number of former rebels, William B. Jones found himself (along with just three hundred or so of Virginia's wealthiest residents) excluded from that pardon due to the fact that he was a man in possession of a great fortune and therefore must have come into it through slavery, through support of the rebellious Confederate government, or both.

The lack of pardon made it impossible for William B. Jones to conduct business. It put all his property at risk of confiscation and made him a subject of deep suspicion to the Union occupiers who controlled Richmond. In August 1865, William B. Jones wrote a letter to President Andrew Johnson, requesting a full pardon, claiming he went to work as a contractor for the "so called Confederate States" only to "keep out of the late so-called Confederate States army."[24]

Given the reports of William B. Jones's wealth after the conclusion of the war, we must consider what it might have been prior to the war's end. A crushing blow was delivered to his personal fortune on the afternoon before the evacuation fire, when Richmond's town fathers decided to destroy all the liquor in town in order to prevent a drunken ravaging of their city. As it turned out, a great quantity of the alcohol destroyed that day belonged to William B. Jones. He spent several years in court trying to recover his losses from the city.[25] By 1871, forty-three-year-old William B. Jones was dead, having failed to see a single penny from the city of Richmond in compensation for his losses.[26]

Some Richmonders blamed the destruction of the evacuation fire on "speculators" who hoarded provisions—especially the vast stockpiles of alcohol—in the city's warehouses during the war.[27] The fact that William Ellis Jones's father and cousin William B. Jones were guilty on both counts (speculation in general, with alcohol in particular) must have been deeply humiliating for him.

It can be assumed William judged his cousin harshly, evidenced by the fact that he neglected to communicate to his children or grandchildren that cousin William B. Jones ever existed. The man was eliminated from the Jones family history as it was handed down to succeeding generations. The erasing of William B. Jones was clearly an intentional act of forgetting.

As previously noted, William Ellis Jones said and wrote very little about his own father, simply recalling him to his children and grandchildren as a stern, conservative man of the Old World who disapproved of his son's "sensitive nature"[28] and of the company William kept. William did not tell his children that his father was a prominent secessionist in Richmond or a relation and partner to an infamous blockade-runner and wartime speculator who contributed to the riots and evacuation fire that destroyed Richmond on April 2 and 3, 1865. Perhaps William hoped that as memories faded, so would the reputation that members of his immediate family had earned during the war years.

Postwar

The Civil War and its aftermath changed everything in Richmond, from the landscape of the city to the composition of its population. William and his fellow veterans returned to their civilian lives humbled to the extreme and unsure of what would become of their lives under Federal occupation.[29] No one would have called them a "rollicking, fun-loving crowd" in the summer of 1865. They were wizened beyond their years, shell-shocked, and exhausted from conflict. Some were deeply embittered, but all of them were profoundly aware of the narrowness of their escape.

For some former soldiers like John C. Goolsby and the bugler Billy Burgess, the best option for moving forward meant escaping the devastation of their homeland and heading north, where there were still opportunities, even for ex-Confederates.[30] For William and the majority of the men with whom he served, starting over meant rebuilding their lives, their prewar professions, and their prewar relationships from the ground up, brick by brick, friend by friend.

In 1866, as soon as Gary & Clemmitt, Printers opened for business, William reported to the rebuilt printing shop, put on his compositor's smock, and sat down at his board. Among the first lines of type he set were these neatly, even beautifully arranged words:

WHAT IS OUR TRUE POLICY?
It is Herein Considered.[31]

As it appears in the finished book-length work, the title is set in a vertically elongated font, which was contemporary in its day. The page is airy in its composition, a style William would more fully develop in the coming years, rendering most of his books as readily identifiable as a signature. If William read the manuscript before he sat down at the composing table—which he almost certainly did—he read a remarkable treatise written by Nathaniel Tyler, then publisher of the *Richmond Enquirer*.

What Is Our True Policy? proffered a solution to begin to heal the wounds of institutionalized slavery and cure the injustice of two hundred years of inequity. By the standards of the twenty-first century, the treatise is far from perfect in all it assumes and offers, yet it is an amazing thing to read considering it was conceived and published in 1865–66, while Richmond was still a ruined city under Federal occupation. This book, despite its flaws, is a high-minded and progressive piece of social, economic, and moral accounting. It offers healing and opportunity. It offers repentance, reconciliation, and, more significantly, financial, social, and civil *reparations* in the form of real property—not to the Union but to the newly freed slaves of the former Confederate states.

It is heartening to consider this was likely the first substantial project William read, set, proofed, and then printed upon his return to work after the bloody and bitter Civil War. On first consideration it seems incongruous that a man like Nathaniel Tyler—longtime editor of one of Richmond's more conservative newspapers (the *Enquirer* was termed the "Democratic Bible" by Dabney in his 1976 biography of Richmond) and a Confederate veteran (he served as lieutenant colonel in the 20th Regiment, Virginia Infantry) whose newspaper was forced to operate under the rigid scrutiny of Federal occupiers—could conceive of a progressive work of reconciliation such as *What Is Our True Policy?*

In the first months after the war ended, many white Southerners feared a reign of terror and retribution at the hands of their "Yankee occupiers." As Reconstruction took shape, they discovered an altogether different circumstance. War veteran and Richmond resident Edward Pollard, whom Peter Carmichael describes as "a fiery pro-Confederate writer of [Jubal] Early's ilk," noted in *Lippincott's Magazine* in 1870, "Reconstruction has been a miracle of generosity." For men like Nathaniel Tyler, William Clemmitt, and William Ellis Jones, the truth of Reconstruction is that it offered Richmond an opportunity to realize the prewar dream of progressivism and prosperity that had been stifled by the plantation elite and backward-looking traditionalists. While many in white Richmond privately bristled under the authority of occupation, the progressives within that society saw their situation as an opportunity to accomplish two things. The first was to rid the state of Federal troops and return Virginia to home rule. The second was to set in motion economic reforms and infrastructure improvements that would vault Virginia into the modern, industrialized era.[32] Progressives like Nathaniel Tyler understood the best way to accomplish these tasks was to accept their defeat, embrace the New South as envisioned by their occupiers, and cooperatively transition to free labor.

Tyler's *What Is Our True Policy?* was a work of shrewd strategy designed to demonstrate to Federal occupying forces in his city, as well as to their commanders in Washington, DC, that Virginians were capable of accepting the new order and were—even at this early date—contemplating creative ways to make the new order work for all Virginia's citizens, white and black.

In *The Last Generation*, Peter Carmichael addresses the question of how these defeated veterans of a failed rebellion so completely accepted the death of their dream of an independent Southern nation while embracing their conquerors' vision of a New South. His answer is, "This group of veterans largely reconstructed their lives without having to reconstruct their intellectual worlds. A generational critique of antebellum Virginia society, which included a call for sweeping economic reforms and new development, provided the framework for their New South vision. The industrial might of Northern armies did not awaken the last generation to a vision of economic innovation and development; they had advocated such a course before Fort Sumter. . . . Reconstruction provided a second chance to reform Virginia character and instill the state with a spirit of innovation and prosperity."[33] This approach, taken up by many of William's generation, worked well. Virginia was re-admitted to the Union and returned to home rule in 1869, long before most other states in the former Confederacy.

In the decade following the publication of *What Is Our True Policy?*, public proclamations of reconciliation and reunionism continued to build, reaching a critical apex in 1877 when veterans from both sides of the Civil War gathered on the battlefield at Gettysburg. The event marked a thoroughly well-documented moment in history when ex-Confederates took to the podium and proclaimed the justness of the Confederate cause and the nobility of its soldiers—*and were permitted to do so by their Northern peers without quarrel.* Rather, Union veterans applauded the bravery of their former foes, romanticizing and sanitizing the nature of their motivations.[34]

This public vindication generally highlights the period in American history when the roots of the Lost Cause first found fertile soil, when those who had lived in the antebellum South and those who never experienced it began to aggressively reinvent history, creating a sentimental, romanticized fiction of a Southern way of life that had never really existed.[35] Following the war and the end of Virginia's brief Reconstruction period, William Ellis Jones played an important role in the collection, creation, and dissemination of much of this Lost Cause ideology.

* * *

After the war, William stuck close to the lifelong friends with whom he once scoured the streams and gullies of Shockoe Valley, looking for relics in the mud.

Ned Valentine returned to Richmond after studying and traveling abroad for the duration of the war. The city he found must have produced a bracing, heartbreaking spectacle when considered against his recollections of his boyhood home. Ned was a gifted artist who was offered opportunities to go to New York or return to Europe, where he might have earned fame and fortune. Instead he remained in Richmond, practicing his art among a generally uncultivated society. He spent his life memorializing in stone, bronze, and clay the heroes of the Lost Cause.[36] Today his small sculpture studio is a popular tourist attraction, attached to the museum his brother, Mann S. Valentine Jr., built and later bequeathed to the city of Richmond.

Edgar Alonza Smith survived the war, although his family's home and fortune were ruined, never to be recovered. After the war, Edgar became a waterworks engineer who traveled between Richmond and the Peninsula on a variety of projects for the state of Virginia.[37] In 1865, William Ellis Jones and Edgar's sister Florence were married. Tragically, Florence died a year later. She was just twenty years old. Despite his loss, William continued close relations with the Smith family. In 1874, eight years after the death of his first love, he married Florence's younger sister, Ella Cordelia, who was only thirteen years old when the Civil War ended. The couple named their first child after William's first wife and Ella's older sister. Florence Ellis Jones (a boy) was born in 1875.

William bought out his business partner, William H. Clemmitt, in 1878,[38] becoming the sole proprietor of William Ellis Jones, Steam Book and Job Printer. By then, he was blessed with a growing family, and his firm was the preferred publishing company for the *Southern Historical Society Papers*, the Virginia Historical Society, the Robert E. Lee Camp #1 (precursor to the Sons of Confederate Veterans and the United Daughters of the Confederacy), and a host of other historical organizations, all focused upon preserving the personal stories and the official and unofficial histories of the Civil War, as recalled from the white Southerner's peculiar perspective.

As William matured and Richmond grew, his circle of friends expanded to include a group of newcomers, men who possessed a somewhat different point of view from many who were born and reared in the city. Among them was the Reverend Thomas Grayson Dashiell, a man recognized in his own generation as one of the great social reformers in Virginia. Dashiell worked tirelessly throughout his career to create economic and educational opportunities for former slaves and their children. He helped establish and fund numerous schools and higher education institutions for African Americans, using his position as a ranking officer in the Episcopal Diocese of Virginia to provide cover and leverage for his social justice work.[39] William Ellis Jones admired Dashiell so much that he named his second son after him. Thomas Grayson Jones was born August 14, 1877. The Reverend T. Grayson Dashiell baptized his namesake and served as his godfather.

Robert Alonzo Brock, one of William's dearest friends since childhood, dedicated himself entirely to his passion for history, collecting, and writing.[40] Brock served as secretary to the *Southern Historical Society Papers* and the Virginia Historical Society and edited countless independently authored manuscripts for publication. After 1880 the lion's share of Brock's work passed through William's presses. While Brock was a collector of manuscripts on a wide variety of topics, much of the work he chose to publish about the Civil War era was distinctly pro-Confederate in its sympathies. The *Southern Historical Society Papers* in particular, provide a uniquely subjective, highly romanticized view of the Confederate perspective of the Civil War experience. The series is generally regarded as among the earliest at establishing the mythology of the Lost Cause, reshaping the way Southerners born after the Civil War viewed their ancestors—not as defeated traitors who risked their lives to defend slavery, but instead as patriotic defenders of Southern honor, Christian gentility, and states' rights. Despite their overt bias, the *Southern Historical Society Papers* still serve as valuable source material for Civil War historians.

While most of William's projects were commercial—for manufacturing, transportation, agricultural interests, and government—his reputation was made by the vast amount of historical and specifically Civil War–related titles that issued from his presses. (See the list of publications published by William Ellis Jones, online at www.siupress.com/spiritsofbadmenlinks.) In general, William worked with local authors and editors he knew very well. Most of the historical work regarding the Civil War era he published was created by authors or assembled by editors with a distinct pro-Confederacy bias. After Reconstruction, a cottage industry of mythmaking around the Confederacy emerged, replacing the reality of mechanized brutality and industrial-scale warfare. William and his printing and publishing concern stood at the leading edge of that cottage industry. It was quite a departure from his first postwar project, *What Is Our True Policy?*

By 1880, with his printing and publishing business growing and with his household numbering six souls—his wife, Ella Cordelia Smith; eldest son, Florence Ellis Jones; second son, Thomas Grayson Jones (and another child on the way, Fairfax Courtney Jones, born 1881); sister-in-law Lemira Smith Gibbs and her husband, Dr. William H. Gibbs—the family and William's ever-expanding personal library had outgrown their Shockoe Hill home.

Ella and her sister Lemira, who was like a second mother to William's sons, convinced him it would be better to raise the boys in the country, far away from the rabble and dirt of town. William saw the sense in constructing a country house spacious enough to accommodate his impressive library as well as entertain his long list of friends and business associates. He commissioned the building of a rambling, old-style country house in the Dumbarton community of Henrico County, far north of the noise and pollution of Richmond.

The house, completed about 1882, was christened "Summerfield."[41] It sat on a substantial agricultural and woodland tract where William installed an extensive orchard and gardens, the latter of which became Ella and Lemira's pastime project. The most prominent feature of Summerfield was its library. This room occupied one full wing of the lower floor of the house, and it became William's private retreat. It served as sanctuary to his collection of more than three thousand volumes, each one of which, it is promised by his contemporaries, he read. He was not just a collector. According to one prominent Richmonder, "He was one of the best-informed Virginians of his generation."[42]

By 1888 William's life appeared the model of excellent reputation, high social standing, and business success. He was happily married with three thriving sons under his wing. He was a member of Richmond's branch of the Odd Fellows Society, the Knights Templar, the Freemasons' Metropolitan Lodge Number 11, the Pegram's Battalion Association; treasurer of his church's executive committee; and the president of Typothetea, the primary organization representing printers and publishers in Richmond.

His business flourished while his beloved city of Richmond emerged from the ruins. Modernized industry, expanded railroads, tobacco manufacturing, and new and expanded colleges transformed the city into a better incarnation of its former self, a teeming, productive capital with tremendous upside potential. The city even began to produce a generation of nationally acclaimed historians, artists, and authors.

But there were heartbreaking setbacks. In 1888, William's rambling house, Summerfield, built for his growing family and expansive library, burned to the ground. History has not recorded how this tragedy occurred, only that the house was a total loss and all but a few dozen volumes from the extensive library were destroyed. William never completely recovered from this loss. He reconstructed the house, an exact replica of the original, and began the daunting task of rebuilding his library. The original collection contained an unknown number of volumes his father brought from Wales. These books could not be replaced at any price. The loss was tragic and a significant financial blow.[43]

Nevertheless, William pressed on.

His three sons were reared in the old Virginia tradition. Unlike their father, they all benefited from excellent educations at Richmond's best private schools.[44] After spending a few terms at Virginia Polytechnic Institute, Florence Ellis Jones followed in his father's footsteps, becoming a partner in the publishing business while also serving as a writer and editor at the *Richmond Journal*. A talented fiction author, F. Ellis Jones (as he styled himself) also published short stories in *The Argosy*,[45] as well as other literary periodicals of the day.

In 1898 F. Ellis Jones married Addie Gray Bowles, the daughter of a prominent old Virginia family who, like the Smiths, saw their fortunes nearly devastated by the war's outcome. Addie Gray, who was likened to Ruth of the Old Testament by her mother-in-law, became the rock of the family as the nineteenth century passed into the tumult of the twentieth.

On August 7, 1899, William Ellis Jones, the fourth in the family line to be honored with that name, was born. Like his father, F. Ellis Jones, before him, early in life he was given all the benefits of an excellent education, the proud heritage of a family of accomplishment, status, and the loving embrace of many blood kin who doted upon him.[46]

On April 18, 1910, William Ellis Jones, the irreverent Civil War diarist who matured into one of Richmond's most respected citizens, died at his home at Summerfield; he was seventy-one years old. He was buried at Shockoe Cemetery in the John Walton Smith family plot (his wife's family), not far from where his father's questionable tombstone stands and where his mother, Margaret White Jones, was interred half a century earlier.

Along with a lengthy obituary appearing in the *Richmond Dispatch*, word of William's passing was published widely, with multiple announcements coming from a variety of sources, including the Virginia Historical Society;

F. Ellis Jones on behalf of William Ellis Jones, Steam Book and Job Press; the Robert E. Lee Camp #1; the Freemasons; St. Mark's Episcopal Church; and a prominent display advertisement placed by the Pegram Battalion Association requesting all members to attend the funeral "by order of W. Gordon McCabe, President of the Association."[47]

At the time of his death, William employed all three of his sons in his printing business. In addition to owning the printing company, William owned a spacious brownstone at 1006 West Avenue and the rebuilt country home, Summerfield, in the Henrico County community of Dumbarton. His library, diminished considerably by the fire at Summerfield in 1888, was restored over the twenty-two years between the fire and the time of William's passing. It numbered about 2,500 volumes at the time of his death. In his will, William gave explicit instructions that the library was to pass intact to his eldest son, F. Ellis Jones, and then to his grandson.[48]

During the summer of 1935, William Ellis Jones (the grandson of the Civil War diarist) began to collect and record his family's history. He penned the following recollection of his grandfather:

> Of all the individuals named . . . my grandfather leaves the most vivid impression on my mind. The earliest memory of my childhood is of him. It is purely a picture-memory, as are most recollections of babyhood, and there are no events leading up to it, or sequel. He is seated by the library fireplace with a leather-bound book open on his knees and he is smiling at me. I must have been playing on the floor. His expression is as clear to me today as though it happened yesterday, and I still feel the security that his smile gave to a very small boy.
>
> At the time he was a man well on in his years, and his serene and manly character had traced itself plainly on his face. As a child at "Summerfield" I looked upon him as the all-powerful governor of the universe. I was raised in a religious household and was taught about God; but until I was seven I considered the importance of God greatly exaggerated. It seemed to me that my grandfather ran the world and did a very competent job of it. And today, after the passing of forty years, I still think he was the greatest man I ever saw.

Whether or not William Ellis Jones was "the greatest man" his grandson ever saw, it must be stated that like most other white Southern males of his generation, he fought for the Confederacy because he believed in the righteousness of slavery and the justice of white male supremacy. After the war, he dedicated a large portion of his professional career to the dissemination of Lost Cause mythology. He was a lifelong, ardent supporter of the Democratic Party when that equated to a return to white supremacy, disenfranchisement of blacks, segregation, and wholesale racial injustice.

On May 29, 1890—twenty years after the last Federal troops left Virginia, returning it to home rule—more than one hundred thousand Southerners (many of them veterans of the failed rebellion) gathered in Richmond for the dedication of the monument to Robert E. Lee. Archer Anderson, son of Joseph R. Anderson of Tredegar Iron Works, the largest supplier of iron, steel, and arms to the Confederacy, took to the stage to deliver the dedication address.

Anderson spoke to the crowd for more than two hours. He opened his remarks with the following observation about the day and the circumstances that brought them all together.

At the end of the first quarter of a century after the close of a stupendous civil war, in which more than a million men struggled for the mastery during four years of fierce and bloody conflict, we should see the Southern States in complete possession of their local self-government, the Federal Constitution unchanged save as respects the great issues submitted to the arbitrament of war, and the defeated party—whilst in full patriotic sympathy with all the present grandeur and imperial promise of a reunited country—still not held to renounce any glorious memory, but free to heap honors upon their trusted leaders, living or dead—all this reveals a character in which the American people may well be content to be handed down to history.[49]

What Anderson stated, and what everyone in attendance that day understood, is that while the Confederacy was defeated in 1865, every principle for which it stood had endured and would persist.

William Ellis Jones stood among his fellow veterans with the Pegram Battalion Association while Anderson delivered his oratory. Anderson's speech was popular, and there was a large demand for its publication. The original issue of Archer Anderson's *Robert Edward Lee. An Address Delivered at the Dedication of the Monument to General Robert Edward Lee at Richmond, Virginia, May 29, 1890*, bears the following imprint on its title page: "Richmond: Wm. Ellis Jones, Printer. 1890."

For Southern whites, the creation of the Robert E. Lee monument and its grand presentation to the city of Richmond was the final element required to permanently enshrine the myths of the Lost Cause for all time. This event demonstrated to the entire nation that while the Confederacy was no more, the Confederates themselves were very much in power and intended to remain so.

As his diary demonstrates, William Ellis Jones was a thoughtful, intelligent man who was unrestrained in pointing out the moral failings of others. Whether he acknowledged failings in himself is difficult to say. What can be stated with certainty is that William had ample opportunity to publish his own story. Instead, he chose to keep silent about his wartime experience, and he chose to keep to himself his opinions on the reshaping of history to fit a romanticized narrative that transformed defenders of slavery and white supremacy into noble sons of liberty.

Perhaps he understood that a critical reading of his wartime journal, when juxtaposed against the actions of the latter half of his life, would reveal facts challenging to the fictional narrative he helped cultivate. Because he saved the diary and passed it down to his grandson, it is possible to believe he would not entirely disapprove of the careful study that has gone into understanding his life and motivations. He might even be gratified by the attention. Whether William would appreciate that the myths of the Lost Cause are finally unraveling under the spotlight of solid scholarship or that the monuments to the leaders of that flawed society are finally coming down or being reinterpreted in their proper context is less certain.

Whatever William's opinions of this project might have been, in terms of scholarship and comprehensiveness, I hope I have done justice to his life and words.

Over the course of this journey, I have come to understand William realistically. He and his contemporaries took up a bad cause, savagely fought for it while sacrificing hundreds of thousands of lives and unaccountable treasure, and in so doing nearly broke the Union in two. Unwilling to swallow the bitter pill of defeat and unable to admit their cause was horribly wrong, they spent the rest of their lives reframing the nature of their rebellion, embracing the pejorative term "rebel" while conflating its meaning with honor and manliness. He and his contemporaries hoped succeeding generations would accept without question and even celebrate their reimagined prewar society, the war itself, and the carefully cultivated image of the honor-bound, noble Confederates who brought it on.

He is, in his own words, "the spirit of bad men made perfect." That perfection, however, is a fiction. Getting to truth is a more complicated process than creating fiction, yet its results are far more instructive. To not repeat the mistakes of history, we must first know what they are and acknowledge the true cost of them. That accounting is something William never attempted, leaving the job for his children and grandchildren. Perhaps it was just too much to take on following the war, after losing so many friends and family members, after the devastation of the evacuation fire, after rebuilding everything from the ground up. Perhaps he and his generation needed to retreat into the comfort of a fictionalized past.

Throughout the war, William Ellis Jones faced incredible challenges and threats to his very survival. Despite it all, he persevered. His legacy is the diary he left to our consideration. His words, his accomplishments, and the facts of his life will survive long after the fiction he helped create and proliferate has faded from memory.

Appendix

Additional Online Appendixes

Notes

Bibliography

Index

Appendix

One June 21, 1864, shortly after the conclusion of the Battle of Spotsylvania Court House, a letter appeared in the *Richmond Whig*, purporting to be from a member of William Pegram's artillery battalion.[1] It is worth noting that by this late date in the conflict, editorials appearing in the *Whig* had become vehemently critical of the Jefferson Davis administration. This newspaper served as a common outlet for the expression of opposition views on the conduct of the rebellion.

While it is impossible to prove the letter was penned by William Ellis Jones as he recuperated in Richmond following the Battle of Spotsylvania Court House, there is good circumstantial evidence supporting the case. Following the letter, which has been reproduced below in its entirety (except where noted *illegible* due to the condition of the scan available), I provide a detailed justification for my conclusion that Jones is the author.

Pegram's Battalion

Turkey Hill, July 11, 1863[2]
[Correspondence of the *Whig*]

It has been decreed that those who are emulous of the praises of their country in this strife shall be the heralds of their own deeds. From this edict, there shall be no appeal. The bed of Procrustes is the common couch for all; those weary in the conflict must here recline, or else depart unknown and unrefreshed. Therefore, whilst the journals of the day are the especial record of the deeds of the day, it is not only the privilege but the duty of all to vindicate their title to an honorable mention. Nor is it from this reflection alone that I am impailed[3] to solicit a notice of the part borne by Pegram's Battalion in this war; but I am urged by the consideration that, heretofore, nothing whatever has been published in this connection of a general comprehensive character. The very few communications to the press have been made by members of companies with relation to the services

183

of their respective companies, and have been of a merely local and transient nature. It is my intention to speak of our career as a battalion.

—It is most that the people of Richmond be jealous of the reputation of this command. In a peculiar manner she is our foster-mother. Three of our companies are hers. Under the shadow of her temple were they consecrated to her service, and along the walks of their childhood, and against the portals of their homes went they forth to the long struggle. Another company is from Fredericksburg, who watches just without her walls. The remaining company is from South Carolina.

One word further as to our particular organization. The Purcell Battery was formerly commanded by Capt. R. L. Walker, now commanding the artillery of the Third Corps. After his first promotion it was under the command of Wm. J. Pegram, now the commanding officer of the battalion. Subsequently it was under the commanded by Capt. Joseph McGraw, who, as Major of our battalion, lost his arm at Spotsylvania Court House. At the same place, its Captain, Geo. M. Casey, was dangerously wounded. Lieut. Charles. E. Crow, who succeeded Capt. Casey in command, was also wounded, and Lieut. Thos. R. Wersham, temporarily assigned the command from the Letcher Artillery, was very severely wounded by the fracture of the lower bone of his left jaw.

The Letcher Artillery, Capt. Thos. A. Brander, was formerly under the command of Capt. Greenlee Davidson, of Lexington, Va., who fell at the battle of Chancellorsville. It would occupy too much space and weary your readers, to dwell upon the action of our companies in detail. It will suffice to speak briefly of the general action of our whole command, in which with general rivar each company has steadily held its own. The Crenshaw Battery, for a long time under the command of Capt. —— Crenshaw was subsequently commanded by Capt. James Ellett, who fell at Fredericksburg. It is now commanded by his brother, Capt. Thos. Ellett.

The Fredericksburg Artillery was formerly commanded by that gallant and efficient officer, Capt. C. M. Braxton, who is now commanding a battalion of artillery in Ewell's Corps. It has been for a long time under the command of Capt. Edward A. Marye.

The Pe(*e*)dee Artillery was formerly commanded by Capt. McIntosh, who now commands a battalion in the corps, and was first promoted after the battle of Fredericksburg, at the same time with Pegram and Braxton. After the promotion of Capt. McIntosh, the command devolved upon Capt. Braxton, of S.C.

I will not mention name by name the battles of this army. Col. Pegram's Battalion has never (*missed one*).[4] Not for one moment has been accorded to us the respite which is the need for good service. We have never been in reserve. Though we have five battalions in our Corps and but three divisions, the day of our relief has not yet come. Whether this were the virtue of our Colonel or of our General, whether it were the predominance of enthusiasm over reflection in our officers, or whether it were the will of the gods, may be speculative. That we have known neither respite or repose can be attested by these (*illegible*) (*illegible*) the crows; the vales, from Malvern Hill to Gettysburg and (*illegible*) made yet sadder than Wilderness; (*illegible*) loneliness. We fought with Jackson in the (*illegible*) campaign from Mechanicsville to Shepherdstown; again we were with him at Fredericksburg, and when the spring was (*illegible*) again we went with him through Chancellorsville, and to Gettysburg. Did I say "on to Gettysburg?"—I had forgotten. That chieftain had again (*illegible*) march so rapidly that whilst hurried on with thoughts of Jackson, I had ever (*illegible*) (*illegible*) (*illegible*); for he never rested. No! Not (*illegible*) (*illegible*)

> *Fought his fight,*
> *Fulfilled his labor,*
> *Stilled his manly breast.*[5]

Then having done enough for glory and for time, he shook off the dust of battle and the long, long marches, and, crossing over the river, he rested under the shade of the trees.

After the battle of Gettysburg the army was generally undisturbed until this Spring. Our Battalion was among the first to go forward at The Wilderness; and through all the tedious and unceasing fighting was engaged throwing up works; we have been toiling and are toiling still.

I have spoken too hurriedly in this desultory sketch. I could wish that I had been more concerned, and that I could have narrated faithfully how our men have striven and how they have suffered; how *undis———gly* they have gone to the conflict, and how ungrudgingly they have borne the sacrifices and disciplines of a strange and severe life; and how they have borne this for years. The reward resulting from this flows from a source I would not profane. The private has not the accessories of name and place and notice but he has that prouder prerogative of doing all and daring all for the consciousness of rectitude and duty. 'Tis here he is unknown by the many; but he strives on for the love and homage of the few; and whilst now his reward is not so manifest, the end is not yet; and there remaineth, for him the same pride and the same triumph in the disenthraiment[6] of our land and the vindication of our cause.

M. S.

[The above letter has been on file for several days.]

While many eminently qualified historians may take issue with my claim that William Ellis Jones penned this letter, I will welcome their arguments and will hear them with an open mind. If it ever becomes possible to either prove or disprove the point, I promise to hear all the evidence and accept the conclusions of those with more expertise in the matter than I will ever be able to claim. That said, I have my reasons for boldly claiming William Ellis Jones was the author.

While the letter in question is far more composed and formal than what appears in William's Civil War journal, this is to be expected. The journal is a private document, while the letter appearing in the *Richmond Whig* was presented to the public, necessitating a more expository approach to both the prose style and the letter's purpose. Despite these differences, there are several notable similarities in style and content lending credence to my claim.

The most obvious commonality that struck me when I first read the letter was the phrase "The bed of Procrustes is the common couch for all; those weary in the conflict must here recline, or else depart unknown and unrefreshed." Throughout his journal, William frequently punctuates his prose with references to Greek and Roman deities and myths. Like many educated men of his era, he was well versed in classic literature and mythology. Most educated men of the era managed to restrain themselves (at least when writing for the general public) from drawing upon truly arcane references that would have escaped the common reader. William, as several of the entries in his diary reveal, appears somewhat self-conscious in his use of these allusions. While it is true he was well educated, his education was an informal one given at home through books, begun and concluded at his father's knee. Instead of going on to pursue a more formal education at university like many of his close friends and his battalion commanders, William became a printer's apprentice and then pursued a trade rather than a profession.

With the preamble, the author is aiming his editorial at an audience a notch or two above the common reader. He is trying *very hard* to inform this audience that he should be taken seriously (because, as it becomes clear in later paragraphs, he feels he and his fellow soldiers have not been shown the respect they deserve). This is a trait persistent throughout William's journal—the idea that he is superior to his superiors and yet is not given the credit due him. The reference to "The bed of Procrustes" reveals an author who wants everyone to believe he is well educated and therefore deserves to be heard and respected.

The author states, "Under the shadow of her temple were they consecrated to her service, and along the walks of their childhood, and against the portals of their homes went they forth to the long struggle." It has already been established that most of the men of Crenshaw's Battery were Richmond natives who worked in the printing trades and as clerks in Shockoe businesses. William, since his early adolescence, worked on "printers' row" in Richmond "under the shadow of her temple" (the capitol building), and its cobbled streets were the very familiar "walks of their [his] childhood."

Concerning the vocabulary used in the letter, there is a similar desire on the author's part to demonstrate a command of uncommon Latin terms as well as arcane or secondary definitions of common words. For example:

- He uses the term "rivar" when "reach" would be understood by more of his readers.
- He uses the term "disentrainment" when simple "withdrawal" or "removal" would do nicely.
- The selection of the word "jealous" in the line "It is most that the people of Richmond be jealous of the reputation of this command" carries an implied definition of "suspicious" or "watchful."

This sentence has one meaning in contemporary parlance ("covetous") and an altogether darker implication when "suspicious" is exchanged for "jealous."

- Similarly, the use of the term "impalement" in the context of "requirement" or "obligated" is a stretch. The author is trying to demonstrate his scholarship. At best, he is demonstrating he is a young man with a great many books in his head and a great deal to say but hasn't yet learned that sometimes it is better to say less.
- The signature "M. S." is a common Latin abbreviation for *manuscriptum*, literally translating "manuscript" or "written by hand." "M.S." was a copy notation common to those in the nineteenth-century printing trades as an indication of a document ready for publication. It is worth noting that an examination of the entire roster for Pegram's Battalion revealed only one individual with the initials "M. S.": Malcolm Seaton, a moulder by trade, recorded as absent from the battalion in September and October 1863 and absent again from May 1864 through February 1865. It is unlikely that Mr. Seaton was the author. The best conclusion was that the initials were offered as a pseudonym.

In the closing paragraph of the letter, the author states, "The private has not the accessories of name and place and notice." He singles out "the private," the rank at which William remained from the beginning of his service to the bitter end. While there is nothing particular about his statement, its presence given the context further backs up the supposition that the author of this letter is particularly sensitive to his inferior status. He does not have a well-known name (especially if he is a "Jones") to distinguish him. He does not have an ancestral home that he can point to as proof of his claim to certain rights (an especially painful point for the children of recent immigrants, who were often treated as aliens themselves). And he does not have "notice," that is, any particular profession or expertise that distinguishes him to those whose attention he aspires. This statement defines William and the tenor of his journal. He constantly sought recognition and was never happier than when he received it from those of status. When he did not receive what he felt was his due, he often became bitter and critical, resorting to the language of sarcasm and personal attack.

True to form, we see this author make the following statement regarding the motivations of his battalion's officer corps: "Whether this were the virtue of our Colonel or of our General, whether it were the predominance of enthusiasm over reflection in our officers, or whether it were the will of the gods, may be speculative." He uses the word "virtue" sarcastically, implying a blinding "righteousness" (an alternative definition of "virtue") that speaks directly and critically to battalion commander William R. J. Pegram.

Pegram, a fiercely religious man, believed that God and the Confederacy were one and that everything that happened on the battlefield was God's will.[7] Therefore Pegram, according to the criticism implied here, saw no conflict whatsoever with sending his men into an outnumbered, outgunned assault on the enemy or marching them until they were exhausted and half-starved. God, according to Pegram's belief system, would protect and provide. It is clear that the author of this letter had a slightly different opinion. (Pegram, who had a habit of riding to the very front in the thick of incoming enemy fire, was eventually killed as a result of his belief that God would somehow protect him from his own reckless decisions.)

The author accuses the battery's various officers of "predominance of enthusiasm over reflection" regarding their decision-making processes. The implication is that they are either stupid or vainglorious but certainly not reflective, as intelligent and careful leaders of men ought to be. This is brutal criticism and not a popular position to proffer when Richmond's citizens were clamoring to find heroes, maintain faith, and believe that the Confederate cause was in good hands.

In his diary, William Ellis Jones takes similar swipes at the officers in his battalion. He reserves a very special, vigorous disdain for his battery commander, William Graves Crenshaw. It is telling that the author of this letter to the *Whig* carefully identifies the full names, ranks, and exploits of all the officers in the battalion except for Crenshaw. I interpret this purposeful omission of Crenshaw's first and middle name, as well as the omission of any comment about him or his service, as evidence that this letter's author found the name of this person so distasteful that he could not even bring himself to speak (or in this case, write) his name in full. In this, as William Ellis Jones demonstrated numerous times in his Civil War diary, he is of exactly the same opinion as the letter's author.

Beyond all this, there are still a few more shreds of evidence pointing toward William Ellis Jones as the author of the letter.

First, when I examined the whole letter in detail and considered how much (or how little) its creator wrote about a specific battery and about geographic places in general, I am left with the positive opinion that the author was certainly a member of one of the Richmond batteries (Purcell, Letcher, or Crenshaw). He expounds on the city of Richmond and admonishes its citizens to care about the welfare of its soldiers because, after all, Richmond is their "foster-mother." He says very little about Fredericksburg, home of the Fredericksburg artillery, except that it has been shelled to rubble. He says almost nothing at all about South Carolina, home of the Pee Dee Artillery.

The next item that struck me as bearing similarity to William's previous style is the bit of flowery prose employed to describe Stonewall Jackson and his death. William Ellis Jones had an opportunity to get a close look at Jackson, which he noted in his diary. While Jackson is not the only officer to receive a kind word in William's Civil War journal, he is the only officer to receive so many kind words, so consistently throughout. William's opinion of Jackson never wavered, unlike his opinions of other commanders he describes. The author of this letter, while lambasting the leadership of Pegram's Battalion, is making it clear to his readership that he still has his Confederate heroes, even if they are dead.

Not only does he have heroes, but he is moved, as was William on numerous occasions, to call upon a snippet of poetry to describe his ardor for General Jackson and his sacrifice. William Ellis Jones was no stranger to employing a bit of poetry or even a popular song here and there in order to emphasize his depth of feeling for a subject. The choice of John Reuben Thompson, a Richmond native and then editor of the *Southern Literary Messenger*, is a further demonstration by the author that he is not only well read but also loyal to local talent, arguably marking him as a Richmond resident. Further, there is some evidence that William Ellis Jones and the poem's author knew one another, as William was the first publisher to put John Reuben Thompson's work into print after the conclusion of the war (outside his early appearance in the *Southern Literary Messenger*). (See the list of materials published under the imprint of William Ellis Jones, available online at www.siupress.com /spiritsofbadmenlinks.)

In closing his letter, the author states, regarding the limited expectations of the rank private, "He has that prouder prerogative of doing all and daring all for the consciousness of rectitude and duty. 'Tis here he is unknown by the many; but he strives on for the love and homage of the few."

As we see in his journal, William Ellis Jones gave up trying to make sense of or to argue with the contradictions and inequities of life as a soldier. I propose he also gave up (generally speaking) on his belief in a Confederate victory or a return to the old feudal system. I proffer the idea that rather than leave the service and face dishonor, William chose to remain alongside his comrades—not because he was fighting for the Confederate cause but because he finally came to the wisdom that his comrades needed him as much as he needed them. This letter's author makes that point in the quote above. He states that he is not expecting the recognition of the "many" but only "strives on for the love . . . of the few."

By writing this letter, the author is certainly seeking recognition by the "many," while his heart is still quite attached to the "few," that is, his comrades still toiling in the battlefield, still very much in harm's way. The author notes his location as "Turkey Hill." This is now better known as the place where the Battle of Cold Harbor was fought. While William lay in Richmond recuperating from his wounds, his comrades in Crenshaw's Battery participated in this horrific battle that, though shorter, rivaled Spotsylvania for the brutality of the encounter and grotesqueness of the suffering of the participants.

The author of the letter to the *Richmond Whig*, whether it was William Ellis Jones or a similarly inclined spirit, had a great many well-justified reasons to call for an examination of the war effort and of the officers conducting it. From the rank soldier's perspective, there was very little noble or honorable about the way the Civil War was carried out or in the way hundreds of thousands of men were uselessly sacrificed. It was, as the author of the letter to the *Richmond Whig* would agree, a cruel, reckless, and tragic waste of potential and of resources that more reflective men might have found a better way to resolve, had they been less enthusiastic for glory or profit.

Additional Online Appendixes

1. William Ellis Jones, Steam Book and Job Press

This exclusive, online-only content provides a chronological listing of the surviving known books, periodicals, pamphlets, and other materials published under the various imprints associated with William Ellis Jones throughout his career, as well those published posthumously under his imprint, after his sons carried on the business. www.siupress.com/spiritsofbadmenlinks

2. The Next Generations

William Ellis Jones was a firsthand witness to the greatest conflagration in American history. He survived the conflict, married, started a family, operated a prosperous business, became a pillar of Richmond society, and reportedly assembled an impressive personal library that was the envy of his friends and acquaintances. After his death in 1910, William's library passed intact to his eldest son, Florence Ellis Jones. This chapter, which is available only online, traces the progress of William Ellis Jones's sons and their descendants, following the library down through the generations into the twenty-first century. www.siupress.com/spiritsofbadmenlinks

Notes

2. Stumbling in the Shadows of Giants

1. J. E. Jones, *Gwyddfa y Bardd*, xi–xx; I. Jones, *Printing and Printers in Wales and Monmouthshire*, 152–63.
2. Williams, *Wales through the Ages*, 16–23.
3. I. Jones, *Printing and Printers in Wales and Monmouthshire*, 152–63.
4. I. Jones, 152–63; J. E. Jones, *Gwyddfa y Bardd*, xi–xx; L. Lloyd, "Merioneth Family"; *Address to Electors Accusing William Buckeley Hughes of Bribery*; E. Lloyd, *Curate*.
5. W. E. Jones, family papers; U.S. Census, Henrico County, Virginia, Population Schedule, Richmond Ward 1, 160–61, Thomas Jones and Margaret Jones, William Ellis Jones and Mary Jones; digital image, Ancestry.com, http://ancestry.com (accessed December 2, 2015).
6. J. E. Jones, *Gwyddfa y Bardd*, xi–xx; W. E. Jones, family papers; I. Jones, *Printing and Printers in Wales*, 152–63.
7. J. E. Jones, *Gwyddfa y Bardd*, xi–xx.
8. I. Jones, *Printing and Printers in Wales*, 152–63; L. Lloyd, "Merioneth Family"; "North Wales Circuit–Beaumaris, July 23," *London Express*, July 26, 1817.
9. L. Lloyd, "Merioneth Family."
10. L. Lloyd, "Merioneth Family"; L. Jones, family papers.
11. L. Jones, family papers.
12. "Andrew J. Byrne," *Virginia State Journal*, January 10, 1871.
13. Ellyson, *Richmond Directory*, 158; "The Firm of Jones & Co.," *Richmond Daily Dispatch*, January 12, 1861; "Joles, Hams, Breasts and Shoulders," *Richmond Daily Dispatch*, February 13, 1861.

3. Before Dixie

1. W. E. Jones, family papers.
2. T. N. Jones, purchase contract between Bernhard and Sally Briel (seller) and Thomas Jones (buyer), April 28, 1840.
3. T. N. Jones, declaration of intent to become a United States citizen, June 1, 1840; T. N. Jones, citizenship naturalization papers, June 21, 1843. Both documents are in the possession of the author.
4. U.S. Bureau of the Census, "Population of the 100 Largest Urban Places."

5. Dabney, *Richmond*, 113.

6. Little, *Richmond*, 133.

7. Little, 133–34.

8. Kimball, *American City*, 31–33.

9. Dabney, *Richmond*, 61, 80.

10. Kimball, *American City*, 17–21.

11. Kimball, 86–88.

12. Kimball, 65.

13. Kimball, 23, 27–30, 43, 65–66, 117, 131–34, 164–66, 173–74, 248, 258.

14. Trammell, *Richmond Slave Trade*, 88.

15. Trammell, 86–88.

16. W. E. Jones, family papers.

17. Ellyson, *Richmond Directory*, 216.

18. W. E. Jones, family papers.

19. L. Tyler, *Encyclopedia of Virginia Biography*, 68–71.

20. Mordecai, *Virginia*, 25–31; L. Tyler, *Encyclopedia of Virginia Biography*, 68–71.

21. L. Tyler, 16–18.

22. L. Tyler, 3–4.

23. Thomas Ellis Jones (son of William Ellis Jones, great-grandson of William Ellis Jones the diarist) in discussion with the author prior to December 31, 1997.

24. Carmichael, *Last Generation*, 20.

25. Carmichael, 19–34.

26. Carmichael, 9.

27. Carmichael, 27.

28. Carmichael, 8–13.

29. Crofts, *Reluctant Confederates*, 66–89; Naragon, "Ballots, Bullets, and Blood," 154–64.

30. "Marine News," *Richmond Daily Dispatch*, August 14, 1855.

31. Kimball, *American City*, xxii.

32. Kimball, 100–109.

33. Dabney, *Richmond*, 148–61; Kimball, *American City*, 108–9.

34. Kimball, 175–82.

35. Goldfield, *Urban Growth*, 256–61; De Bow, "General Walker's Policy in Central America," 173–82.

36. "The Executive Committee of the Central Southern Rights Association of Virginia," *Richmond Daily Dispatch*, January 2, 1860.

37. Kimball, *American City*, 174–76; Dew, *Ironmaker to the Confederacy*, 23–28, 31, 129.

38. Goldfield, *Urban Growth*, 258–60; Kimball, *American City*, 100.

39. Kimball, 60, 86; Bowman, *At the Precipice*, 160–82.

40. Goldfield, *Urban Growth*, 194.
41. Scott, *History of Orange County*, 184–85.
42. Dabney, *Richmond*, 164.
43. Sanchez-Saavedra, "Beau Ideal of a Soldier," 1–3, 23–71, 133–72; Eicher and Eicher, *Civil War High Commands*, 210, 629.
44. "Local Matters—Underground Operations," *Richmond Daily Dispatch*, April 29, 1854; "Effect of the Underground Railroad," *Richmond Daily Dispatch*, April 1, 1854.
45. Johnson, *University Memorial*, 496–514.
46. Kambourian, "Slave Traders in Richmond"; Smathers, "Birth of the SBC Foreign Mission Board."
47. Tunnell, "Confederate Newspapers in Virginia during the Civil War."
48. "Personal," *New York Times*, August 18, 1860; Capehart, "Beginnings of American Journalism," 40.
49. Hadfield, "Reader Voices."
50. Fontaine, *My Life and My Lectures*, 18.

4. A True Virginian

1. Dabney, *Richmond*, 113. See the following from the *Richmond Daily Dispatch*: "To the Public," February 16, 1852; "The Fight of the Factions," February 20, 1852; "County Police," July 12, 1853; "Throwing Stones," May 21, 1855; "Throwing Stones," November 18, 1856; "The Fight of Stones," April 27, 1860.
2. "William H. Clemmitt, Oldest Active Printer," 714.
3. Dabney, *Richmond*, 129–31.
4. "William H. Clemmitt, Oldest Active Printer," 714.
5. W. E. Jones, family papers.
6. "New Hams," *Richmond Daily Dispatch*, November 10, 1857. These types of advertisements appeared weekly throughout the 1850s, ending during the first few months of the Civil War.
7. Thomas Ellis Jones in discussion with the author prior to December 31, 1997. Note that I recall specifics of the conversation having to deal with an arrowhead and stone collection assembled by William Ellis Jones and Ned Valentine, as my father made a specific point of noting that the Valentine Museum may never have come into being had it not been for the "Indian archaeology" practiced by the "boys of Richmond." My father, like his father before him (William Ellis Jones, grandson of the Civil War diarist), worked as a young man at the Valentine Museum and maintained social connections with a new generation of the Valentine family as late as the 1950s, a benefit he claimed was a result of the deep connection developed in boyhood between Ned Valentine and William Ellis Jones.

8. W. E. Jones, family papers.

9. Ellyson, *Richmond Directory*, 216. (Prior to 1856, advertisements placed by Thomas Norcliffe Jones listed "Thomas Jones" as the proprietor. After 1856 and until 1862, advertisements reflected the proprietors' name as "Thomas Jones & Co.")

10. Ellyson, 216.

11. I have scoured the prewar Richmond newspaper social and business sections and have been unable to locate even the scarcest mention of William B. Jones. Thomas Norcliffe Jones was mentioned occasionally, and William Ellis Jones and members of his family were (after the war) mentioned frequently. The only conclusion to be drawn is that for whatever reason, William B. Jones kept a low profile and did not put himself forward either to join any of the popular social or fraternal organizations or private clubs or to attend any of the public or social functions that should have warranted his participation. I was able to locate mentions of him in the "Marine News" sections, which covered businessmen and private citizens traveling by ship in and out of the ports of Norfolk and the Chesapeake region.

12. In the *Richmond Daily Dispatch*: "State Elections," May 18, 1860; "Political Notices," October 10, 1860; "Local Matters," October 11, 1860.

13. Carmichael, *Last Generation*, 41.

14. W. E. Jones, family papers; "Died. At the Residence of Her Husband," *Richmond Daily Dispatch,* June 2, 1859.

15. W. E. Jones, family papers. Eventually William Ellis Jones moved his membership to St. Mark's.

16. W. E. Jones, family papers.

17. "Died. At the Residence of Her Husband," *Richmond Daily Dispatch*, June 2, 1859.

18. "Genteel Household Furniture," *Richmond Daily Dispatch*, June 9, 1859.

19. "Died. In Halifax Nova Scotia," *Richmond Daily Dispatch*, October 13, 1864. The line in this announcement "leaving a wife and five children" leaves the date of marriage uncertain. Given the number of children indicated, they must have been married immediately after Margaret White Jones's death. No record of the marriage has been located to date. Neither has the wife's name been identified. Their place of residence is unknown. Thomas Norcliffe Jones does not appear on Richmond's 1860 census. The Jones family (with first wife Margaret) did appear on both the 1840 and 1850 censuses.

20. "Very Valuable Improved Real Estate," *Richmond Daily Dispatch*, July 1, 1859.

21. Simpson, *Good Southerner*, 219–51.

22. Dabney, *Richmond*, 204–5.

23. L. Tyler, *Encyclopedia of Virginia Biography*, 16–18.

24. This statement is based upon three known facts. The first is that there were extreme paper shortages in the South throughout the war, causing many printers to shut down and causing the Confederate War Department no small amount of inconvenience. (See J. B. Jones, *Rebel War Clerk's Diary*, 102, 175.) The second is that William Clemmitt did not cease printing during the war. (For evidence, see the short list of materials published under the imprint of William H. Clemmitt between 1860 and 1864, available online at www.siupress.com/spiritsofbadmenlinks.) Third, Clemmitt made no mention of ceasing business through the war. He stated he was "burned out" by the evacuation fire of April 2–3, 1865. (See "William H. Clemmitt, Oldest Active Printer.")

25. "Selling Off at Reduced Prices to Close Business," *Richmond Daily Dispatch*, March 11, 1862.

26. Kimball, *American City*, 223, 227–28.

27. National Park Service, "Soldier Details. Brock, Robert A."

28. Dabney, *Richmond*, 163.

29. National Park Service, "Soldier Details. Smith, Edgar A."

30. By March 1862, Edgar Alonza Smith was back in Richmond working at Midlothian Coal Company. See "Wanted—Recruits," *Richmond Daily Dispatch*, March 11, 1862. Following his first year of active duty service, Brock was reassigned to Winder Hospital for the balance of the conflict. See L. Tyler, *Encyclopedia of Virginia Biography*, 3–4.

31. "The Firm of Jones & Co.," *Richmond Daily Dispatch*, January 12, 1861.

32. "Joles, Hams, Breasts and Shoulders," *Richmond Daily Dispatch*, February 13, 1861. This is the first of many such advertisements placed in the weeks and months following the dissolution of the old partnership.

33. Lester, *Cases in Law and Equity*, 549–60. (The brown sugar held in warehouses in Atlanta, Georgia, and impressed into service to the Confederate government was valued at $37,336 by William B. Jones.) Thomas Johnson Michie, "Jones & Company vs. The City of Richmond," in *Virginia Reports*, 699–701; W. B. Jones, applications for pardon submitted to President Andrew Johnson by former Confederates excluded from earlier amnesty proclamations, *Case Files of Applications from Former Confederates for Presidential Pardons*, 1865–67, National Archives Catalog ID: 656621, Record Group 94, NARA M1003, Roll 0063.

34. "Public Arrests," *Richmond Daily Dispatch*, April 22, 1864; "Hustings Court," *Richmond Daily Dispatch*, December 23, 1863; "Hustings Court," *Richmond Daily Dispatch*, November 21, 1863.

35. "Heavy Bond," *Richmond Daily Dispatch*, July 14, 1864; "Sketch of His Life," *Richmond Daily Dispatch*, March 18, 1900.

36. "Substitute Wanted," *Richmond Daily Dispatch*, September 2, 1862.
37. "Lost on Main Street," *Richmond Daily Dispatch*, November 30, 1864.
38. "Sketch of His Life," *Richmond Daily Dispatch*, March 18, 1900.
39. "Administrator's Sale," *Richmond Daily Dispatch*, February 18, 1865; "Large and Attractive Sale," *Richmond Daily Dispatch*, January 7, 1865.

5. Prelude to War

1. The Conscription Act of 1862 was passed by the Confederate Congress on April 16 of that year, making all white males between the ages of eighteen and thirty-five eligible to be drafted into military service. This was the first military draft in American history, predating the Union Conscription Act of 1863, passed by the U.S. Congress on March 3 of that year.
2. "Important Arrests," *Richmond Daily Dispatch*, March 3, 1862; "Martial Law," *Richmond Whig*, March 3, 1862; "The Yankee Prisoners," *Richmond Enquirer*, March 6, 1862; "The Condemned Spies," *Richmond Daily Dispatch*, April 5, 1862; "A Union Man in Richmond. Personal Recollections of the Great Rebellion, by a Man on the Inside," *National Tribune* (Washington, DC), July 27, 1899.
3. Noe, *Reluctant Rebels*, 33–35.
4. Carmichael, *Last Generation*, 20.
5. Young and Ellett, "History of the Crenshaw Battery," 275.
6. "A Union Man in Richmond."
7. "Trial, Sentence, and Execution of Timothy Webster as a Spy," *Richmond Daily Dispatch*, April 30, 1862.
8. Carmichael, *Lee's Young Artillerist*, 15–17, 35.

6. The Civil War Diary of William Ellis Jones, of Richmond, Virginia

1. Carmichael, *Purcell, Crenshaw and Letcher Artillery*, 109; Young and Ellett, "History of the Crenshaw Battery."
2. W. E. Jones, form for a retiring soldier.
3. Scott, *History of Orange County*, 184–85; Young and Ellett, "History of the Crenshaw Battery."

PART 1. FIRST MUSTER AT RICHMOND THROUGH MANEUVERS AROUND FREDERICKSBURG, VIRGINIA MARCH 14–MAY 23, 1862

1. Carmichael, *Purcell, Crenshaw and Letcher Artillery*, 109; Young and Ellett, "History of the Crenshaw Battery."
2. "Camp Lee," where Crenshaw's Battery performed squad drill on March 18, 1862, was located on the "new fairground," behind what is now the Richmond

Science Museum. See 1865 map of Richmond in the U.S. National Archives, Record Group 77, Map G 204, #51.

3. This entry was penned on May 3, 1862. It and all others written between May 3 and June 27, 1862, were copied into the leather-bound notebook after William found it on the battleground after the Battle of Gaines' Mill. The book originally belonged to William R. Daugherty, believed to be a Union soldier. To date I have been unable to locate any information identifying this individual with certainty.

4. "Trial, Sentence, and Execution of Timothy Webster as a Spy," *Richmond Daily Dispatch*, April 30, 1862.

5. "... when we were ordered out of the Fair Grounds ..."—The execution took place at Camp Lee, otherwise referred to as the "new fairgrounds," north of Richmond. See note 2 just above, diary entry dated March 18, 1862.

6. "We reached Summit, which is about six miles from Fredericksburg ..."— The artillery disembarked and unpacked at Guinea Station, about thirteen miles from Fredericksburg and about one mile from Summit Station. See Carmichael, *Purcell, Crenshaw and Letcher Artillery,* 62; and Farrell, diary.

7. "...Nature's restorer, balmy sleep."—A misquote of a line from Edward Young's *Night Thoughts*: "Tired nature's sweet restorer, balmy sleep!" Young was an eighteenth-century Romantic poet who was a favorite of Goethe and his acolytes.

8. "... 'hard road to travel.'"—"Richmond Is a Hard Road to Travel" was a popular song among soldiers and civilians alike in the early days of the Civil War. It was sung to the tune of Daniel Emmett's minstrel tune "Jordan Am a Hard Road to Travel." Its lyrics roasted the lengthy list of Union generals who tried and failed to conquer Richmond, from the First Battle of Manassas in July 1861 to the Battle of Fredericksburg in December 1862. See Civil War Poetry, "Poetry and Music of the War between the States."

9. Misspelling of Brigadier General Maxcy Gregg, made often throughout the diary. Gregg served as a major with the U.S. Army during the Mexican War without seeing any direct conflict. Following his service there, he returned to his South Carolina law practice, where, as the sectional crisis began to build, he functioned as a member of the state's secession convention. At the outset of the Civil War, he served in a number of leadership positions in the Confederate army, eventually assigned to A. P. Hill's division in May 1862. Gregg was wounded at Second Bull Run and was killed later the same year during the Battle of Fredericksburg while trying to regroup and rally his men, following a Union break of the Confederate lines. See Sifakis, *Who Was Who in the Confederacy*, 114.

10. "... *manuel* of the piece ..."—Training and drills on how to operate the guns of the artillery.

11. "... dinner ..."—In the vernacular of the era, dinner was always the midday meal. The evening meal was supper.

12. Farrell, diary. Farrell also documented this event in his diary, recording the date as May 8, 1862.

13. Misspelling of "Massaponax." The new Massaponax Church building was less than ten years old when the Civil War began. In 1863, the church was instructed to give letters of dismissal to all black members of the congregation. The war, lasting four years, brought church services to a standstill, as the building was used alternately by both Confederate and Union armies.

14. "He informed us that he had five sons in the army ..."—While I have so far been unable to locate the Mr. Bullock of this entry or his farm, I was able to locate several individuals in the neighborhood who are likely among his five sons. Private James Edgar Bullock (b. 1837), who enlisted on June 14, 1861, was mustered into F Company, "Bowling Green Guards," Virginia, 30th Infantry, as a private. James Edgar Bullock died on July 26, 1907, at Guinea Station, Caroline County, Virginia. According to his obituary, which appeared in the *Fredericksburg (VA) Daily Star* on July 29, 1907, he was interred in the "estate" at Locust Hill, Cosby Cemetery, Guinea Station, Caroline County, Virginia. Private Thomas Slaughter Bullock mustered into M Company, "Bowling Green Guards," Virginia, 30th Infantry, as a private on March 13, 1862. Thomas Bullock was likely the brother of James Edgar Bullock, as both are listed as hailing from Caroline County, Virginia. He died in the Robert E. Lee Soldiers' Home, Richmond, and is interred in Hollywood Cemetery, Confederate Soldiers Section. See Find a Grave Memorial, "Pvt. Thomas Slaughter Bullock."

15. "... guard mounting ..."—Refers to ceremonial changing of the guard, usually highly choreographed and formal.

16. "... Gray-eyed Morn smiled at frowning Night ..."—A slightly misquoted line from act 2, scene 3, of Shakespeare's *Romeo and Juliet*.

17. "'Eastern View' was a high hill from which place you had an extensive and varied view towards the East ..."—What William calls "Eastern View" is known today as Prospect Hill. It is accessible near Old Hamilton's Crossing in Spotsylvania County, Virginia, on the southernmost part of the Fredericksburg National Battlefield Park.

18. Rable, *Damn Yankees!*, 37–38.

19. "Tempus fugit ..."—From the Latin; "Time flies."

20. "Went to the cars ..."—The battery was camped very close to the railway at Summit Crossing, which is where the mail was offloaded from the trains during the war.

21. "... cousin from Richmond ..."—William refers here to his cousin William B. Jones, who served as the mail carrier contracted to the Confederate War

Department, working between Fredericksburg and Brunswick Hall, Brunswick County, Virginia. See W. B. Jones, applications for pardon submitted to President Andrew Johnson by former Confederates excluded from earlier amnesty proclamations, *Case Files of Applications from Former Confederates for Presidential Pardons*, 1865–67 (see chapter 4, note 33).

22. "... tattoo ..."—A drumbeat or bugle call that signals the soldiers to return to their quarters.

23. "Nous verrons!"—From the French; "We'll see!"

24. Meier, *Nature's Civil War*, 33, 12–113, 134.

25. National Park Service, "Major General Benjamin F. Butler"; Smith, "Benjamin F. Butler (1818–1893)." Butler's "infamous proclamation" can be found in the *Private and Official Correspondence of General Benjamin F. Butler*, "General Orders No. 28, May 18, 1862."

26. "Captain" refers to Captain William Graves Crenshaw. See Scott, *History of Orange County*, 184.

27. "Second Lieutanant" refers to Senior Second Lieutenant Andrew Bell Johnston. Prior to the war, Andrew Bell Johnston was a clerk at William Graves Crenshaw's Woolen Mills in Richmond and was active in the first recruiting efforts for forming Crenshaw's Battery in February and March 1862. He enlisted on March 14, 1862, with the battery as a second lieutenant and was promoted to first lieutenant on December 13, 1862. On July 6, 1863, he was injured at Gettysburg. In October 1863 he requested a transfer from the battery, writing, "I have had many years of experience as a book keeper & clerk & am quick and correct at figures." His request was denied, as the postwar ledger states that Johnston served until the surrender. He was paroled at Richmond on May 12, 1865. See Carmichael, *Purcell, Crenshaw and Letcher Artillery*, 115; and "Light Artillery," *Richmond Daily Dispatch*, February 18, 1862.

PART 2. THE PENINSULA CAMPAIGN
MAY 24–JULY 28, 1862

1. "... sunrise we reached Jarrett's Mill in Caroline County ..."—The location referenced here is Jerrell's Mill, not Jarrett's Mill.

2. Hanover Junction is now Doswell, Virginia.

3. "Slashes of Hanover" is the original name of the community now known as Ashland, Virginia.

4. Robert Q. Strother enlisted on March 14, 1862, and served with Crenshaw's Battery until March 17, 1864, when he transferred to Company E, First Engineers Regiment. In 1900 he was still alive and active with the Robert E. Lee Camp #1 (a Confederate veterans' group). William Ellis Jones was also a member of this organization, which spawned the establishment of the

Sons of Confederate Veterans and the United Daughters of the Confederacy. See Carmichael, *Purcell, Crenshaw and Letcher Artillery*, 118; and Virginia Historical Society, "United Confederate Veterans."

5. ". . . flea in his ear."—Much irritation.

6. Somnus was the Roman god of sleep.

7. Meier, *Nature's Civil War*, 50–52, 130–31.

8. ". . . that the fight occurred at Hanover Court House the previous evening and that our forces were compelled to retreat . . ."—According to Robert Krick, former chief historian of Fredericksburg and Spotsylvania National Military Park, on the afternoon of May 27, 1862, a medium-sized battle occurred about four miles south of Hanover Courthouse. Union sources usually refer to this event as the Battle of Hanover Courthouse. In the south it is referred to as the Battle of Slash Church. The Confederate force (with Crenshaw's Battery included within it) moved south from Fredericksburg toward Ashland and Richmond, operating under the vague idea of reinforcing Confederate forces already in place east of Ashland near Hanover Courthouse.

9. Misspelling of Brigadier General Charles William Field.

10. Morpheus was the Roman god of dreams, son of Somnus, the Roman god of sleep.

11. For information on approximate location of J. Bacon Crenshaw's residence, see the map on page 67. This information was generously supplied by Robert Krick, former chief historian of Fredericksburg and Spotsylvania National Military Park.

12. Bears, *Dictionary of Virginia Biography*, 550–51.

13. "Physician came to see me, prescribed brandy and laudanum . . ."—Brandy was prescribed by Civil War–era physicians to combat the painful bowel cramps associated with dysentery, while laudanum was prescribed for pain and to slow the stools. See Flannery, *Civil War Pharmacy*, 120, 221.

14. Flannery, 23.

15. This is the day of the Battle of Seven Pines.

16. "We were halted about a mile this side of the bridge that spans the Chick-ahominy."—The battery's Record of Events cards note that in the last week of May it crossed the river at Meadow Bridge. Today this is approximately where Route 627 crosses the river. This information was generously provided by Robert Krick, former chief historian of Fredericksburg and Spotsylvania National Military Park.

17. This is a misspelling.; The reference is to Stuart's flying artillery, commanded by General James Ewell Brown "J. E. B." Stuart.

18. "Orderly Scott . . ."—This probably refers to William C. Scott. Prior to the war Scott resided in Orange County. He enlisted with the battery on March

14, 1862, as an ordnance sergeant. He was commissioned a captain on January 23, 1863, in the Quartermaster's Department. See Carmichael, *Purcell, Crenshaw and Letcher Artillery*, 118.

19. ". . . bottle of misture . . ."—This statement is too general to precisely pin down as to product or ingredients; however, it probably refers to a precipitate of opium (or laudanum) in an alcohol base.

20. ". . . some banquet hall deserted . . ."—This is a line from "Oft in the Stilly Night" by the Irish poet Thomas Moore.

21. "We reached our new camp ground late in the afternoon . . ."—The men of the battery, according to John O. Farrell, called this new site "Camp Quicksand." (See the John O. Farrell diary.)

22. "Some of the boys ran the blockade . . ."—This would have involved crossing the Confederate blockade lines rather than any Union lines, as might be implied. The risk of being fired upon was minimal; however, the risk of being caught by scouts looking for straggling soldiers was high, which, as is documented in upcoming entries, incurred serious consequences.

23. The men referred to in this entry are:

> Private John A. Mayo—Enlisted with the battery on March 14, 1862. On July 3, 1863, he was slightly wounded at Gettysburg but returned to duty. On April 26, 1865, he was paroled at Richmond.
>
> Private Marion Knowles—Prior to the war he resided on Canal Street in Richmond and worked as a printer. He enlisted with the battery on March 14, 1862. On June 27, 1862, he was severely wounded at the Battle of Gaines' Mill and disabled. After his recovery he was detailed to the Post Quartermaster's Office. He took the Oath of Allegiance to the Union on April 15, 1865.
>
> Private John Cunningham Goolsby—A native of Richmond, he enlisted with the battery on March 14, 1865. He was wounded at Chancellorsville on May 3, 1863, but returned to service. On July 14, 1863, he was captured at Falling Waters. On December 24, 1863, he was paroled and exchanged at Point Lookout. On April 10, 1865, after the fall of Richmond, prior to the formal surrender, he was listed among the Union-held prisoners at Libby Prison. After the war Goolsby worked as a proofreader for Everett Waddey Printing Company in Richmond. In 1900 Goolsby wrote an account of the history of Crenshaw's Battery for the *Southern Historical Society Papers*, which appeared in volumes 28 and 29. He married Ida J. and died in Newark, New Jersey.
>
> Private Thomas J. Mallory—Mallory was born in Orange County. He enlisted with the battery on March 14, 1862, and was severely

wounded in the neck at the Battle of Gaines' Mill on June 27, 1862. On July 23, 1863, he deserted and was captured at Front Royal, saying he was *"desirous of going to Washington or Alexandria. Tired of the War."* He was sent to Point Lookout and released on March 14, 1864, after taking the Oath of Allegiance.

Private Thomas H. Burroughs (or Burruss)—Enlisted with the battery on March 14, 1862. On May 3, 1863, he received three gunshot wounds in the chest at Chancellorsville. He was absent with medical leave for most of the war but returned to duty on January 20, 1865. On April 10, 1865, he was listed among Confederate soldiers remaining in U.S. military prisons.

For further details, see Carmichael, *Purcell, Crenshaw and Letcher Artillery*, 112, 114, and 116.

24. Captain John B. McCarthy was a native of Montgomery, Alabama, and an officer in the 6th Alabama Infantry.; He was killed at the Battle of Seven Pines. See Willis Brewer, *Alabama*, 599.

25. The Montgomery, Alabama, connection is interesting in that William's cousin Richard Evan Jones (brother of William B. Jones), who emigrated from Wales in 1843, was then serving in the Gulf City Guard, which would become part of the Alabama Artillery in the Confederate army. It's probable that William knew he had a cousin in Alabama, and it's possible he knew John B. McCarthy through a relationship with his cousin Richard. See National Park Service, "Soldier Details. Jones, Richard E."; and W. E. Jones, family papers.

26. The men who were tied to the guns include:

Corporal Edward Strother Ferneyhough (or Fernerhough) Jr.—Born in 1846 and a resident of Richmond. Prior to the war he resided at 4th and Byrd Streets and worked as a clerk. He enlisted with the battery on March 14, 1862, and on November 14, 1863, he was promoted to corporal. He was wounded during the Mine Run Campaign and went AWOL. On April 12, 1865, he took the Oath of Allegiance to the Union. After the war he was a member of the Pegram Battalion Association and was active with the Robert E. Lee Camp #1.

Private Ralph E. Allen—He was born in Richmond and prior to the war worked as a printer. He enlisted with the battery on March 14, 1862. He received a medical discharge prior to war's end.

Private William. D. Snead—Prior to the war he resided at the corner of 2nd and Main Streets in Richmond and worked as a printer. He enlisted with the battery on March 14, 1862, and was promoted to corporal on May 6, 1864. On April 22, 1865, he took the Oath of Allegiance to the Union in the Henrico County District (of Richmond). After the war he was a member of the Pegram Battalion Association. He died on December 8, 1930, and is buried at Hollywood Cemetery.

Private Benjamin F. Burgess—Enlisted with the battery on March 14, 1862. On December 13, 1862, he was wounded at the Battle of Fredericksburg. He was absent on medical leave for much of the war but returned to duty on January 2, 1865.

Private William Ellis Jones—The subject of this biography.

For further details on the above men, see Carmichael, *Purcell, Crenshaw and Letcher Artillery*, 112, 114, 115, 118.

Private Joseph H. Colquitt—Colquitt served in Crenshaw's Battery, Ellett's Company, Virginia Light Artillery. See National Park Service, "Soldier Details. Colquitt, Jr., Joseph H."

There is a fascinating and lengthy account of this man, or perhaps his father, appearing in the autobiography of Henry "Box" Brown, a slave narrative that became an international bestseller in the years immediately prior to the Civil War. It's worth reading but not necessarily relevant to this text. See Brown, *Narrative of the Life of Henry Box Brown*, 33–34.

27. "... one additional one this morning, W. E. Jones, a name-sake of mine."— This is a confusing entry. There was no other "W. E. Jones" in Crenshaw's Battery, and to my knowledge, William had no kinsmen who would have been "name-sake" among his comrades. There was a Private William Gregory Jones. It seems possible that William inadvertently wrote "E." instead of "G." and intended the "name-sake" comment as humor. William Gregory Jones enlisted with the battery on March 14, 1862. According to diarist John O. Farrell, Jones spent some time in the guardhouse for being absent without leave. He was present on the final roll call in February 1862. See Farrell, diary; and Carmichael, *Purcell, Crenshaw and Letcher Artillery*, 116.

28. "... forgot to state that Jones was strapped to the gun . . ."—It is likely that William was referencing W. G. Jones in this entry, as with the June 8, 1862, entry above (note 27).

29. Sergeant Alpheus G. Newman enlisted with the battery on March 14, 1862. On June 28, 1863, he was captured at Fountaindale. From July 1863 to January 1865, he was a prisoner of war at Point Lookout. On February 18, 1865, he was exchanged, only to be captured again on April 1, 1865, at Five Forks. He was released from Point Lookout Prison on June 2, 1865, after taking the Oath of Allegiance to the Union. See Carmichael, *Purcell, Crenshaw and Letcher Artillery*, 117.

30. "... dumb agues . . ."—High fever and sore throat.

31. Quinine was a remedy most often prescribed for the symptoms of malaria (headache and fever). See Flannery, *Civil War Pharmacy*, 132–51.

32. Royal Society of Chemistry, "Search for Blue Mass Medicine"; Felter and Lloyd, *King's American Dispensatory*, 1007–9; Potter, *Compendium of Materia Medica*, 78–80; Kress, "Massae Pilularum"; Flannery, *Civil War Pharmacy*, 129, 132–42.

33. Langford and Ferner, "Toxicity of Mercury."

34. "We reached Dr. Friend's farm . . ."—See the map on page 67 for the location of Dr. Friend's farm. This information was generously provided by Robert Krick, former chief historian of Fredericksburg and Spotsylvania National Military Park.

35. See diary entry dated Wednesday, June 11, 1862, note 32.

36. ". . . the calomel acting with talismanic effect on my liver."—Nineteenth-century physicians (and those before them), along with their patients, believed improper liver function was at the root of many afflictions and that by balancing biliary secretions they could cure the disorder. This notion was wrong on nearly every account, as was the treatment prescribed. For more detail on this subject, see Flannery, *Civil War Pharmacy*, 135–37.

37. Langford and Ferner, "Toxicity of Mercury," 651–56.

38. Langford and Ferner, 651–56.

39. ". . . masked batteries . . ."—Large artillery guns (cannon) placed so as not to be seen by an enemy until it opens fire.

40. ". . . water battery . . ."—Either a group of cannon mounted on the edge of a body of water or a battery mounted on ship's deck.

41. Rable, *Damn Yankees!*, 38.

42. Organized in April 1862 at Richmond, Virginia, Dabney's Battery saw action in the Seven Days' Battles, then moved to North Carolina. It was stationed at Goldsboro, North Carolina, with two officers and thirty-one men. Later the battery was assigned to E. F. Moseley's battalion of artillery, Department of Richmond. Early in 1864 the battery disbanded. Captain William J. Dabney was in command. See Crute, *Units of the Confederate States Army*, 398.

43. ". . . Long Tom . . ."—It was common for the armies on both sides of this conflict to name their guns, as they became intimately familiar with each cannon's individual personality and operation. Confederate forces captured many guns during the early part of the war. This cannon was captured at the First Battle of Manassas in 1861. It served in many battles and was moved around as needed. The addition of this gun and one other brought Crenshaw's Battery to a total of eight guns. See Cole and Foley, *Collett Leventhorpe*, 76.

44. ". . . Laughing Charlie . . ."—This gun, like "Long Tom," was captured at the First Battle of Manassas in 1861. See Cole and Foley, 76.

45. "... General Hill..."—Ambrose Powell (A. P.) Hill Jr. was a native Virginian from a prominent old Culpeper County family who pursued a career in the U.S. military. A. P. Hill was killed during the Union army offensive at the Third Battle of Petersburg on April 2, 1865. See Robertson, *General A. P. Hill*, 4–5, 36, 317–24.

46. Private William Robertson Burgess—"Billy" Burgess, as he was known familiarly within the battery—was born in Richmond on December 12, 1845. He enlisted with the battery on March 14, 1862, as a bugler. He is distinguished among his comrades in that he was present for every roll call of the battery, meaning that he was never absent due to sickness, injury, or personal leave or absent without leave. His name is included on a list of soldiers paroled, but no date is given. He died on April 20, 1912, in Washington, DC. See Carmichael, *Purcell, Crenshaw and Letcher Artillery*, 112.

47. "... carried before General Pender..."—William Dorsey Pender was born near the town of Tarboro, in Edgecombe County, North Carolina. Pender resigned from the U.S. Army and was appointed a captain of artillery in the Confederate States Army. Robert E. Lee rated Pender among the most promising of his commanders, promoting him to major general at twenty-nine years of age, the youngest of that rank in the Confederate military. Pender's distinguished career ended at the Battle of Gettysburg on July 1, 1863, where he was mortally wounded and died shortly thereafter. See Wills, *Confederate General William Dorsey Pender*, 7, 51–53, 66–68, 129–34, 234–38, 244.

48. First Lieutenant Charles Lewis Hobson was born in Virginia about 1836 and worked in Richmond as a tobacconist in 1860. He enlisted with the battery on March 14, 1860, as a lieutenant. From December 1862 until April 1863, he was detailed by the secretary of war and sent to England. In April 1863 he was lost at sea. See Carmichael, *Purcell, Crenshaw and Letcher Artillery*, 115.

49. Private R. S. Herndon of Crenshaw's Battery died on this date. Private Herndon enlisted with the battery on March 14, 1862. His cause of death is not recorded, but it is unlikely it was due to battlefield injuries, as the battery had not seen any serious action up to this date. He died in the hospital at Camp Winder, in Richmond. See Carmichael, *Purcell, Crenshaw and Letcher Artillery*, 115.

50. The officer referred to here is Lieutenant Virginius Dabney of the 48th Virginia Regiment.

51. The Purcell Artillery, a light artillery company, was established on April 20, 1861, in Richmond through the efforts of Daniel Hagerty. The battery was named for John Purcell, a wealthy Richmond merchant who financed the majority of its hardware. Lieutenant William R. J. Pegram became the commander of Purcell's Battery and was considered one of the Confederacy's most

distinguished artillerists. When William Ellis Jones wrote, "Purcell Battery won an enviable fame. They had thirty killed and wounded," he was being more than mildly sarcastic. It is doubtful that he, or anyone, envied their "accomplishment" that day. Historians have described the result alternately as "decimated" and "destroyed." John O. Farrell recorded in his diary that Purcell's battery "received a heavy loss." See Carmichael, *Purcell, Crenshaw and Letcher Artillery*, 1–57.

52. Burton, *Extraordinary Circumstances*, 58–81; Carmichael, *Purcell, Crenshaw and Letcher Artillery*, 76.

53. James Longstreet was one of the foremost Confederate generals of the American Civil War and the principal subordinate to General Robert E. Lee. Following the war, Longstreet enjoyed a successful postwar career working for the U.S. government as a diplomat, civil servant, and administrator but suffered under withering criticism from former Confederates due to his endorsement of Grant for president and advice to Southerners to support Reconstruction. See American Battlefield Trust, "Biography James Longstreet"; and Sifakis, *Who Was Who in the Confederacy*, 176–77.

54. Crenshaw's Battery members wounded or killed during the June 27, 1862, Battle of Gaines' Mill:

> Private Benton V. Graves—Lost a leg, permanently disabled. Graves was born in Spotsylvania County and was a farmer prior to the war. He enlisted with the battery on March 14, 1862, and served until his injury at Gaines' Mill.
>
> Private Marion Knowles—See note 23 above for diary entry dated June 5, 1862.
>
> Private Daniel M. Lancaster—Died July 3, 1862, from wounds received at the Battle of Gaines' Mill. Lancaster enlisted with the battery on March 14, 1862.
>
> Mordecai Thomas Rider—Wounded, recovered. Enlisted with the battery on March 14, 1862. After being shot with a minié ball he was sent to the Female Institute (hospital) in Richmond and later transferred to Bedford County Hospital. From November 1863 to December 1864 he was detailed "extra duty" as a harness maker. On April 25, 1865, he was paroled in Richmond. He was a member of the Pegram Battalion Association. He died on August 13, 1912, at the Confederate Soldiers' Home in Richmond. He is buried at Hollywood Cemetery.
>
> Sergeant Sidney Strother—Died June 28, 1862, following the Battle of Gaines' Mill. Strother was born c. 1841 and was a resident of

Richmond, where he owned a mercantile business. He enlisted with the battery on March 14, 1862. Following his injury on June 27, he was immediately sent home to his family at Richmond, where he died. The battery members attended his interment several days later at Hollywood Cemetery, as is documented in William's diary entry of June 29, 1862.

Private Robert. N. Hines—Killed. Enlisted with the battery on March 14, 1862. At Gaines' Mill he was killed instantly by a shot to the head. On June 28, 1862, William noted in his diary that members of the battery brought the body of Hines to his family's home in Richmond.

Private George S. Young—Recovered. Enlisted with the battery on March 14, 1862. After returning to duty following his injury at Gaines' Mill, he was promoted to corporal on December 12, 1862. He was later wounded at Cold Harbor on June 27, 1862, when shrapnel shot passed entirely through his neck. He was wounded again at Gettysburg on July 3, 1863. He died May 30, 1864, at Jackson's Hospital in Richmond from wounds received at Jericho Ford on May 23, 1864.

Private Thomas J. Mallory—See note 23 above for diary entry dated June 5, 1862.

Corporal William B. Allen—Recovered. Allen enlisted with the battery on March 14, 1862. After recovering from his wound at Gaines' Mill, he was promoted to sergeant. On July 3, 1863, he was wounded at Gettysburg. On November 14, 1863, he was promoted to lieutenant. On March 9, 1865, he resigned from duty. In 1900 he was living and was affiliated with the Robert E. Lee Camp #1 in Richmond. His brother was Ralph E. Allen; see note 26 above for diary entry dated June 7, 1862.

Private Matthew Alex Caldwell—Recovered. Prior to the war, Caldwell resided in Craig County. He enlisted with the battery on March 14, 1862, and was only slightly injured at Gaines' Mill. On September 17, 1862, he was wounded at Antietam. On July 3, 1863, he was wounded at Gettysburg and remained absent until November 12, 1863. He was absent without leave on March 4, 1865. On April 15, 1865, he was paroled at Lynchburg.

Private Alonzo K. Phillips—Recovered. Phillips was born in Norfolk in 1843. He enlisted with Crenshaw's Battery on March 14, 1862. After recovering from his wound at Gaines' Mill, he was promoted to corporal. On May 18, 1864, he was shot in the face at Spotsylvania Court House. He was admitted to General Hospital #9 in Richmond on June 4, 1864. He was present at roll call on January 2, 1865. He died on May 3, 1893.

For further details see Carmichael, *Purcell, Crenshaw and Letcher Artillery,* 112, 114–19.

55. See note 54 for entry dated June 27, 1862.

56. From the notes of William Ellis Jones, the grandson of Civil War diarist William Ellis Jones: "My grandfather never completely recovered from this infection. As long as he lived the eruption broke out on him in the summer and at the slightest contact with poison ivy his entire body would become infected. I remember as a child that when the ditch banks at Summerfield were burned, my grandfather had to go away for the day because the smoke was able to bring the poison of the burning plant to him." From W. E. Jones, family papers.

57. "Dr. Thomas"—According to Civil War Richmond, "Richmond City Business Directory, 1860," there was a Doctor H. L. Thomas in Richmond, with either his residence or his office located on Broad Street, between 1st and 2nd Streets. A Dr. Thomas was also listed as assistant surgeon at General Hospital #1. A report to him, existing in the U.S. National Archives (Record Group 109.8.4, ch. VI, vol. 764), titled "Reports of Resection Cases, General Hospital No. 1. 1862–64," is labeled "Dr. H. L. Thomas," who is probably the recipient of the reports contained therein. With this information in mind, William's complaint does seem to carry weight. While Dr. Thomas may not have been "regular army," he was almost certainly commissioned with the care of a great many Confederate soldiers.

58. The officer who gave William a pass to go home was Senior Second Lieutenant Andrew Bell Johnston; see part 1, note 27, for diary entry dated Friday, May 23, 1862.

59. Private Daniel M. Lancaster died this day (or possibly July 4, 1862) from wounds received at the Battle of Gaines' Mill. See note 55 above for diary entry dated June 27, 1862. See also Young and Ellett, "History of the Crenshaw Battery"; and Carmichael, *Purcell, Crenshaw and Letcher Artillery,* 116. (Carmichael states that Lancaster died on July 4, 1862.)

60. "Wanted—Recruits for Thomas's Artillery," *Richmond Daily Dispatch,* March 11, 1862.

61. Private W. W. Smith—Enlisted with the battery on March 14, 1862, and was promoted to corporal on December 31, 1862. On June 11, 1863, his rank was broken to private, no reason recorded. After a period of sick leave, he returned to duty on January 2, 1865, and served until the surrender. See Carmichael, *Purcell, Crenshaw and Letcher Artillery,* 118.

62. Senior First Lieutenant James D. Ellett—Prior to the war, Ellett was clerk of circuit court in Richmond. He enlisted with the battery on March 14, 1862, as a lieutenant. He was killed in action at Fredericksburg on December 13, 1862.

His brother Robert Ellett served in Company F until Crenshaw's Battery was formed, when he joined on March 14, 1862. Another brother Thomas R. Ellett also enlisted with Crenshaw's Battery. Thomas is the only one of the three brothers to survive the war. See Carmichael, *Purcell, Crenshaw and Letcher Artillery,* 113.

63. John Cunningham Goolsby—See note 23 above for diary entry dated June 5, 1862.

64. Private Taliaferro P. Loving (or Long)—Enlisted with the battery on March 14, 1862. He is listed as "Absent sick" on July 12, 1862; July 1863 (dysentery); September 1863 (rheumatism); and November 12, 1863. He was detailed as a wagoner on an ordnance train on March 10, 1863, and again in February 1864. On March 18, 1864, he was discharged. See Carmichael, *Purcell, Crenshaw and Letcher Artillery,* 116.

65. Corporal then later Private A. S. Hackley—Enlisted with the battery on March 14, 1862, as a corporal. In December 1863, he was detailed to "extra duty" as clerk at the Quartermaster's Office, through February 1865. See Carmichael, *Purcell, Crenshaw and Letcher Artillery,* 114.

66. *War of the Rebellion: A Compilation of the Official Records of the Union and Confederate Armies,* series 1, vol. 12, pt. 3, 896 (hereafter cited as *OR*).

67. Colonel Reuben Lindsey Walker was a Virginia native, a graduate of the Virginia Military Institute, and an engineer by training and profession. At the outset of the war, Walker organized an artillery battery, the Purcell Artillery, and quickly moved up in the ranks, ultimately becoming the commander of artillery in A. P. Hill's Third Corps, Army of Northern Virginia. Walker, who earned the rank of brigadier general before war's end, was distinguished by the fact that he served in every battle his division and the Third Corps participated in during the entirety of the war (excluding the Seven Days' Battles, due to illness) and was never wounded (a fact he apologized for). Following the war, Walker returned to private life, farming and working as an engineer. See Sifakis, *Who Was Who in the Confederacy,* 294–95.

68. Union Hill is one of the oldest neighborhoods in Richmond. This camp location is probably the same or nearly the same one where the battery camped on June 28, 1862, as they refitted after Gaines' Mill.

69. The young lady referenced here is Miss Florence M. Smith, sister of Edgar Alonza Smith.

PART 3. MARCH TO JOIN JACKSON AND ON TO SECOND MANASSAS
JULY 29–SEPTEMBER 1, 1862

1. While "Dixie" is a familiar song, particularly to anyone with Southern roots or interest in the Civil War, "Maryland, My Maryland," written by James Ryder Randall, is less well-known. Written in 1861 and set to the tune of

"O Tannenbaum," the ballad became the official state song in 1939. While the song refers to Maryland's geographic beauty and rich history, it calls for Maryland to fight the Union, and it quickly became a Civil War battle hymn. See Dabney, *Richmond*, 169.

2. "Learned today that we had been transposed from General Grigg's to General Pender's brigade . . ."—The transfer noted here is from Brigadier General Maxcy Gregg's brigade to General William Dorsey Pender's command of North Carolinians. For further information on General Pender, see note 47 in part 2.

3. ". . . speech from our 'Profitt' . . ."—The soldier referenced here is Private Willis Washington Proffitt. He enlisted with the battery on March 14, 1862. After a period of illness, he was detached as a nurse at Chimborazo Hospital in Richmond on February 12, 1864, having been pronounced "unfit for active duty in the field" by a medical examination board. On January 2, 1865, he was listed as a deserter. On May 15, 1865, he was paroled in Louisa County. He died on February 18, 1902, of heart disease. See Carmichael, *Purcell, Crenshaw and Letcher Artillery*, 117.

4. ". . . would be voted in toto."—In total or comprising all the members of the battery.

5. National Park Service, "Soldier Details. Cabell, James Caskie."

6. Thomas Ellis Jones (son of William Ellis Jones, great-grandson of William Ellis Jones the diarist) in discussion with the author prior to December 31, 1997.

7. "The roll was called and the men counted, when 78 were found to be present."—On March 14, 1862, when the Crenshaw Battery was formed, 139 men were on the original roster. Between that date and the date of this entry, at least 1 man died prior to the battery seeing any action, 5 died due to injuries sustained at the Battle of Gaines' Mill, and another 6 were injured in the same battle or in camp accidents. That leaves 49 men unaccounted for, due to illness, straggling, or desertion. This absentee rate represents almost 44 percent of the battery.

8. Cynthia was originally an alternative name of the Greek goddess of the moon, Artemis, who according to legend was born on Mount Cynthus.

9. For additional information regarding Central America and the expansion of slavery into that realm, see De Bow, "General Walker's Policy in Central America."

10. "We crossed the Rapidan at Barnett's Ford where there was a pretty good skirmish last night . . ."—Based on the known route taken as documented in the diary, and with comparison to other period documents, including a map produced by J. E. B. Stuart in support of his August 1862 report on the

advance of the army toward the Rappahannock, the nearest approximate location of Barnett's Ford is shown on the map on page 93.

11. "We crossed Robinson's River in the middle of the day . . ."—This crossing probably took place due north of Barnett's Ford. See the map on page 93 for approximate location.

12. "We reached Mrs. Pettit's farm about four or five o'clock . . ."—According to a 1937 survey and report made by the Virginia Works Projects Administration, Historical Inventory Project, sponsored by the Virginia Conservation Commission under the direction of its Division of History, this farm was located eight miles southwest of Culpeper, Virginia, on what is now Highway 15 (James Madison Highway). According to the survey description, the house was built in 1740. It was a two-story, L-frame construction that was then (1937) in possession of the Crittenden family. According to John Hennessy, National Park Service chief historian with the Fredericksburg and Spotsylvania National Military Park, the house was on the east side of the road. See Library of Virginia Online Catalog, "Byrd Eastham Place, Cloverdale."

13. A misspelling of Charles Sidney Winder. Winder was a native of Maryland who began his military career at the U.S. Military Academy at West Point, graduating in 1850. Winder resigned his U.S. Army commission on April 1, 1861, and was appointed a captain and then major of artillery in the Confederate army. On August 9, 1862, Winder led his men into battle at Cedar Mountain. He was personally directing the fire of a battery when a Union shell struck him in his left side. Borne to the rear on a stretcher, Winder died later that evening. Krick, *Stonewall Jackson at Cedar Mountain*, 17–19, 376–78.

14. Union brigadier general Henry Prince was a West Point graduate and career army man with substantial combat experience. On August 9, 1862, during the Battle of Cedar Mountain, he was captured by the Confederate army. General Prince remained a prisoner until December, when he was paroled in an exchange. See Krick, *Stonewall Jackson at Cedar Mountain*, 117, 287–89; and Eicher and Eicher, *Civil War High Commands*, 441.

15. Socially well-connected, decidedly antislavery in his political ideology, and close to President Lincoln in both proximity and view of how the war should be prosecuted, General John Pope was appointed commander of the newly constituted Union Army of Virginia in June 1862, following the disaster of Jackson's Shenandoah Valley Campaign and the resounding defeat of all three Union armies. Unlike McClellan, who was conservative politically as well as on the battlefield, Pope expressed a willingness to aggressively bring the war to the civilian population in order to "perish" slavery. While many prominent Northern newspaper editors declared that Pope was just the man to quickly reverse the timidity and failures of his predecessor, he was viewed

as impulsive and pompous by many of his peers and subordinates. From almost the first moment of his appointment he managed to insult both his fellow officers and his soldiers with the issuance of an order demanding a "bolder spirit" that was to set the tone for his relationships within his own command for the tenure of his command. As the fighting season of 1862 slogged on, Pope and his cheerleaders learned that there were no easy fixes for the imperiled Union army. Following Pope's humiliating entrapment and defeat and the Second Battle of Bull Run, he was relieved of command on September 12, 1862. His Army of Virginia was merged with McClellan's Army of the Potomac, and Pope was sent west to deal with the Dakota War in Minnesota. Hennessy, *Return to Bull Run*, 3–20, 451–54.

16. Mercer Featherston enlisted in Purcell's Artillery in Richmond on February 22, 1862. He was promoted to lieutenant on March 31, 1862, and killed in action at Cedar Mountain ("head shot off"). See Carmichael, *Purcell, Crenshaw and Letcher Artillery*, 48.

17. Misspelling of Barnett's Ford.

18. Misspelling of General James Ewell Brown "J. E. B." Stuart, who served under General Thomas J. Jackson during the Northern Virginia Campaign.

19. "General Hill . . ."—See diary entry dated Saturday, June 22, 1862, in part 2, note 45.

20. Carmichael, *Purcell, Crenshaw and Letcher Artillery*, 116.

21. Misspelling of Raccoon Ford, which is easily accessible today from the Orange County side, just north of Virginia Route 611. See Hennessy, "Exploring Culpeper."

22. "After finishing it I went up on one of the small mountains to look at the Yank's camp on the other side of the Rapidan."—William ventured to the top of Clark Mountain. See the map on page 93 for precise location. Interestingly, less than two years later, General Robert E. Lee would stand on this very same spot and observe the Union army crossing the Rapidan on its march toward Richmond. See Johnston and Buel, *Battles and Leaders of the Civil War*, 118.

23. This is line seven from "The Pleasures of Hope," a poem by Thomas Campbell, a Scottish poet of substantial reputation in his era.

24. *War Trail*, written by Mayne Reid, was a nineteenth-century adventure novel. Most of this author's works were produced for the juvenile market, which might explain why William was unimpressed.

25. Meier, *Nature's Civil War*, 122–46.

26. ". . . we started taking the road to Somerville Ford, across the Rapidan River."—Refer to the map on page 93 for precise location of the ford. See Hennessy, "Exploring Culpeper."

27. "... and took the road to Stevensburg to Culpeper."—It is unlikely the march carried the battery over the road to Culpeper, Virginia, via Stevensburg, as this would have been considerably out of the way. William is probably mistaken.

28. "... meeting J. Herndon at it ..."—The soldier referenced is Private James Cooper Herndon. He was born in Orange County and is noted in the records as "illiterate." He enlisted with the battery on March 14, 1862. From December 1863 through February 1865 he was detailed to "extra duty" as a wagon driver. While there is no further military record of him, he married "Texana" on March 2, 1864, in Orange County. After the war he worked as a watchman on the C&O Railroad. He died on September 15, 1905. See Carmichael, *Purcell, Crenshaw and Letcher Artillery,* 115.

29. "Started this morning for a Ford higher up the river."—Refer to the map on page 93 for approximate location of the ford.

30. William Henry Chase Whiting, originally from Biloxi, Mississippi, entered West Point and graduated at the top of his class in 1845. His career in the U.S. Army, where he served in varying commands in the Army Corps of Engineers, ended as the Civil War erupted.

    Dissatisfied with Whiting's performance at the Seven Days' Battle, General Robert E. Lee replaced him with Brigadier General John Hood. In May 1864 Whiting took over the defenses at Petersburg. In 1865 Whiting was wounded and captured at Fort Fisher, near Wilmington, North Carolina. The general died in prison at the Union military hospital on Governors Island, New York City, on March 10, 1865. See Sifakis, *Who Was Who in the Confederacy,* 303; and Eicher and Eicher, *Civil War High Commands,* 566.

31. General William Booth Taliaferro (pronounced "tah-liver") was a native Virginian born at "Bellville" in Gloucester County. Prior to the Civil War, he attended William & Mary College, graduating in 1841, and Harvard University. He served in the U.S. Army in the Mexican War and later was a member of the Virginia House of Delegates. Taliaferro and Thomas J. "Stonewall" Jackson had a difficult relationship throughout the war, culminating in Taliaferro being given command of Jackson's Division at the Battle of Cedar Mountain, over the objections of Jackson. Following Fredericksburg, he was sent to Charleston, South Carolina, ultimately opposing Sherman's march through the Carolinas. Taliaferro survived the war and died at home in Gloucester County, Virginia, at the age of seventy-five. Eicher and Eicher, *Civil War High Commands,* 521; Sifakis, *Who Was Who in the Confederacy,* 274–75.

32. "Logan, one of the officer's cooks, gave me a piece of bacon ..."—"Logan" is not listed on any of the battery rosters, as either a first or a last name. One

conclusion to be drawn is that "Logan" was a slave in service to one of the brigade officers. This is a safe assumption given that slaves were often assigned the housekeeping tasks of cooking and laundry. This reference is the only named reference in the diary to a slave in company with the battery, although it's likely he was not the only one. It will be interesting to see whether, as time passes, some historian or researcher is able to identify this individual and determine which officer he was attached to and perhaps discover more information on Logan, his family, or any surviving descendants.

33. General Richard Stoddert Ewell was a career U.S. Army officer prior to the opening engagements of the Civil War. He won respect as a commander under Thomas J. "Stonewall" Jackson and Robert E. Lee and was thought an effective leader throughout much of the war, despite being wounded on multiple occasions and eventually losing a leg at the Battle of Grovetown (Brawner's Farm). Toward the end of the war, controversies were raised over his actions (or inaction) during the Battle of Gettysburg and the Battle of Spotsylvania Court House. Robert E. Lee relieved Ewell of his command after the debacle at Spotsylvania, reassigning him to command the Confederate garrison in Richmond. It was likely under Ewell's orders that Richmond was set ablaze in an intentional act of sabotage during the evacuation in April 1865, as Richmond was about to be captured by Union forces. Ewell and his remaining forces were captured by the Union army as they fled the city, and he was sent to prison in Boston until July 1865. After his release he retired to his wife's plantation and lived the remainder of his life as a gentleman farmer. See American Battlefield Trust, "Biography: Richard S. Ewell"; Sifakis, *Who Was Who in the Confederacy*, 89; and Pfanz, *Richard S. Ewell*, 426–27.

34. "... stopped within five miles of Salem."—Salem, Virginia, is now Marshall, Virginia.

35. Hennessy, *Return to Bull Run*, 94–95.

36. Private George A. Arvin—Prior to the war, George Arvin resided in Pennsylvania. He enlisted with the battery on March 14, 1862. He is listed as "Absent Without Leave" for five days on July 8, 1863. On January 2, 1865, he was detailed to the ambulance corps, and on April 14, 1865, he was paroled near Burkesville, Virginia. See Carmichael, *Purcell, Crenshaw and Letcher Artillery*, 112.

37. Cleary, "Stonewall's Bounty"; Hennessy, *Return to Bull Run*, 111–13.

38. "Started early this morning for Manassas Junction where we had a sharp engagement in which our Battery participated ..."—The raid at Manassas Junction, in combination with the previous day's events at Bristoe Station, marked a turning point in the Manassas Campaign, setting the stage for the largest, bloodiest battle to date in the war. See Hennessy, *Return to Bull Run*, 113–30.

39. ". . . Walter R., a noble boy . . ."—Referred to here is Corporal Walter T. Ratcliffe. At sixteen years old, Walter was a clerk in Richmond, probably serving as an apprentice. He enlisted with Crenshaw's Battery on March 14, 1862. On December 31, 1862, he was promoted to corporal. He was wounded at Gettysburg. On July 12, 1864, he was promoted to sergeant. He was wounded during the Spotsylvania Campaign. On April 15, 1865, he was paroled in Richmond. His brother William T. Ratcliffe was a member of the Pegram Battalion Association. See Carmichael, *Purcell, Crenshaw and Letcher Artillery*, 118.

40. "J. H. Campbell was thrown from the caisson . . ."—James H. Campbell was born in Virginia. In 1860 he was listed as age thirty-five. Prior to the war he resided in Richmond and worked as a printer. He enlisted with Crenshaw's Battery on March 14, 1862. On August 27, 1862, he was elevated to the position of corporal, but on November 12, 1862, he was reduced to private. On April 1, 1865, he was captured at Five Forks. On June 24, 1865, he was released from Point Lookout after having taken the Oath of Allegiance to the Union. See Carmichael, *Purcell, Crenshaw and Letcher Artillery*, 112.

41. "It was very well fortified and considered by some almost impregnable."—Today, Centerville is an unincorporated community within Fairfax County, Virginia. It's a densely packed suburb of Washington, DC, with no features recognizable from its nineteenth-century roots. It is one of many important Civil War sites permanently lost to history.

42. "We left it, taking the road to the northwest . . ."—They did not go northwest if they left Centerville, then passed the battlefield of Manassas. Rather, they went southwest. Based on conversations with Manassas historian and author John Hennessy, it's believed William intended here that after leaving the Warrenton Turnpike (present-day Highway 29), the battery turned to the northwest onto what is now Sudley Road and took a position behind the unfinished railroad. See Hennessy, *Return to Bull Run*, 211.

43. ". . . passing over a portion of the battleground of Manassas . . ."—The reference is obviously to the First Battle of Manassas (July 21, 1861), not the Second Battle of Manassas, which took place on roughly the same ground.

44. "We were put in a commanding position on a slight rise in an open field and had to keep a bright lookout for Yanks. We had not been long there before a column of them were seen making their way through a corn field about a hundred yards off . . ."—According to John Hennessy, National Park Service chief historian at the Fredericksburg and Spotsylvania National Military Park, this description places Crenshaw's Battery in position on the high ground near Sudley Church.

45. "After I left, the boys tell me our forces (Branch's Brigade) were driven out . . ."—According to John Hennessy, this statement is incorrect. The brigade that was driven out was Gregg's Brigade, with some of Branch's Brigade mixed in.

46. Hennessy, *Return to Bull Run*, 456–72.

47. ". . . I had a severe attack of cramp colic . . ."—A condition of severe lower intestinal or colon cramps (indigestion). See Meier, *Nature's Civil War*; and Flannery, *Civil War Pharmacy*, 53–54, 59–60, 87.

48. "The Captain sent off and got me some Jamaica Ginger . . ."—Jamaica ginger extract, commonly referred to by the slang name "Jake," was a popular nineteenth-century patent medicine containing about 75 percent ethanol by weight. It was often prescribed for indigestion and lower bowel problems. See Flannery, *Civil War Pharmacy*, 112.

49. ". . . the battle of Manassas being nothing in comparison . . ."—The reference is to the First Battle of Manassas.

50. The reference is to the First Battle of Manassas.

51. Misspelling of Philip Kearny Jr., who was one of the most colorful and well-loved of all the Union commanders during the Civil War. Born in New York City to wealthy parents, his fortunes were derived from vast international holdings in shipping, mills, manufacturing, banks, and investment houses. Kearny's father, Philip Kearny Sr., was one of New York's wealthiest residents. Kearny was noted for urging his troops forward by allegedly declaring, "Don't worry, men, they'll all be firing at me!" His performance during the Peninsula Campaign earned him tremendous respect from both the enlisted as well as the officer corps. After his death on the battlefield at the Second Battle of Manassas, General Lee sent Kearny's body back to Union forces with a condolence note attached. At the time, there were rumors in Washington that President Abraham Lincoln was contemplating replacing George B. McClellan with "Kearny the Magnificent." Kearny's loss was keenly felt on both sides of this tragic conflict. See De Peyster, *Personal and Military History of Philip Kearny*, 29–33, 277, 448, 450–60.

52. Hennessy, *Return to Bull Run*, 450–51.

PART 4. ON TO MARYLAND, HARPERS FERRY, AND ANTIETAM
SEPTEMBER 2–20, 1862

1. This misspelling refers to Dranesville, Virginia.

2. ". . . I met Dick Green, an old friend and Comrade-in-arms . . ."—According to the Civil War Soldiers and Sailors System, maintained at the National Archives and Records Administration and made available by the National Park Service, there are two likely candidates for "Dick Green." The first and most likely candidate is Richard L. Green, private, of the 15th Regiment,

Virginia Infantry, Company E. The 15th Regiment was organized in May 1861, comprising men from Richmond, Virginia, and Henrico and Hanover Counties. This regiment fought from the Seven Days' Battles through the Battle of Fredericksburg. A second likely candidate is Richard A. Green, private, of the 23rd Regiment, Virginia Infantry, Company C. The 23rd was organized in May 1861 at Richmond, Virginia, and included men from Louisa, Amelia, Halifax, Goochland, Prince Edward, and Charlotte Counties.

3. ". . . 'Maryland, my Maryland' . . ."—See diary entry dated Friday, August 1, 1862, part 3, note 1.

4. The correct spelling is "Monocacy."

5. ". . . where the Baltimore and Ohio R.R. crosses."—Refer to the map on page 120 for the location of the bridge.

6. Stover, *History of the Baltimore and Ohio Railroad*, 108.

7. Stover, 108.

8. This misspelling refers to Frederick City, Maryland.

9. This misspelling refers to Boonsboro, Maryland, near the location of the Battle of Antietam, September 17, 1862.

10. In 1862, Martinsburg was located in Virginia. Today it is in West Virginia.

11. National Park Service, "Harpers Ferry–Bolivar Heights."

12. Lieutenant Colonel David Gregg McIntosh was a native South Carolinian and practicing lawyer with little previous military experience prior to the Civil War. Upon South Carolina's secession, McIntosh offered his services, and on July 29, 1861, he was appointed captain of Company D, 1st South Carolina Infantry, seeing action at the Battle of Vienna. His company was converted to the "Pee Dee Light Artillery" in 1862, and he saw action in the Peninsula Campaign, the Battle of Harpers Ferry, the Battle of Antietam, and the Battle of Fredericksburg. McIntosh was a brother-in-law to Confederate general John Pegram and his younger brother, William J. Pegram (under whom Crenshaw's Battery served). McIntosh was married to Virginia Pegram, John and William Pegram's sister. After the war ended, McIntosh resumed practicing law in Maryland. See Carmichael, *Lee's Young Artillerist*, 15; Wise, *Long Arm of Lee*, 508, 549, 822; and Sifakis, *Who Was Who in the Confederacy*, 184.

13. Prior to the war Charles Pemberton was a resident of Richmond. He enlisted with Crenshaw's Battery on March 14, 1862. He was mortally wounded at Sharpsburg and died on September 18, 1862. He was buried near the field hospital located on the battlefield. See Carmichael, *Purcell, Crenshaw and Letcher Artillery*, 117.

14. This is a misspelling of Edward N. Lynham. Lynham enlisted with Crenshaw's Battery on March 14, 1862. On September 17, 1862, he was wounded at

Sharpsburg. On August 24, 1864, he was admitted to Chimborazo Hospital in Richmond for dyspepsia. On September 5, 1864, he was transferred to the 1st Virginia Battalion, Infantry. See Carmichael, *Purcell, Crenshaw and Letcher Artillery*, 116.

15. John T. Gray was born in Virginia and in 1860 was listed as a druggist, living in Richmond, age thirty-one and single. He enlisted with Crenshaw's Battery on March 14, 1862. He was slightly wounded at Sharpsburg on September 17, 1862. In 1900 he was listed as living. See Carmichael, *Purcell, Crenshaw and Letcher Artillery*, 114.

16. Davis and Robertson, *Virginia at War*, 140–48; Eicher, *Longest Night*, 268–333; McPherson, *Crossroads of Freedom*, 30–34, 44–47, 80–86; Gallagher, *Antietam Campaign*, 192–222.

PART 5. MEANDERING TOWARD FREDERICKSBURG
SEPTEMBER 21–DECEMBER 14, 1862

1. Kitchens, "Experiences of William Henry Kitchens."

2. Misspelling of "Opequon," which is a creek (a tributary of the Potomac) rather than a river.

3. Due to the breakdown of discipline and the increasing numbers of stragglers and desertions following the Second Battle of Manassas, Lee and Jackson instituted increasingly more draconian reactions to even slight infractions against military discipline. See Hennessy, *Return to Bull Run*, 55–56. Also see my editor's note following the diary entry for August 19, 1862, regarding self-care, straggling, and the risks soldiers ventured to ensure their well-being.

4. Carmichael, *Lee's Young Artillerist*, 70.

5. Goolsby, "Crenshaw Battery"; McCabe, *Annual Reunion of the Pegram Battalion Association*, 1; Carmichael, *Lee's Young Artillerist*, 81–82.

6. "Had a guest from Richmond, Mr. Elmore."—Richmond's 1860 city business directory listed a Mr. John H. Elmore as a grocer, with his business located at the corner of Main Street and 23rd Street. See Civil War Richmond, "Richmond City Business Directory, 1860." Another prominent Elmore who was a resident of Richmond was mentioned by Dabney in *Richmond*. He states, "E. C. Elmore," treasurer for the Confederacy, engaged in a duel with John M. Daniel of the *Examiner* in 1864 over Elmore's criticism of the Confederate government.

7. Misspelling of Darkesville, West Virginia, which is an unincorporated town in Berkeley County.

8. ". . . blue mas . . ."—See part 2, note 32, for diary entry dated June 11, 1862.

9. ". . . quinine . . ."—See part 2, note 31, for diary entry dated June 10, 1862.

10. Smithfield is now Middleway, West Virginia.

11. ". . . a thousand miles off . . ."—It seems likely that William intended to say "yards" but simply used the wrong word.

12. "Nous verrons."—From the French; "We'll see."

13. Boreas is the Greek god of the north wind.

14. "Mirabile dictu."—From the Latin; "Miracle to speak of" or "Wonderful to tell." (In this case, sarcasm.)

15. ". . . grim-visaged war"—This snip is from William Shakespeare's opening lines of *Richard III*.

16. Newtown is now Stephens City, Virginia.

17. Today the old Telegraph Road is now Highway 1, also commonly known as the Jefferson Davis Highway.

18. Richard C. Walden enlisted with the battery on March 14, 1862. Between June 6 and December 2, 1862, he was promoted to corporal but then reduced in rank to private on December 3, 1862. On January 2, 1865, he was listed as present at roll call. After the war he was a member of the Pegram Battalion Association; he was buried at Hollywood Cemetery. See Carmichael, *Purcell, Crenshaw and Letcher Artillery*, 119.

19. O'Reilly, "True Battle for Fredericksburg."

20. ". . . await the onset of Lincoln's myrmidons."—This choice of words represents more of William's dehumanization of the enemy. The term "myrmidons" originates in Greek mythology, notably in Ovid but also in Hesiod. More recently, the *Oxford English Dictionary* indicates a myrmidon is a "hired ruffian" or "a loyal follower, one who unquestioningly and pitilessly executes orders." The term is applied contemptuously. See *Compact Edition of the Oxford English Dictionary* (1971), s.v. "myrmidon," 811–12; Morris and Morris, *Morris Dictionary of Word and Phrase Origins*, 393; and Rable, *Damn Yankees!*, 14–19, 37–38.

21. ". . . Lt. Thomas Elliot . . ."—The person referred to is Lieutenant Thomas Ellett, brother of James Ellett and Robert Ellett. See part 2, note 62, for diary entry dated July 15, 1862.

22. ". . . Sergeant Robert Ellott . . ."—The person referred to is Sergeant Robert Ellett. He was killed at Fort Gregg on April 2, 1865. He was the brother of Thomas Ellett and James Ellett. See part 2, note 62, for diary entry dated July 15, 1862.

23. James Ellett—See part 2, note 62, for diary entry dated July 15, 1862. Also see William Ellis Jones's diary entry of August 4, 1862, also referencing First Lieutenant James Ellett, which takes an entirely different view of this officer. It must be presumed he improved upon dying. This officer was the brother of Robert Ellett and Thomas Ellett.

24. Misspelling of John Payne. Prior to the war, Payne resided in Richmond. He enlisted with Crenshaw's Battery on March 14, 1862. He was killed on the battlefield at Fredericksburg on December 13, 1862. See Carmichael, *Purcell, Crenshaw and Letcher Artillery*, 117.

25. Members of Crenshaw's Battery killed or injured December 11–13, 1862 in the Battle of Fredericksburg:

John A. Payne—Killed at Fredericksburg, December 13, 1862. See note 24 above.

Private Thomas J. Mallory—See part 2, note 23, for diary entry dated June 5, 1862.

Private John L. Douglass—Enlisted with the battery on March 14, 1862. On December 13, 1862, he was wounded in the leg at Fredericksburg and sent to a Richmond hospital. On October 2, 1864, he was admitted to Chimborazo for syphilis and returned to duty three days later. He served until surrender.

Private Benjamin F. Pleasants—Enlisted with the battery on March 14, 1862, and wounded at Fredericksburg on December 13, 1862. On October 14, 1863, he was badly wounded at Bristoe Station. On February 7, 1865, he was wounded at Hatcher's Run and three days later admitted to Chimborazo Hospital, where his leg was amputated. On April 27, 1865, he was paroled at Richmond.

Private Benjamin F. Burgess—See part 2, note 26, for diary entry dated June 7, 1862.

Private James Malcolm Hart—Prior to the war he was a resident of Louisa County. He enlisted with the battery on March 14, 1862. On December 13, 1862, he was shot through the thigh at Fredericksburg and remained absent through June 1863. In August 1863 Hart solicited an appointment at the Treasury Department. His recommendation stated that Hart was "a gentleman worthy of entire confidence, & who will faithfully discharge any duties that may be assigned to him." He was absent sick November 12, 1863. On January 2, 1865, he was detailed to Lindsay Walker's headquarters. On April 26, 1865, he was paroled at Ashland. His wartime letters are in the James Hart Collection at the University of Virginia.

Private John J. Wheeler—Enlisted with the battery on March 14, 1862. He was slightly wounded on December 13, 1862, at Fredericksburg and wounded again on May 3, 1863, at Chancellorsville. He was absent because of wound through November 12, 1864. He served until surrender.

Private Richard S. Seeley—Born in Kentucky. In 1860 he was a student living at home in Richmond, age seventeen. His father was Reverend Lyman and his mother was Sarah. He enlisted with the battery on March 14, 1862. From June 27, 1862, through October 1862 he was absent without leave. He returned to duty on November 12, 1862.

On December 13, 1862, he was slightly wounded at Fredericksburg. On May 10, 1864, he was badly wounded at Spotsylvania and absent through February 1865 as a result.

Corporal Jefferson R. Ruffin—Born in Richmond on November 6, 1842, and enlisted with Crenshaw's Battery on March 14, 1862, as a corporal. After July 20, 1862, his rank is listed as a private. On December 13, 1862, he was slightly wounded at Fredericksburg. On August 18, 1863, he was admitted to Charlottesville General Hospital with scabies. On September 7, 1863, he returned to duty. On November 25, 1863, he transferred to Rockbridge Artillery. After the war he was a member of the Pegram Battalion Association. On December 18, 1899, he died in the Richmond Soldiers' Home and was buried at Monticello Cemetery, Albemarle County, Virginia.

For further details on the above, see Carmichael, *Purcell, Crenshaw and Letcher Artillery,* 112–19.

26. O'Reilly, *Fredericksburg Campaign,* 498–99; *OR,* series 1, vol. 21, 142, 562.
27. O'Reilly, *Fredericksburg Campaign,* 494–506.

PART 6. MARCH TO WINTER QUARTERS
DECEMBER 15–31, 1862

1. Misspelling of Guinea Depot.
2. Misspelling of Milford.
3. Misspelling of Woolfolk. The farm referenced in this entry is Mulberry Place plantation, home of the Jourdan Woolfolk family of Bowling Green, Virginia. See chapter 7 for more information.

7. A Strange and Severe Life

1. Vera Palmer, "Old Mulberry Place—Woolfolk Ancestral Home, Caroline County, Virginia," *Richmond Times Dispatch,* January 2, 1938.
2. Wingfield, *History of Caroline County,* 487–89.
3. Woolfolk, family papers, series 1, 2, and 3, Special Collections Research Center, Swem Library, College of William & Mary.
4. Carmichael, *Lee's Young Artillerist,* 81–82.
5. Carmichael, 1–6.
6. Carmichael, 80.
7. Chamberlayne, *Ham Chamberlayne,* 154.
8. The remnants of the artillery battalion's winter quarters were viewed by the author on May 13, 2014, while on a tour of Mulberry Place, conducted by the property owners, Dr. and Mrs. Trahos of Bowling Green, VA.
9. Chamberlayne, *Ham Chamberlayne,* 156.

10. Kitchens, "Experiences of William Henry Kitchens." William Henry Kitchens served in Company F, 45th Georgia Regiment, Thomas Brigade, Wilcox Division, Stonewall Jackson's Brigade, Army of Northern Virginia.

11. Carmichael, *Purcell, Crenshaw and Letcher Artillery*, 113–17.

12. "Military Execution," *Richmond Dispatch*, February 23, 1863.

13. Young and Ellett, "History of the Crenshaw Battery," 283.

14. Young and Ellett, 283.

15. Rhea, *Battles for Spotsylvania Court House*, 296–99. See William Pendleton's report in *OR*, vol. 36, pt. 1, 1045.

16. Young and Ellett, "History of the Crenshaw Battery," 288.

17. U.S. National Park Service, *Battle of Spotsylvania Court House, May 10, 1862*, maps 6–8.

18. Goolsby, "Crenshaw Battery," 360.

19. Goolsby, 360.

20. Fox, *Regimental Losses in the American Civil War*, 541.

21. A. Young, *Lee's Army during the Overland Campaign*, 236.

22. Rhea, *Battles for Spotsylvania Court House*, 267–72, 293.

23. Background is drawn from material presented by John Hennessy (author and National Park Service chief historian at the Fredericksburg and Spotsylvania National Military Park) at "City of Hospitals," a lecture presented at Fredericksburg Baptist Church in commemoration of the 150th anniversary of the Battle of Spotsylvania Court House, May 9, 2014.

24. Carmichael, *Lee's Young Artillerist*, 121.

25. Rhea, *Battles for Spotsylvania Court House*, 267–72, 293; Matter, *If It Takes All Summer*, 329–49.

26. "Pegram's Battalion," *Richmond Whig*, June 21, 1864.

27. The words shown in parentheses, "(missed one)," were illegible in the scanned version of the newspaper that I had access to. After carefully examining the visual image as well as considering the surrounding text for context, I believe I have correctly guessed, or at least come very close to the author's original intent.

28. See diary entries dated June 8, 18, July 19, and August 4 in chapter 6 as examples of William's difficulties with authority. Author and historian Peter S. Carmichael called William's relationship with his commanding officer "a feud." See Carmichael, *Purcell, Crenshaw and Letcher Artillery*, 80.

8. Bad Men Made Perfect

1. "Local Matters," *Richmond Daily Dispatch*, January 16, 1865.

2. "Administrator's Sale," *Richmond Daily Dispatch*, February 18, 1865; "Administrator's Sale," *Richmond Daily Dispatch*, February 22, 1865.

3. Thomas Johnson Michie, "Jones & Company vs. The City of Richmond," in *Virginia Reports*, 699–701.

4. *OR*, series 1, vol. 46, pt. 1, *Reports, Section 2*, 264.

5. "The Evacuation—The Conflagration—The Surrender—Scenes," *Richmond Whig*, April 6, 1865.

6. "The Evacuation—The Conflagration—The Surrender—Scenes."

7. "The Evacuation of Richmond by the Confederate Army—Its Occupation by Federal Forces—Great Fire—The Entire Portion of the Business Section Destroyed—Etc. Etc," *Richmond Whig*, April 4, 1865; "The Evacuation—The Conflagration—The Surrender—Scenes"; "Our Richmond Mobs—Some Experiences in This City with Unruly Masses," *Richmond Daily Dispatch*, December 16, 1888.

8. Ewell and Brock, "Evacuation of Richmond," 247.

9. J. W. M., "Fall of Richmond—Evacuation of the Capital of the Confederacy as Seen by a Boy," *National Tribune*, July 12, 1900; Putnam, *Richmond during the War*, 270.

10. Pickett, *What Happened to Me*, 162.

11. "Killed by the Magazine Explosion," *Richmond Whig*, April 7, 1865; J. W. M., "Fall of Richmond—Evacuation of the Capital of the Confederacy as Seen by a Boy"; "The City Magazine," *Richmond Whig*, April 27, 1865; W. E. Jones, family papers.

12. Semmes, *Service Afloat*, 812.

13. U.S. Naval War Records Office, *Official Records of the Union and Confederate Navies in the War of the Rebellion*, series 1, vol. 12, 191.

14. American Battlefield Trust, "Reaction to the Fall of Richmond, Virginia." The source credits Frank Lawly of the *London Times* from April 1865.

15. "The Evacuation—The Conflagration—The Surrender—Scenes"; Lankford, *Richmond Burning*, 144–45.

16. American Battlefield Trust, "Reaction to the Fall of Richmond, Virginia."

17. Lankford, *Richmond Burning*, 144–45.

18. "Grant: Richmond Ours," *New York Herald*, April 4, 1865.

19. "Prisoners," *Richmond Whig*, April 22, 1865; "Taking the Oath," *Richmond Whig*, May 2, 1865.

20. "William H. Clemmitt, Oldest Active Printer"; "The Evacuation of Richmond by the Confederate Army—Its Occupation by Federal Forces—Great Fire—The Entire Portion of the Business Section Destroyed—Etc. Etc."; Lankford, *Richmond Burning*, 2–3, 144.

21. "The Evacuation of Richmond by the Confederate Army—Its Occupation by Federal Forces—Great Fire—The Entire Portion of the Business Section Destroyed—Etc. Etc."

22. Dabney, *Richmond*, 203–4.

23. "William H. Clemmitt, Oldest Active Printer."

24. W. B. Jones, applications for pardon submitted to President Andrew Johnson by former Confederates excluded from earlier amnesty proclamations, *Case Files of Applications from Former Confederates for Presidential Pardons*, 1865–67 (see chapter 4, note 33).

25. Michie, "Jones & Company vs. The City of Richmond."

26. "Andrew J. Byrne," *Alexandria (VA) Daily State Journal*, January 10, 1871; Michie, "Jones & Company vs. The City of Richmond."

27. Dabney, *Richmond*, 181–82.

28. W. E. Jones, family papers.

29. Carmichael, *Last Generation*, 216–17.

30. Carmichael, *Purcell, Crenshaw and Letcher Artillery*, 112, 114.

31. N. Tyler, *What Is Our True Policy?*

32. Carmichael, *Last Generation*, 222–26.

33. Carmichael, 215–16.

34. For deeper inquiry into the romanticism of the white Southern cause and the price paid for reunion, see Blight, *Race and Reunion*; McConnell, *Glorious Contentment*; and Silber, *Romance of Reunion*.

35. Carmichael, *Last Generation*, 235–36; Blight, *Race and Reunion*, 255–99.

36. L. Tyler, *Encyclopedia of Virginia Biography*, 16–18.

37. "Notice. Bids are requested . . . ," *Richmond Daily Dispatch*, February 2, 1907.

38. "William H. Clemmitt, Oldest Active Printer." See the list of materials published under the imprint of Clemmitt & Jones, then William Ellis Jones, between 1877 and 1878 (demonstrating Jones's takeover of the company in 1878), available online at www.siupress.com/spiritsofbadmenlinks.

39. Norman, "T. Grayson Dashiell."

40. L. Tyler, *Encyclopedia of Virginia Biography*, 3–4.

41. W. E. Jones, family papers.

42. Thomas Ellis Jones (great-grandson of William Ellis Jones) in discussion with the author prior to December 31, 1997. According to my father, this quote is attributable to James Branch Cabell. At the time of the conversation, I had no idea who Cabell was. My recollection of the conversation is based upon the fact that my father communicated the anecdote, remarking that the library at Virginia Commonwealth University was named in honor of Cabell. Therefore, there is some evidence to suppose the alleged quote is attributable to Cabell, as William published a number of Cabell's genealogy works. The men obviously knew one another fairly well, and they shared a deep love of literature and genealogy. (See the list of publications authored

by James Branch Cabell, published by William Ellis Jones, online at www.
siupress.com/spiritsofbadmenlinks.)

43. W. E. Jones, family papers.
44. W. E. Jones, family papers. All three of William Ellis Jones's sons attended
   the prestigious McGuire's School of Richmond.
45. W. E. Jones, family papers. I have been fortunate enough to come into possession of one issue of *The Argosy* containing a short story authored by F. Ellis
   Jones.
46. "The fifth birthday of Master William Ellis Jones," *Richmond Times-Dispatch*,
   August 9, 1904, 6.
47. "Headquarters Pegram Battalion Association," *Richmond Times-Dispatch*,
   April 19, 1910, 11.
48. The library, assembled by William Ellis Jones, passed first to his eldest son,
   Florence Ellis Jones, and passed again just a few months later to his grandson,
   William Ellis Jones, who added to it significantly over the course of his life.
   Upon the death of William Ellis Jones, the library passed to his son Thomas
   Ellis Jones. Thomas Ellis Jones proved a poor custodian, abandoning the library
   to storage in a building owned by his former wife's parents. While a small number of volumes were cherry-picked and saved by Thomas's underage children,
   the bulk of the library was destroyed by fire in 1990, a fire that was planned
   by a relative and carried out by the local fire department as a training exercise.
   The book's owners (Thomas Ellis Jones's children) were not given notice and
   were made aware of the destruction only after it was carried out. Fewer than
   200 volumes were spared. They are now in the possession of the author.
49. Anderson, *Robert Edward Lee*, 3–4.

Appendix

1. "Pegram's Battalion," *Richmond Whig*, June 21, 1864.
2. "1863"—This is a typographical error, of which there are several in this composition. The actual date should have been rendered "1864." It is worthwhile
   to note that the majority of Richmond's printers and compositors (trained
   since childhood on the art and craft of setting type and preparing copy for
   print) enlisted en masse in Crenshaw's Battery in March 1862. If William
   Ellis Jones was, in fact, the author of this letter, it must have irked him to
   no end to see so many careless mistakes in his carefully drafted missive.
3. The correct spelling is "impaled." The somewhat arcane definition in this
   usage is implied to mean "required" or "obligated."
4. ". . . *(missed one)*."—In the original scan of this newspaper, these two words
   were illegible. By examining the word length and the context, I have made an

educated guess as to what the author wrote, or at least intended. While I may not have identified precisely the exact words, I am certain, after examining the Pegram Battalion's service record for 1862, 1863, and 1864, that I have captured the essence of the author's intent.

5. The quote from this poem "Ashby" is from John Reuben Thompson, a Richmonder who edited the *Southern Literary Messenger*. After a sojourn in London for his health, he became editor of the *New York Evening Post*. He was a fan and student of Poe. Thompson also wrote "The Death of Stuart."

6. Incorrect spelling. The correct spelling of this word is "disentrainment," the meaning of which is "withdrawal" or "removal."

7. Carmichael, *Lee's Young Artillerist*, 15–16, 35.

Bibliography

Unpublished Materials

Farrell, John O. Diary of John O. Farrell. Museum of the Confederacy, Eleanor Brockenbrough Library, Richmond, VA.

Jones, Lewis Evan, Sr. Family papers. Papers are in the possession of Doug Bond, Raleigh, NC.

Jones, Thomas Norcliffe. Citizenship naturalization papers. Richmond, VA, June 21, 1843. Papers are in the possession of Constance Hall Jones, Raleigh, NC.

———. Declaration of intent to become a United States citizen. Richmond, VA, June 1, 1840. Papers are in the possession of Constance Hall Jones, Raleigh, NC.

———. Purchase contract between Bernhard and Sally Briel (seller) and Thomas Jones (buyer), April 28, 1840. Document is in the possession of Constance Hall Jones, Raleigh, NC.

Jones, William B. Applications for pardon submitted to President Andrew Johnson by former Confederates excluded from earlier amnesty proclamations. U.S. National Archives. Washington, D.C.

Jones, William Ellis. Civil War diary of William Ellis Jones. 1862. Clements Library, Schoff Civil War Collection, University of Michigan, Ann Arbor.

———. Family papers. Unpublished manuscript and family papers are in the possession of Constance Hall Jones, Raleigh, NC.

———. Form for a retiring soldier, February 1, 1865. Papers are in the possession of Constance Hall Jones, Raleigh, NC.

Kitchens, William Henry. "Experiences of William Henry Kitchens in the Civil War—Written by Him on or about the year 1915 at Griswoldville, Twiggs County, GA." Unpublished manuscript provided by Frances Lee Kitchens Jr., Winston-Salem, NC.

Naragon, Michael Douglas. "Ballots, Bullets, and Blood: The Political Transformation of Richmond, Virginia, 1850–1874." PhD diss., University of Pittsburg, 1996.

Sanchez-Saavedra, Eugene M. "The Beau Ideal of a Soldier: Brigadier General Charles Dimmock." Master's thesis, University of Richmond, 1971.

Thomas, Dr. H. L. "Reports of Resection Cases, General Hospital No. 1. 1862–64." U.S. National Archives. Washington, D.C.

Woolfolk, Jourdan. Family papers. Special Collections Research Center, Swem Library, College of William & Mary.

Newspapers and Journals

Alexandria (VA) Daily State Journal
Editor and Publisher and Journalist
Fredericksburg (VA) Daily Star
Inland Printer
Journal of Human Hypertension
London Express
National Tribune (Washington, DC)
New York Herald
New York Times
Richmond Daily Dispatch
Richmond Enquirer
Richmond Times–Dispatch
Richmond Whig
Royal Society of Chemistry
Salt Lake City Deseret News
Southern Historical Society Papers
Virginia State Journal

Official Compilations and Government Sources

U.S. Bureau of the Census. Henrico County, Virginia, Population Schedule, Richmond, Ward 1, 160–161. Washington, DC: Bureau of the Census, 1840.

———. "Population of the 100 Largest Urban Places: 1840." June 15, 1998. https://www.census.gov/population/www/documentation/twps0027/tab07.txt.

U.S. National Archives. Applications for pardon submitted to President Andrew Johnson by former Confederates excluded from earlier amnesty proclamations, 1865–1867. Washington, D.C.

———. 1865 map of Richmond. Contributors Nathaniel Michler and Peter S. Michie. Washington, D.C.

U.S. National Park Service. *Battle of Spotsylvania Courthouse, May 10, 1862.* Maps. Researched by Frank O'Reilly, Melissa Decour, Elizabeth Getz, and Kelly O'Grady. Illustrated by Steve Stanley. Fort Washington, PA: Eastern Publishing, 2000.

———. Civil War Soldier and Sailor Database. https://www.nps.gov/civilwar/soldiers-and-sailors-database.htm.

War of the Rebellion: A Compilation of the Official Records of the Union and Confederate Armies. 130 vols. Washington, DC: Government Printing Office, 1890–1901.

War of the Rebellion: A Compilation of the Official Records of the Union and Confederate Navies. Series 1, vols. 1–27, and series 2, vols. 1–3. Washington, DC: Government Printing Office, 1894–1922.

Works Projects Administration. Historical Inventory Project. Virginia Conservation Commission Historical Inventory Project. 1937.

Articles and Pamphlets

Address to Electors Accusing William Buckeley Hughes of Bribery. Caernarfon, Wales: Lewis Evan Jones, 1841.

Anderson, Archer. *Robert Edward Lee. An Address Delivered at the Dedication of the Monument to General Robert Edward Lee at Richmond, Virginia, May 29, 1890.* Richmond, VA: Wm. Ellis Jones, Printer, 1890.

Capehart, Richard. "The Beginnings of American Journalism: *The Richmond Enquirer.*" *Editor and Publisher and Journalist* 12, no. 29 (January 1913).

De Bow, James Dunwoody Brownson, ed. "General Walker's Policy in Central America." *De Bow's Review and Industrial Resources, Statistics & etc., Devoted to Southern Institutions, Commerce, Agriculture, Manufactures, Internal Improvements, Political Economy, Education and General Literature,* 28 (1860).

Ewell, General R. S. "Evacuation of Richmond." Edited by Robert Alonzo Brock. *Southern Historical Society Papers* 13 (1885): 247–59.

Goolsby, John Cunningham. "Crenshaw Battery. Pegram's Battalion. Confederate States Artillery." Edited by Robert Alonzo Brock. *Southern Historical Society Papers* 28 (1900): 336–76.

Langford, N. J., and R. E. Ferner. "Toxicity of Mercury." *Journal of Human Hypertension* 13 (1999): 651–56.

Lloyd, Evan. *The Curate.* Wales: Arvonian Press, Lewis Evan Jones, for Owen Owen Roberts, 1832.

Lloyd, Lewis. "A Merioneth Family of Printers in Wales and the U.S.A." *Journal of the Merioneth Historical and Records Society* 12, no 4 (1997).

McCabe, W. Gordon. *Annual Reunion of the Pegram Battalion Association.* Richmond: William Ellis Jones, 1886.

Stevenson, Christopher M. *Burial Grounds for Negroes, Richmond, Virginia: Validation and Assessment.* Virginia Department of Historic Resources, June 25, 2008.

"William H. Clemmitt, Oldest Active Printer." *Inland Printer* 47 (April–September 1911): 714.

Young, Charles P., and Thomas Ellett. "The History of the Crenshaw Battery, with Its Engagements and Roster." Edited by Robert Alonzo Brock. *Southern Historical Society Papers* 31 (1903): 275–91.

Online Resources

American Battlefield Trust. "Biography: James Longstreet." https://www.battlefields .org/learn/biographies/james-longstreet. Accessed May 1, 2019.

————. "Biography: Richard S. Ewell." https://www.battlefields.org/learn /biographies/richard-s-ewell. Accessed May 1, 2019.

————. "Reaction to the Fall of Richmond, Virginia." https://www.battlefields .org/learn/articles/reaction-fall-richmond. Accessed May 1, 2019.

Civil War Poetry. "Poetry and Music of the War between the States." http:// www.civilwarpoetry.org/confederate/songs/richmond.html. Accessed May 1, 2019.

Civil War Richmond. "Richmond City Business Directory, 1860." http://www. civilwarrichmond.com/written-accounts/city-directories/21-richmond-city -business-directory-1860. Accessed May 1, 2019.

Cleary, Ben. "Stonewall's Bounty." *Opinionator* (blog). *New York Times*, August 26, 2012. https://opinionator.blogs.nytimes.com/2012/08/26/stonewalls-bounty/.

Find a Grave Memorial. "Pvt. Thomas Slaughter Bullock." December 6, 2008. http://www.findagrave.com/cgi-bin/fg.cgi?page=gr&GSln=Bullock&GSfn =Thomas&GSmn=Slaughter&GSbyrel=all&GSdyrel=all&GSst=48&GScntry =4&GSob=n&GRid=31997028&df=all&.

Hadfield, Kathleen Halverson. "Reader Voices: LDS Church's Welfare Plan Was Pattern in a 1930s Virginia Community." *Salt Lake City Deseret News*, February 5, 2012. http://www.deseretnews.com/article/700221860/Reader -Voices-LDS-Churchs-welfare-plan-was-pattern-in-a-1930s-Virginia -community.html?pg=all.

Hennessy, John. "Exploring Culpeper and Orange—Somerville and Raccoon Fords." Mysteries and Conundrums, November 27, 2013. http://npsfrsp .wordpress.com/2013/11/27/exploring-culpeper-and-orange-somerville-ford/.

Kambourian, Elizabeth. "Slave Traders in Richmond." *Richmond Times-Dispatch*, February 24, 2014. https://www.richmond.com/slave-traders-in-richmond /table_52a32a98-9d56-11e3-806a-0017a43b2370.html.

Kress, Henriette. "Massae Pilularum—Pill Masses." Henrietta's Herbal Home-page. http://www.henriettesherbal.com/eclectic/kings/massae-pilu.html. Ac-cessed May 1, 2019.

Library of Virginia Online Catalog. "The Byrd Eastham Place, Cloverdale: 1936 March 24 (research made by J. P. Thompson)." Survey report. http://image .lva.virginia.gov/VHI/html/07/0187.html. Accessed May 1, 2019.

National Park Service. "Harpers Ferry—Bolivar Heights." December 12, 2017. https://www.nps.gov/places/harpers-ferry-bolivar-heights.htm.

————. "Major General Benjamin F. Butler, Fort Monroe National Monument." November 16, 2018. https://www.nps.gov/people/benjaminfbutler.htm.

————. "Soldier Details. Brock, Robert A." https://www.nps.gov/civilwar /search-soldiers-detail.htm?soldierId=AACF3686-DC7A-DF11-BF36 -B8AC6F5D926A. Accessed May 1, 2019.

————. "Soldier Details. Cabell, James Caskie." https://www.nps.gov/civilwar/search-soldiers-detail.htm?soldierId=D0C4138A-DC7A-DF11-BF36-B8AC6F5D926A. Accessed May 1, 2019.

————. "Soldier Details. Colquitt, Jr., Joseph H." https://www.nps.gov/civilwar/search-soldiers-detail.htm?soldierId=6FC82C8F-DC7A-DF11-BF36-B8AC6F5D926A. Accessed May 1, 2019.

————. "Soldier Details. Jones, Richard E." https://www.nps.gov/civilwar/search-soldiers-detail.htm?soldierId=7EA282AD-DC7A-DF11-BF36-B8AC6F5D926A. Accessed May 1, 2019.

————. "Soldier Details. Smith, Edgar A." http://www.nps.gov/civilwar/search-soldiers-detail.htm?soldierId=F1C2A0D2-DC7A-DF11-BF36-B8AC6F5D926A. Accessed May 1, 2019.

Norman, Worth E., Jr. "T. Grayson Dashiel: Secretary and Envoy." *Living Church*, January 13, 2012. http://livingchurch.org/t-grayson-dashiell-secretary-and-envoy.

O'Reilly, Frank. "The True Battle for Fredericksburg." American Battlefield Trust. https://www.battlefields.org/learn/articles/true-battle-fredericksburg. Accessed May 1, 2019.

Royal Society of Chemistry. "Search for Blue Mass Medicine That Made Abraham Lincoln Lose His Cool." September 10, 2009. http://www.rsc.org/AboutUs/News/PressReleases/2009/BlueMass.asp.

Smathers, Jason. "The Birth of the SBC Foreign Mission Board. May 08, 1845 Meeting Minutes." Witnesses unto Me, March 18, 2010. http://www.witnessesuntome.com/2010/03/the-birth-of-the-sbc-foreign-mission-board-may-08-1845-meeting-minutes/.

Smith, Michael Thomas. "Benjamin F. Butler (1818–1893)." *Encyclopedia Virginia*, June 28, 2014. https://www.encyclopediavirginia.org/Butler_Benjamin_F_1818-1893.

Tunnell, Ted. "Confederate Newspapers in Virginia during the Civil War." *Encyclopedia Virginia*, 2013. http://www.encyclopediavirginia.org/Newspapers_in_Virginia_During_the_Civil_War_Confederate.

Virginia Historical Society. "United Confederate Veterans. R. E. Lee Camp, No. 1." May 28, 2003. http://www.vahistorical.org/collections-and-resources/how-we-can-help-your-research/researcher-resources/finding-aids/united.

Books

Baring-Gold, Sabine. *A Book of North Wales*. London: Methuen, 1903.

Bears, Sara. *Dictionary of Virginia Biography*. Vol. 3. Richmond: Caperton-Daniels, Library of Virginia, 2006.

Bill, Alfred Hoyt. *The Beleaguered City: Richmond, 1861–1865*. New York: Alfred A. Knopf, 1946.

Blight, David W. *Race and Reunion: The Civil War in American Memory.* Cambridge, MA: Belknap Press of Harvard University Press, 2001.

Borrow, George. *Wild Wales: Its People, Language and Scenery.* Great Britain: Nelson and Sons, undated.

Bowman, Shearer Davis. *At the Precipice: Americans North and South during the Secession Crisis.* Chapel Hill: University of North Carolina Press, 2010.

Brewer, Willis. *Alabama, Her History, Resources, War Record, and Public Men: From 1540 to 1872.* Montgomery, AL: Barrett and Brown, 1872.

Brown, Henry. *Narrative of the Life of Henry Box Brown, Written by Himself.* Manchester, Eng.: Lee and Glynn, 1851.

Burton, Brian K. *Extraordinary Circumstances: The Seven Days Battles.* Bloomington: Indiana University Press, 2001.

Butler, Benjamin F. *Private and Official Correspondence of Gen. Benjamin F. Butler, during the Period of the Civil War.* Volume 1, *April 1860–June 1862.* Norwood, MA: Plimpton, 1917.

Carmichael, Peter. *The Last Generation: Young Virginians in Peace, War, and Reunion.* Chapel Hill: University of North Carolina Press, 2005.

———. *Lee's Young Artillerist—William R. J. Pegram.* Charlottesville: University of Virginia Press, 1995.

———. *The Purcell, Crenshaw and Letcher Artillery.* Lynchburg, VA: H. E. Howard, 1990.

Chamberlayne, C. G., ed. *Ham Chamberlayne—Virginian: Letters and Papers of an Artillery Officer in the War for Southern Independence, 1861–1865.* Richmond, VA: Dietz Printing Company, 1932. Reprint, Wilmington, NC: Broadfoot, 1992.

Cole, J. Timothy, and Bradley R. Foley. *Collett Leventhorpe, the English Confederate: The Life of a Civil War General, 1815–1889.* Jefferson, NC: McFarland, 2007.

Crofts, Daniel W. *Reluctant Confederates: Upper South Unionists in the Secession Crisis.* Chapel Hill: University of North Carolina Press, 1989.

Crute, Joseph H., Jr. *Units of the Confederate States Army.* Midlothian, VA: Derwent, 1987.

Dabney, Virginius. *Richmond: The Story of a City.* New York: Doubleday, 1976.

Davis, William C., and James I. Robertson, eds. *Virginia at War—1862.* Lexington: University of Kentucky Press, 2007.

De Peyster, John Watts. *Personal and Military History of Philip Kearny, Major General United States Volunteers.* Elizabeth, NJ: Palmer and Co., 1870.

Dew, Charles B. *Ironmaker to the Confederacy: Joseph R. Anderson and the Tredegar Iron Works.* New Haven: Yale University Press, 1966.

Eicher, David J. *The Longest Night: A Military History of the Civil War.* New York: Simon and Schuster, 2001.

Eicher, David J., and John H. Eicher. *Civil War High Commands.* Stanford: Stanford University Press, 2002.

Ellyson, Moses. *Richmond Directory and Business Advertiser for 1856.* Richmond, VA: H. K. Ellyson, 1856.

Faust, Drew Gilpin. *This Republic of Suffering: Death and the American Civil War.* New York: Alfred A. Knopf, 2008.

Felter, Harvey Wickes, MD, and John Uri Lloyd. *King's American Dispensatory, Volume II.* Cincinnati: Ohio Valley Company, 1905.

Flannery, Michael A. *Civil War Pharmacy: A History.* Carbondale: Southern Illinois University Press, 2017.

Fontaine, Lamar. *My Life and My Lectures.* New York: Neale, 1908.

Fox, William F. *Regimental Losses in the American Civil War, 1861–1865.* Albany: Albany Publishing Company, 1889.

Freeman, Douglas Southall, *Lee's Lieutenants: A Study in Command.* New York: Simon and Schuster, 1998.

Gallagher, Gary W., ed. *The Antietam Campaign.* Chapel Hill: University of North Carolina Press, 1999.

———, ed. *The Spotsylvania Campaign.* Chapel Hill: University of North Carolina Press. 1998.

Goldfield, David R. *Urban Growth in the Age of Sectionalism: Virginia, 1847–1861.* Baton Rouge: Louisiana State University Press, 1977.

Hagemann, James. *The Heritage of Virginia: The Story of Place Names in the Old Dominion.* Norfolk, VA: Donning, 1988.

Hennessy, John J. *Return to Bull Run: The Campaign and Battle of Second Manassas.* New York: Simon and Schuster, 1993.

Hoehling, A. A., and Mary Hoehling. *The Last Days of the Confederacy: An Eyewitness Account of the Fall of Richmond, Capital City of the Confederate States.* New York: Fairfax Press, 1981.

Hunter, Jerry. *Sons of Arthur, Children of Lincoln: Welsh Writing from the American Civil War.* Cardiff: University of Wales Press, 2007.

Johnson, John Lipscomb. *The University Memorial: Biographical Sketches of Alumni of the University of Virginia Who Fell in the Confederate War.* Baltimore: Turnbell Brothers, 1871.

Johnston, Robert Underwood, and Clarence Clough Buel. *Battles and Leaders of the Civil War, Volume 4.* New York: De Vinne Press, The Century Company, 1888.

Jones, Ifano. *Printing and Printers in Wales and Monmouthshire.* Cardiff, Wales: William Lewis Printers, 1925.

Jones, John Beauchamp. *A Rebel War Clerk's Diary at the Confederate States Capital.* Bedford, MA: Applewood Books, 1866.

Jones, John Ellis. *Gwyddfa y Bardd; Sef, Gwaith Awenyddol. Y Bardd* (Biography of the Bard, some of his poetry, plus the novel *The Bard*). Caernarfon, Wales: Mr. H. Humphreys, Mr. Ellis Jones, 1851.

Jones, William Ellis. *Darluniad o nos Sadwrn y gweithiwr* (Picture of the Saturday night worker). N.p., n.d. (Probably produced during the period William Ellis Jones was with Josiah Tomas Jones, 1840–48.)

———. *Gormod o heyrn yn y tân Nos Sadwrn y gweithiwr / Cawrdaf* (Too many irons in the Saturday night workers fire, by Cawrdaf). Wales: Mr. D. Jones, n.d. (Probably produced during the period William Ellis Jones was with Josiah Tomas Jones, 1840–48.) Reprint, Llandyssul, Wales: J. D. Lewis, Gomerian Press, 1896.

Kimball, Gregg D. *American City, Southern Place: A Cultural History of Richmond.* Athens: University of Georgia Press, 2000.

Kolchin, Peter, and Eric Foner, eds. *American Slavery: 1619–1877.* New York: Hill and Wang, 1993.

Krick, Robert K. *Stonewall Jackson at Cedar Mountain.* Chapel Hill: University of North Carolina Press, 1990.

Lankford, Nelson. *Richmond Burning: The Last Days of the Confederate Capital.* New York: Viking Penguin, 1999.

Lester, George N. *Cases in Law and Equity, Argued and Determined in the Supreme Court of Georgia, Containing the Decisions from Macon, June Term, 1861 to Milledgeville, November Term, 1863, Inclusive.* Vol. 33. Macon, GA: J. W. Burke, 1870.

Little, John Peyton. *Richmond, the Capital of Virginia: Its History.* Richmond, VA: Dietz, 1933.

Mackowski, Chris, and Kristopher D. White. *A Season of Slaughter: The Battle of Spotsylvania Court House, May 8–21, 1864.* El Dorado Hills, CA: Savas Beatie, 2013.

———. *Simply Murder: The Battle of Fredericksburg, December 13, 1862.* El Dorado Hills, CA: Savas Beatie, 2012.

Majewski, John. *Modernizing a Slave Economy: The Economic Vision of the Confederate Nation.* Chapel Hill: University of North Carolina Press, 2009.

Matter, William D. *If It Takes All Summer: The Battle of Spotsylvania.* Chapel Hill: University of North Carolina Press, 1988.

McConnell Stuart. *Glorious Contentment: The Grand Army of the Republic, 1865–1900.* Chapel Hill: University of North Carolina Press, 1992.

McPherson, James M. *Crossroads of Freedom: Antietam, the Battle That Changed the Course of the Civil War.* New York: Oxford University Press, 2002.

Meier, Kathryn Shively. *Nature's Civil War: Common Soldiers and the Environment in 1862 Virginia.* Chapel Hill: University of North Carolina Press, 2013.

Michie, Thomas Johnson. *Virginia Reports, Jefferson—33 Grattan. 1730–1880, Volumes 1–2*. Charlottesville, VA: Michie Company, Law Publishers, 1901.

Mordecai, Samuel. *Virginia, Especially Richmond in Bygone Days*. Richmond, VA: George M. West, 1856.

Morris, William, and Mary Morris. *Morris Dictionary of Word and Phrase Origins*. New York: Harper and Row, 1977.

Noe, Kenneth W. *Reluctant Rebels*. Chapel Hill: University of North Carolina Press, 2010.

O'Reilly, Francis Augustín. *The Fredericksburg Campaign*. Baton Rouge: Louisiana State University Press, 2006.

Page, Thomas Nelson. *Social Life in Old Virginia before the War*. Sandwich, MA: Chapman Billies, 1892, 1994.

Pfanz, Donald C. *Richard S. Ewell: A Soldier's Life*. Chapel Hill: University of North Carolina Press, 2000.

Pickett, LaSalle Corbelle. *What Happened to Me*. New York: Brentano's, 1917.

Potter, Samuel O. *A Compendium of Materia Medica, Therapeutics, and Prescription Writing*. Philadelphia: P. Blakiston's Son and Company, 1894.

Putnam, Sallie Brock. *Richmond during the War: Four Years of Personal Observation*. Lincoln: University of Nebraska Press, 1996.

Rable, George C. *Damn Yankees! Demonization and Defiance in the Confederate South*. Baton Rouge: Louisiana State University Press, 2015.

Rhea, Gordon C. *The Battles for Spotsylvania Court House and the Road to Yellow Tavern: May 7–12, 1864*. Baton Rouge: Louisiana State University Press, 1997.

———. *The Battles of the Wilderness: May 5–6, 1864*. Baton Rouge: Louisiana State University Press, 1994.

Robertson, James I., Jr. *General A. P. Hill: The Story of a Confederate Warrior*. New York: Vintage, 1992.

Ryan, David D. *Four Days in 1865: The Fall of Richmond*. Richmond: Cadmus/William Byrd Press, 1993.

Scott, W. W. *A History of Orange County, Virginia*. Richmond, VA: Everett Waddey, 1907.

Semmes, Admiral Raphael. *Service Afloat: or, The Remarkable Career of the Confederate Cruisers Sumter and Alabama during the War between the States*. Baltimore: Baltimore Publishing Company, 1887.

Sifakis, Stewart. *Who Was Who in the Confederacy*. Vol. 2 of *Who Was Who in the Civil War*. New York: Facts on File, 1988.

Silber, Nina. *The Romance of Reunion: Northerners and the South, 1865–1900*. Chapel Hill: University of North Carolina Press, 1993.

Simpson, Craig M. *A Good Southerner: The Life of Henry A. Wise of Virginia*. Chapel Hill: University of North Carolina Press, 1985.

Smollett, Tobias, and Lewis M. Knapp, eds., revised by Paul-Gabriel Bouce. *The Expedition of Humphrey Clinker.* Oxford, Eng.: Oxford University Press, 1771, 1988.

Stover, John F. *History of the Baltimore and Ohio Railroad.* West Lafayette, IN: Purdue University Press, 1987.

Trammell, Jack. *The Richmond Slave Trade: The Economic Backbone of the Old Dominion.* Charleston, SC: History Press, 2012.

Tyler, Lyon G. *Encyclopedia of Virginia Biography, Volume IV.* New York: Lewis Historical Publishing Company, 1915.

Tyler, Nathaniel. *What Is Our True Policy? It Is Herein Considered: By a Virginian.* Richmond, VA: Gary and Clemmitt, Printers, 1866.

Williams, W. Ogwen. *Wales through the Ages: Volume II, Modern Wales, from 1485 to the Beginning of the 20th Century.* Edited by A. J. Roderick. Swansea, Wales: Christopher Davies, 1971.

Wills, Brian Steel. *Confederate General William Dorsey Pender: The Hope of Glory.* Baton Rouge: Louisiana State University Press, 2013.

Wingfield, Marshall. *A History of Caroline County, Virginia, from Its Formation in 1727 to 1924.* Baltimore: Genealogical Publishing Co., 2005.

Wise, Jennings Cropper. *The Long Arm of Lee, or The History of the Artillery of the Army of Northern Virginia.* 3 vols. Lincoln: University of Nebraska Press, 1915, 1991.

Wright, Mike. *City under Siege: Richmond in the Civil War.* New York: Cooper Square Press, 1992.

Wynes, Charles E. *Race Relations in Virginia, 1870–1902.* Totowa, NJ: Rowman and Littlefield, 1971.

Young, Alfred C., III. *Lee's Army during the Overland Campaign: A Numerical Study.* Baton Rouge: Louisiana State University Press, 2013.

Young, David. *The Origin and History of Methodism in Wales and the Borders.* Edinburgh, Scotland: Morrison and Gibb, 1893.

Index

Strother, Robert Q., 201
Strother, Sydney, 85, 87, 155, 208
Stuart, James Ewell Brown "J.E.B.,"
 21, 73, 105, 115
Sudley Church, 217
summer complaint. *See* diarrhea
Summit. *See* Guinea Station
Summit Point, 138

Taliaferro, William Booth, 113, 215
temperance, 6
Tennessee, 16
Thomas, Dr. H. L., 87–88, 210
Thompson, John Reuben, 190, 228
Trahos, Michael and B. L., xv, 223
Tredegar Iron Works, 18–20, 166, 178,
 234
Turkey Hill, Virginia, 183, 91
Tyler, Nathaniel, 170–71, 238

Underground Railroad, 20
Union Army: 4th Massachusetts
 Cavalry, 167; V Corps, 127; 118th
 Pennsylvania, 127; Boston Light
 Artillery, 48; Union Army of the
 Potomac, 146, 214
United Daughters of the Confeder-
 acy, 173, 202

Valentine, Mann Satterwhite, Jr., 173
Valentine, Mann Satterwhite, Sr., 15
Valentine, Edward "Ned" Virginius,
 14–15, 25, 27, 30, 173, 195
Virginia: Central Southern Rights
 Association of, 19–20, 26;

Constitutional Convention of 1850,
 18; secession, 17, 19–21, 30, 37;
 suffrage, 10, 18, 24
Virginia Historical Society, 40,
 173–74, 176
*Virginia Magazine of History and
 Biography*, 3

Walden, Richard C., 145, 221
Wales, 4–7
Walker, Reuben Lindsey, 92, 95, 103,
 140, 142, 154, 184, 211, 222
Washington, George, 12
water battery, 79–80, 206
Weitzel, Godfrey, 167
Wersham, Thomas R., 184
Wesleyan, 6
Wheeler, John J., 146, 222
Whig (political party), 16
Whiting, William Henry Chase, 112,
 215
Williamsport, Maryland, 124
Williamsport Pike, 124
Willis, John and Lucy, 44, 101–2
Winchester, Virginia, 132, 140–42
Winder, Charles Sidney, 103, 213
Wise, Henry A., 18, 21, 29, 31, 237
Wise, O. Jennings, 21
Woodstock, Virginia, 142
Woolfolk, Elizabeth, 153
Woolfolk, Jourdan, 50, 153
Wortham, Charles T., 21

Young, Charles P., 36, 54, 156, 231
Young, George S., 85, 209

Constance Hall Jones is an antiquarian book dealer and author working in Raleigh, North Carolina. A graduate of East Carolina University, she follows in the footsteps of seven generations preceding her, carrying on the family business of writing, publishing, and trading in books, while studying the history those volumes preserve for all time.

ENGAGING
—*the*—
CIVIL WAR

Engaging the Civil War, a series founded by the historians at the blog Emerging Civil War (www.emergingcivilwar.com), adopts the sensibility and accessibility of public history while adhering to the standards of academic scholarship. To engage readers and bring them to a new understanding of America's great story, series authors draw on insights they gained while working with the public—walking the ground where history happened at battlefields and historic sites, talking with visitors in museums, and educating students in classrooms. With fresh perspectives, field-tested ideas, and in-depth research, volumes in the series connect readers with the story of the Civil War in ways that make history meaningful to them while underscoring the continued relevance of the war, its causes, and its effects. All Americans can claim the Civil War as part of their history. This series helps them engage with it.

Chris Mackowski and Brian Matthew Jordan, Series Editors

Queries and submissions
emergingcivilwar@gmail.com